The House
without the Door

The House without the Door

A Study of Emily Dickinson
and the Illness of Agoraphobia

Maryanne M. Garbowsky

Rutherford • Madison • Teaneck
Fairleigh Dickinson University Press
London and Toronto: Associated University Presses

All rights reserved. Authorization to photocopy items for internal or personal use, or the internal or personal use of specific clients, is granted by the copyright owner, provided that a base fee of $10.00, plus eight cents per page, per copy is paid directly to the Copyright Clearance Center, 27 Congress Street, Salem, Massachusetts 01970. [0-8386-3331-5/88 $10.00 + 8¢ pp, pc.]

Associated University Presses
440 Forsgate Drive
Cranbury, NJ 08512

Associated University Presses
25 Sicilian Avenue
London WC1A 2QH, England

Associated University Presses
P.O. Box 488, Port Credit
Mississauga, Ontario
Canada L5G 4M2

The paper used in this publication meets the requirements
of the American National Standard for Permanence of Paper
for Printed Library Materials Z39.48-1984.

Library of Congress Cataloging-in-Publication Data

Garbowsky, Maryanne M.
  The house without the door.

  Bibliography: p.
  Includes index.
  1. Dickinson, Emily, 1830-1886 — Biography —
Psychology. 2. Poets, American — 19th century — Biography.
3. Agoraphobia — Patients — United States — Biography.
4. Poets — Psychology. 5. Agoraphobia in literature.
6. Fear in literature. 7. Psychoanalysis and literature.
I. Title.
PS1541.Z5G37 1989   811'.4[B]   87-46361
ISBN 0-8386-3331-5 (alk. paper)

Doom is the House without the Door—
'Tis entered from the Sun—
And then the Ladder's thrown away,
Because Escape—is done—

Contents

Foreword		9
Preface		17
Acknowledgments		23

1	The Impression: "An Excess of Tension and an Abnormal Life"	27
2	"My Life Was Made a Victim"	34
3	"The World Looks Staringly"	39
4	"I Love So to Be a Child"	45
5	"What If They Die When I'm Gone?"	49
6	"Newton Is Dead. The First of My Own Friends"	57
7	"I Have Never Seen Anyone That I Cared for as Much as You"	62
8	"I Had a Terror—Since September"	67
9	"I Told My Soul to Sing"	75
10	"A Prison Gets to Be a Friend"	79
11	"A Thing So Terrible"	90
12	"I Dropped Down and Down"	103
13	"Blank—and Steady Wilderness"	112
14	"Then—Close the Valves of Her Attention Like Stone"	133
15	"Alone, I Cannot Be"	140
16	"The Soul Achieves—Herself"	147

Notes	153
Bibliography	173
General Index	183
Index of First Lines	187

Foreword

In the presence of almost any nineteenth-century artistic genius, Emily Dickinson, one imagines, could easily have held her own. For sheer brilliance and intellectual power she had few equals; indeed, it is hard to think of one in any century who surpassed her. Yet she spent her life sequestered among ungifted people, primarily family members or in-laws — and suffered for it. Not that Edward, her father, or Austin, her brother, or his wife, Susan, were blockheads. Rather, like most of her intimates, they were undeniably superior: keen witted, quick thinking, discerning, well read. Only in comparison with the poet do they appear dull and prosaic. Although she loved these people who were, on the whole, very good to her, she nevertheless longed for the recognition of the superlatively endowed and accomplished — that is, of people more like herself. She intensely admired Emily Brontë and followed from afar with passionate interest the creative careers of Elizabeth Browning and George Eliot. The thought must often have crossed her mind how delightful and gratifying it would be to approach these geniuses, become one of their circle, share her mind with them.

What prevented it? Not distance, certainly, nor lack of connections, nor family opposition, nor lack of financial resources, nor frail health, nor domestic commitments, nor any of the other hundred and one objective hindrances that keep human beings from going where they please and approaching those to whom they feel akin. Why then did Emily Dickinson yearn for acceptance of her work and consequent fame for herself (as most Dickinson specialists think she did) and make so few and feeble efforts to achieve them?

Feminists, with more than a little justification, place the blame on nineteenth-century American society and its hostility to women. They claim that Emily Dickinson could never have struck out on her own and conquered the world; there was simply too much going against her. Short of teaching school or managing a shop, she could not have supported herself, they say, and such work was of course grotesquely removed from what interested her. Here, I believe, they overlook the fact that her father was extremely well-off financially, supported her all her life, and would undoubtedly have done so under any circumstances. If she had somehow arranged to go to Europe to meet Mrs. Browning, say, and was determined to go, it is hard to imagine Edward Dickinson's refusing his permission, although he might have insisted that Austin accompany her.

9

The idea is not far fetched. The career of Helen Fiske, Emily's friend from childhood when they were next-door neighbors on Pleasant Street, shows how easily such as expedition could be managed, despite the undeniably intense pressure to keep women at home.

Helen Fiske Hunt Jackson and Emily Dickinson—what a contrast! Yet their backgrounds were very similar, so similar, in fact, that their lives present almost what a scientist would consider a natural experiment. The constants, pertaining equally to both women, were nineteenth-century culture in general with its male chauvinism and suppression of women, the mores of Amherst in particular, with its provincialism and puritanism and, even more specifically, the conservative religious and secular values of the Fiske and Dickinson families, which, in this regard, were also very like each other.

What then is the variable? The answer: the personality characteristics of the two women.

Consider the likenesses in their backgrounds. The Dickinsons were a long-established, distinguished New England family. So were the Fiskes; the first who came to Massachusetts from England, a descendant of John Locke, arrived in Watertown in 1642. Like the Dickinsons, Helen's family were Whigs and Calvinists. Both families were solidly upper middle-class. Nathan, Helen's father, graduated first in his class from Dartmouth College and later from the Andover Theological Seminary where he made Phi Beta Kappa. Edward Dickinson went to Yale and was a good student even though he was not, as Cynthia Griffin Wolff and others have asserted, the valedictorian of his class. Nathan Fiske ultimately became professor of languages and rhetoric at Amherst College, while Edward Dickinson embarked on a successful political and legal career in the same town and became a lifelong trustee of that institution.

The maternal sides of the two families were also comparable and of similarly old New England stock, although Helen's mother, Deborah Vinal, may have been a little better educated than Emily's mother, Emily Norcross. Deborah attended Joseph Emerson's finishing school, considered one of the best, and later went to the Adams Female Seminary in New Hampshire. Joel Norcross, a well-to-do farmer who believed in education even for women, sent his daughter Emily to boarding school in New Haven. She was still there at least until midyear 1823 when she had already reached her nineteenth birthday. Any woman of that era who attended school to that advanced age had every reason to regard herself as unusually well educated. Even the medical histories of the families on the maternal side shared important similarities. Tuberculosis stalked both Vinals and Norcrosses, and Helen's parents both died of the disease.

The similarities continue. Helen Fiske and Emily Dickinson were almost exact contemporaries. Helen was born on 15 October, 1830, Emily two months less five days later. Helen died in 1885, Emily in 1886. Their educations were similar, although Helen's was more disrupted. Helen, like Emily, first was sent to the Amherst Academy; Emily stayed to graduate while her friend went on to a number of comparable schools, including the Ipswich Female Seminary, also attended by Emily's sister, Lavinia.

Yet, despite these common influences, how their lives diverged (and converged again before their close)! By the time she was twenty-one, Helen had visited or lived in New York City, Albany, Cincinnati, Baltimore, Washington, Roxbury, New Haven, and other cities. Emily, by then, had been no further from home than South Hadley where for a year or so she had attended Mount Holyoke Female Seminary. By age twenty-five, Helen was in Newport and making friends with artists John LaFarge and William M. Hunt, the actress Charlotte Cushman (who knew George Sand), and Henry and William James. She attended soirees at the home of Mrs. Vincenzo Botta, where she was very popular, and whither also came Poe, Longfellow, Margaret Fuller, Lydia Marie Child, William Cullen Bryant, Horace Greeley, Charles A. Dana, Harriet Beecher Stowe, Thomas Wentworth Higginson, William Dean Howells. . .the list is endless. While Emily was gradually becoming an inaccessible recluse in her father's house, Helen continued to expand her geographical and social horizons. Before she turned forty she had visited or resided for various lengths of time in almost all the major cities of Europe. She also traveled extensively by train throughout the United States, on one such occasion introducing herself unhesitatingly to another passenger, Ralph Waldo Emerson, who, in time, came to regard her as a great poet. In the 1860s she became friends with Harriet Hosmer, the sculptress, who was on intimate terms with Emily's idol, Elizabeth Barrett Browning, and her husband Robert. In the meantime, Helen had married twice, been widowed once, and had given birth to two sons, both of whom died in childhood. She had also become a famous author, her poems and travel essays appearing in *Scribner's Monthly, The Atlantic, Hearth and Home, Harper's The Independent*, and other widely circulated periodicals. Late in life she became a celebrated reformer in the cause of the Indians and a world-famous novelist. Her romance, *Ramona*, eventually became the subject of a wildly successful motion picture.

Now I am not by any means suggesting that it would have been well for Emily Dickinson to have followed in Helen Jackson's restless and boisterous footsteps. My point is to emphasize the one thing that utterly barred her from doing so — her personality. It was Emily Dickinson's cognitive and emotional makeup, that and that alone, and not her culture, or her family, or her education, or her religion, or financial constraints, that blocked her access to the kindred spirits she admired from afar, and that kept her from the recognition and appreciation she craved.

External hindrances may have played a secondary role, of course. But all explanations that invoke them as the ultimate cause of her reclusion and

lifelong obscurity are bound to fail. The reason they fail is that other exceptional women of her place and era, with far less intelligence, talent, and
material advantages than were at Emily Dickinson's command, overcame
each and every one of them and made a place for themselves in the world,
just as Helen Jackson had done. Incidentally, I am not here suggesting that
Helen was the more successful artist! Quite the contrary is true.

When we turn our attention, as we must, to Emily Dickinson's life and
work and ask ourselves what precisely it was in her makeup that held her
back, we are faced with the same peripheral clues and "omitted center" that
we encounter in her more obscure verses. Her poems and letters, and the
remarks of contemporaries, are replete with undeniable reflections of emotional turmoil. We find references to anxiety in superabundance, and also
to depression, irrational fears, nervous exhaustion, psychological collapse—
even disturbances in thinking and lapses of rationality. But, for all this
evidence, we are still far from having a complete picture. It is not fashionable
today to think of Emily Dickinson as a "patient," especially a psychiatric
one, as though the great have no business being ill. Yet it is impossible to
imagine any psychiatrist well acquainted with the poet's biography and body
of work who would not come to the conclusion that she had some kind of
psychological disorder of significant magnitude. The difficult question is not
whether there was a diagnosable infirmity present—for it is clear that there
was—but what was its essential nature. Here we come to the omitted center
and the divergency of possible explanations.

The historical record reveals a great deal about Emily Dickinson's symptoms. What we do not know is their exact hierarchical ranking in terms of
severity, duration, and time of onset and which were the more central symptoms, which the more peripheral. The American Psychiatric Association's
official *Diagnostic and Statistical Manual of Mental Disorders* (*DSM* III) con-
tains a number of diagnoses that suggest themselves as to some extent ap-
plicable to Emily Dickinson, depending on what strikes one as the primary
core of her trouble. These include the following: the Adjustment Disorders,
Avoidant Personality Disorder, Brief Reactive Psychosis, Cyclothymic
Disorder, Depersonalization Disorder, Dysthymic Disorder, Generalized Anxiety Disorder, Hysterical Personality Disorder, Major Depressive Episode,
Schizoaffective Disorder, Schizotypal Personality Disorder, and Social
Phobia. The diagnosis that seems most appropriate depends, of course, on
the precise weight one assigns to each bit of evidence and to each symptom.

In the present book, Maryanne M. Garbowsky presents her reasons for
believing that Emily Dickinson suffered from agoraphobia. That the poet,
who shrank from stepping outside her home for the latter half of her life,
suffered from the *symptom* agoraphobia, there can be little doubt. But that
she was afflicted with Agoraphobia with a capital *A*—that is, not as a
peripheral factor associated with one of the other possible diagnoses, but

as the primary diagnosis, is a new idea which forms the substance of Dr. Garbowsky's closely argued thesis. I will leave it to the individual reader to decide just how ably she makes her case. I will, however, vouch for Dr. Garbowsky's psychological sophistication, command of the psychiatric literature, and straightforward honesty in her marshaling of the abundant evidence for the existence of Emily Dickinson's affliction.

Certainly, in examining the symptomatology, Dr. Garbowsky has bravely looked into one of the most problematic and troubling aspects of the poet's life. It does not solve the problem to sweep it under the rug, as even the most distinguished of Dickinson specialists tend to do. Perhaps, in the last analysis, the most important contribution of a work of this kind is not that it furnishes a definitive label for Emily Dickinson's illness, but that it reopens a window on the life, a window needlessly closed and shuttered. It accepts the illness as a fact, inconvenient as that is for biographers, and takes it seriously as an important reality of her existence. The book thus constitutes a necessary counteractant to the dissertations of those who ignore the offending window and who would, if they could, permanently brick it up.

Aside from concerns about the roots of Emily Dickinson's reclusion, one comes away from this book with questions about its function or, if that is too teleological a word, its ultimate consequences. One is led to consider what her life might have been had she been free of the inhibitions imposed by her illness and to look for insight into the lives of comparable artists who lacked such constraints. It seems undeniable, for instance, that her anxieties had a protective effect and safeguarded not only the poetry, but her person as well. Certainly there is reason to believe that life in the open world can be highly dangerous to artists, and the higher the voltage of their emotions (and in Emily Dickinson it was high indeed) the riskier it appears to be. Female poets, but male ones also, seem especially vulnerable, and disastrous lives often ending in suicide strike one as alarmingly frequent.

In this regard it is interesting to compare Emily Dickinson's fate with that of another genius, Delmira Agustini, Uruguay's foremost woman poet, for there are striking resemblances. Both were astonishingly gifted in the verbal realm, both highly emotional, both matured under extremely sheltered conditions, and, up to a point, Delmira Agustini was as reclusive as Emily Dickinson. Both had psychiatric symptoms: Delmira's personality was radically unintegrated and had at least two, possibly three, dissociated manifestations. In one, she was "Baby" an infantile, dependent self; in another, Delmira the poet — visionary, ecstatic, and ravished by fantasies of sex and death. Both poets dressed symbolically, Emily Dickinson in white, Delmira Agustini in red. Both suffered inner conflicts of agonizing intensity — but Agustini left home and Dickinson did not. And that made all the difference.

Delmira Agustini was born in Montevideo in 1886, five months after Emily Dickinson's death. Her formative years were as secluded as her parents could make them. Delmira was not allowed to go to school at all and was educated at home by her mother who had been a teacher. Because Señora de Agustini suffered from constant headaches, the house had to be kept utterly and permanently quiet. Delmira herself had intractable insomnia and seems almost never to have slept. Sequestered in her silent room late at night she wrote poems of breathtaking intensity and powerful sexual symbolism. At twenty-one, she published her first book of verse, which brought her instant notoriety and scandalized the community. Families of the upper middle-class, to which the Agustinis belonged, forbade their offspring to have anything to do with her, thereby reinforcing her isolation. With fame, however, came opportunity to escape the prison-nest. Entirely lacking Dickinson's inhibitions, Agustini by age twenty-two was out in the world and, a beautiful woman, was soon engaged to be married. As Delmira the poet she continued to pour out superb, passionate poems, entirely beyond her actual experience, which she created in trancelike states. As the naive child, she wrote baby talk in her letters to her fiancé (who had rejected her sexual advances to reserve them for after their marriage), signing her letters "Baby" or, sometimes, "Baby, Delmira and I." The competing claims of the different sides of her personality and her esurient sensuality, which seems to have been overwhelming, conspired to produce a condition of increasing psychic tension. Yet she postponed her marriage until she was twenty-eight, in the meantime publishing two more volumes of poetry, each one superior to the last. In August 1913 she at least married her fiancé, Enrique Reyes, an unsuitable choice. Reyes whose middle name, appropriately, was Job, was an auctioneer with no interest in literature, whose appeal for her seems to have been compounded only of physical desire and fantasy. Five weeks later she fled him and filed for divorce (then almost unheard of in Catholic Uruguay) on the grounds of his "vulgarity." She continued to dally with him, however, as the intermittent contact without possession fed her fantasies. In conflict over her raging sexual impulses she began to dress in symbolic red. One day Señor Reyes, desperate to get her back, arranged a secret tryst, taking along his gun. Exactly what transpired between them is not known except that he ended by shooting her dead and killing himself. Delmira was only twenty-nine.

A posthumous book was published, *Stars of the Abyss*. Of this work critic Sidonia C. Rosenbaum says "...one would feel, reading these palpitating verses of the last period, that one is face to face with a naked soul that vibrated with passion bordering on the pathological. Enriched by superb imagery and erotic imagination, prodigious in its intensity, these poems reach heights that reveal her as a woman mature with passion..." (*Americas* 39, no. 1 [January–February 1987]: 38–41).

One would like to think that Emily Dickinson, had she had the inner freedom to leave Amherst, would have possessed the balance, focus, and wit to avoid the pitfalls that trapped Helen Jackson and Delmira Agustini.

Helen, it cannot be denied, frittered away much of her time and talent and only began to concentrate her creative energies toward the end of her life. On her deathbed she intensely regretted not having settled down to serious work earlier, for she had felt it within her to become a novelist of consequence. Delmira Agustini's difficulty, by contrast, was not that she fell victim to the distractions of a social butterfly and neglected her poetry. Rather, she found that she could not do without the structure and routine imposed by her mother. Once she lacked these constraints she discovered she could not control herself. Her mighty imagination and unbridled emotions took her over completely, and they, combined with her ignorance of men and the world, did the rest.

They are extreme cases, of course: on the one hand, dissipation of creative concentration and running off in all directions; on the other, complete domination by the irrationalities of impulse and fantasy. We can never know if Emily Dickinson would have succumbed to either of these fatalities, but it is not impossible to imagine.

But we do know some things beyond a shadow of a doubt. We know that Emily Dickinson stayed at home, that home sheltered her and provided a haven for the exercise of her creative gift, and that as a result she was able to enrich the world by a body of magnificent poetry. We also know that what kept her at home in the first place were her anxieties and insecurities — whatever their nature.

JOHN CODY

Preface

The mystery of Emily Dickinson has captured the imagination of general readers and scholars alike. Even before her death, the community speculated about her odd behavior, and stories began to circulate. As early as 1854, her friends worried that the people of Amherst "wholly misinterpret her."[1] It is little wonder, for the life of Emily Dickinson reads like a fairy tale, with the air of a dream clinging to it — a young woman dressed in white confined to her father's house. We read the life and ask what kept her secluded. Every reader tries to answer this question, to discover the secrets hidden in the dark corners of that Amherst house. Was there some shame from which she hid? Was it a nervous breakdown, an illness, or simply an occurrence, a "happen," as the poet's sister claimed?

Whether coy or extremely private, Dickinson never revealed why she began to withdraw from life in the mid-1850s and remained within her father's house for the last twenty years of her life. Despite the poet's reticence, theories proliferate. They range from a belief that the poet had a secret though rejecting male lover, an affair with a married man, or a homosexual liaison, to — most recently — a marriage and an abortion. In each case, the author bases his or her argument on a kernel of truth, although the whole of it may be far from correct. In the chapter "Problem of the Biographer," Richard Sewall considers the far-reaching theories that have arisen to fill the gaps in Dickinson's life and admits that "even the wildest may have a grain of truth in it."[2]

One might ask, how could someone who left more than seventeen hundred poems and a thousand letters be elusive? This seeming paradox drives the student of Dickinson to plow and replow the same field of inquiry hoping to uncover an answer. Many critics have used psychoanalysis to find answers.

In the early 1970s such an approach was taken by psychiatrist John Cody. *After Great Pain*, a brilliant and painstaking study, argues convincingly that Dickinson suffered a nervous breakdown during the crisis years of 1861–63, a psychosis brought on by her mother's early rejection of her. Cody examines the letters and outlines the stages of Dickinson's psychosis recorded within the poetry. However persuasive his argument, it is flawed in two ways. For one, he does not discuss the poetry chronologically, but by the "process" of the breakdown: "In my analysis no effort will be made to review the poems in the chronological order of the composition. Instead, they will be arranged

17

in a sequence that corresponds to the gradually developing clinical picture of an actual psychotic illness. What justifies this approach is the fact that it is the only way to render the process understandable."[3] He maintains that the chronology is "more or less irrelevent" to his study because "the poems evoked by her illness must largely have been written in retrospect" not at the time the poet was experiencing these effects.[4]

This was in 1971 before the appearance of Ralph W. Franklin's *The Manuscript Books of Emily Dickinson*, which arranged the poems in the order the poet left them. Sections of Cody's book were written as early as 1967, the year Franklin's *The Editing of Emily Dickinson* first appeared with its revision of the Johnson variorum order. If we consider Franklin's establishment of "the internal sequence of the forty bound fascicles," we have some important clues to the work habits and chronology of the poems. According to Franklin, "The year of composition for a poem—that is, the date of the worksheets now destroyed—may not have been the year it was transcribed onto a fascicle sheet. Some lag is to be expected, and there are examples to suggest it...."[5] "The pool of worksheets from which she was selecting poems for the fascicles may, thus, have had a range of dates greater than the year in which she was copying poems. On the other hand, the infrequency of such repetition and the lack of worksheets for poems during the years continuously covered by the fascicle sheets, through the mid-1860s, suggest that her copying was systematic and may have kept up fairly well with her poetic production."[6]

Cody speculates further that Dickinson's psychosis probably began in the fall of 1861—the "terror" she described to Higginson—or even as early at 1857.[7] However, if the breakdown began then and ran its course until 1864, how is it possible that Dickinson wrote the poems she did at the height of the crisis years? "A large percent of Emily Dickinson's poems could not have been written at the time the poet was living through the circumstances they depict. Obviously, a person depressed to the point of immobility, or one whose thought processes are unable to follow a rational sequence, cannot write a coherent poem. Emily Dickinson's poems are, almost without exception, perfectly coherent. Therefore, the poems evoked by her illness must largely have been written in retrospect."[8]

The forty fascicles, as compiled and ordered by the poet between 1858 and 1864 and recently reassembled by Franklin, contradict this assumption. If we take several poems Cody uses to describe the sequence of Dickinson's illness, poems like "The First Day's Night" or "The Soul has Bandaged Moments," we find that the evidence of the fascicles dates these poems in early 1862 (which means the poems may have been written earlier, although not later than 1862). How is it possible that Dickinson, undergoing a violent mental upheaval, would be able to clinically and objectively describe it? The fact that the poet's most intense experiences are recorded in fascicles 15, 16, and 17 and gathered in 1862 brings into question Cody's premise that her poems were written after the experience. It is more likely that the poems were written at the same time. The evidence of the chronology must be considered, especially in light of Franklin's reconstruction.

The second problem is Cody's belief that the poet suffered a psychosis.[9] It can logically be argued that Dickinson was neurotic rather than psychotic. Cody addresses this issue in a footnote: "It is useful to think of the various 'neuroses' and 'psychoses,' including the many 'schizophrenic' subgroups, not as fixed states, but as representing points on a continuum from a hypothetical completely 'normal' extreme to a hypothetical completely disorganized extreme."[10] Cody places Dickinson at the furthest extreme— as completely disorganized. Yet looking at the evidence of the fascicles, we note that it was precisely during this time from 1858 to 1864, when Cody believes the poet was in a state of nervous collapse, that Dickinson bound her work together. "With the annus mirabilis of 1862 her practice became regular. . . . Emily Dickinson may have stopped binding because, once she had survived the crisis and drive of 1861–63, her need for self-publication declined."[11] Thus, according to Franklin, the fascicle making shows that rather than experiencing a "reason-disrupting, prostrating psychosis" as Cody believes,[12] Dickinson was instead organizing her work in her own private act of "publication."[13] Richard Sewall finds scant evidence in the poet's letters or in family records to support the hypothesis of her breakdown but is struck instead by "how firmly she kept her faculties under control during" this time.[14]

Before Cody, critic Clark Griffith psychoanalyzed the poet, looking for the secret of Dickinson's seclusion in her poetry. He dismisses a secret romance as the cause of Dickinson's behavior because "the affair fails to square with much of what she wrote,"[15] Instead he attributes the poet's retreat and tragic outlook to personal and metaphysical causes: the fact that Dickinson felt spurned by God was a result of Dickinson's "child-parent relationship."[16] Griffith blames her "cold and forbidding father"[17] for the poet's desire to withdraw and hide herself from public view. "Out of these relations, I believe, there emerged the warped notions of God and man, the morbid idea of a masculine Nature, the deep distrust of love and marriage, and the neurotic spinsterism, all of which are among the ubiquitous features of Emily Dickinson's later life and poetry."[18] Like Cody, Griffith ignores chronology, finding "few marked year to year variations in techniques or idea."[19]

As a "poet of dread," Griffith writes that Dickinson was a "recorder of nervous fears"[20] and that she "wrote poetry in order to gain relief from great personal tensions," that her "only solace" came "from the sheer magic of creativity."[21] He believes that the poems "fathom the last thirty years of Emily Dickinson's life"[22] and that these "letters to the world" are "likewise. . . her explanation."[23] However, his belief that Dickinson's "quest to shed a public identity" was "predominant in the poet's need for seclusion"[24] has to be reconsidered. This position, more directly stated by Thomas Johnson among others and espoused by contemporary feminist critics, maintains that the poet voluntarily withdrew from life and that her isolation was by choice. "The home in which Emily was born she elected to make in a physical sense exclusively her life."[25] However, this position is deceptive and leads to a misinterpretation of Dickinson's life.

The overemphasis on the life of Dickinson and its secrets has led critics to distrust biographical studies. In her recent study *Emily Dickinson*, Cynthia Wolff urges readers "to dispel the melodramatic aura that has attended so many accounts of...Dickinson's life"[26] and to focus on "that Voice of the verse, for it was in her poetry and not in the world that...Dickinson deliberately decided to 'live.'"[27] Yet before turning to the poetry, Wolff herself succumbs to the biographical (and psychoanalytical) temptation, claiming that it was the failure of Dickinson's early relationship with her mother that prompted her " 'Fall into Language,' verbal discourse seeming a second-best alternative to some other, loosely defined, transcendent intimacy."[28]

Earlier, David Porter argued that "biographical inquiry based on the poems... is unsubstantial business." Although this type of study is "irresistible," "the root of the fallacy is the seemingly ineradicable belief still fostered in literary study that most poetry is essentially an expression of the poet's emotions."[29] Quoting Dickinson, "When I state myself as the Representative of the Verse, it does not mean—me—but—a supposed person,"[30] Porter points out that "Dickinson lived in the primacy of the written word not just as any poet...but in the extreme state created when she took the words inside to live with her, away from reality, and made them perform in her deliberate handwriting on odd shapes of paper."[31] Thus for Porter, Dickinson's poetry is "performance," "demonstration," disconnected from the life of the poet. "She disengaged poetry from the complicated network of exterior existence, making the art self-conscious, private, momentary."[32] "Highly personal it [the poetry] drew on no authority outside its immediate ends"—"the 1775 brief poems written through all those years face one another closed and independent, subject to no other family claims or the check of a comprehensible philosophy."[33]

To envision the poet as Porter does—a caged bird singing in a language unrelated to reality—is difficult. The poetry is not a "parable of incomprehension" as he claims. Thought is representative. It is the emotion at the root of the words that animates them. Without that spark or current of feeling, the words lie limp on the page, a brilliant alphabet meaning nothing. Whether as readers we reach into our own experience or delve into the mysteries of Dickinson's life, the words take on life. This is why scholars continue to confront what Porter calls "the biographical fallacy"[34] and to search for the literal and emotional connections that make the words discover meaning. Although the poet was a recluse, she did not live in a vacuum. Withdrawn from the outside world, she participated in its activities through her family, her reading, and her correspondence. Sewall urges readers to change their "usual notion of" Dickinson as someone isolated from the world. "It is not right to think of her as detached from the affairs of the nation and the world. She was a devoted reader of magazines, and it is said that she never missed a day of *The Springfield Republican*, Bowle's paper. One of her surest ways of keeping in touch with the world was through her more adventurous friends."[35]

Dickinson was involved in the fabric of a larger life that she reflected in her poetry. Brilliant demonstration though her poems are, they are the product of a controlling artistic voice. The privacy with which personal details were treated in her lifetime and within her own family necessitated her statement that the person speaking was not herself. In his essay "Art and Neurosis," Lionel Trilling writes that "the more a writer takes pains with his work to remove it from the personal and subjective, the more—and not the less—he will express his true unconscious."[36] Cody also wonders if "even a poet ... can portray a feeling state that he has not himself undergone. And if one grants that this is possible, what could possibly motivate a person to attempt to express what he never felt?"[37] Higginson's comment that "almost all these poems are strangely impersonal"[38] does not dismiss the fact that these poems sprang from various circumstances or events in the poet's life. They are gnomic only insofar as we do not perceive their roots. Even though the life is "opaque" and the "door" to Dickinson's life "as tightly closed upon herself as ever it was closed in the upstairs bedroom,"[39] we cannot turn our backs on "the only alternative route" into "the poet's mind."[40] Dickinson's poems have a larger context that clarifies them and allows the reader to see the poet "at the White Heat"[41] when life becomes art.

Trilling's essay is one of numerous studies that probe the connection between neurosis—or what might have been called madness in an earlier day—and creativity. Interest in this connection, according to Trilling, goes back to the nineteenth century and the "beginning of the Romantic Movement."[42] What is the relation between mental health and the creative process? What influence does it have on achievement? *Creative Malady*, a study of such famous men and women as Charles Darwin and Florence Nightingale, questions the role that illness played in their lives. Charles Darwin became a recluse within two years of his famous *Beagle* voyage; Florence Nightingale, a recognized heroine at thirty-six, became an invalid a year after her work in the Crimea. In each instance, author George Pickering finds "a psychological illness with a purpose":[43] "It became evident to me that an illness that is not debilitating or disabling, or threatening to life, may provide the ideal circumstances for creative work."[44] Psychological illness "develops to meet a need in a particular set of circumstances and so long as those remain more or less stable, the illness does its job."[45] Trilling came to a similar conclusion, emphasizing that the one part of the artist "that is healthy, ... is that which gives him the power to conceive, plan, to work, and to bring his work to a conclusion."[46]

The House without the Door is a new synthesis, a reevaluation of the only certain information we have, the letters and the poems. It theorizes that Dickinson was reclusive due to an agoraphobic syndrome that left her in fear of the outside world. Although the terms *phobic* and *agoraphobic* have been used to describe the poet before, there has been no extended study of the impact of the illness on her life and poetry. Two factors make such a study possible today: one is the publication of Franklin's *The Manuscript Books of Emily Dickinson*, which permits a close look at the fascicles, and the other is the availability and accessibility of information about agoraphobia.

By juxtaposing the medical facts of agoraphobia with the poet's life, we see how the agoraphobic syndrome affected Dickinson's life-style, how she changed from a normal, outgoing person to someone afraid to leave the "safe" confines of her father's house. Turning to representative poems within the fascicles, we find the record of that life: the grip of fear, the pattern of flight, and the habit of denial. In selected fascicles written during the critical year 1862, we come face to face with the poet's psychic torment: the terror of panic attack with its accompanying fears of madness and death. We trace the course of agoraphobia as the poet becomes more isolated, depressed, and ultimately calcified into her life-style. The poems not only reveal the seriousness of Dickinson's disorder, but also how the act of composition was therapeutic, releasing her from a life that would otherwise have been impossible to live.

This study does not — and cannot — answer all the questions raised by the poet's life, nor does it intend to. For a poet as rich and complex as Dickinson should never be reduced to a simple formula or portrayed as someone "who did nothing but one joyless thing over and over again."[47] As in all attempts to explain the poet and her work, no matter how rooted in facts, there is always the danger of subjectivity. Given this caveat, I propose another answer to the life and work of Emily Dickinson, one more solution to the riddle at the heart of Dickinson scholarship. Jay Leyda writes that "the worthiest aim for all Dickinson scholarship of the future is to make it easier for her poetry to speak directly and freshly to every reader."[48] A study of the nature of agoraphobia with panic attack that correlates its symptoms, causes, and effects with the life and work of the poet will empower the poetry to speak more "directly and freshly" to us.

Acknowledgments

> but sweeter yet
> The still small voice of gratitude.
>
> — "Ode for Music" (1769)

Thomas Gray's observation rings true, but in my own experience the voice is neither still nor small. It is loud and resonant, reminding me of the many to whom I am grateful. These include my friend and teacher Merrill Skaggs who showed me many years ago how to begin with a grain of sand and build it into pearl. She has guided and encouraged me with her gentle and steady strength. Dr. John Cody, whose work I admire and respect, has become a friend whose opinion I value and trust. His support and encouragement have been invaluable. Harry Keyishian at Fairleigh Dickinson believed in the work and was willing to give it a chance. Editors Beth Gianfagna and Lauren Lepow worked conscientiously to make the manuscript the best it could be. My college administrators and committees helped me complete my work by granting me first a leave and then a sabbatical. The library's loan facilities, under the able guidance of Georgia Hefnawy, Reference Librarian, and her staff offered immeasurable assistance. Drew University library gave me carrel space and special consideration. Union College helped with their word processing facilities. My colleagues in the English Department sustained me with their interest and concern. My friend and colleague in the discipline of psychology, Marge Gelfond, willingly shared her research and her enthusiasm. Pat Wahl helped prepare the manuscript.

Finally—the most important of all—my family for their belief in me, for their patient understanding, and their day-to-day, month-to-month, year-to-year endurance. To my mother who has never wavered in her support, to my daughters Toni and Lara whose joy never dulled, and last but never least, to the man without whose constancy of love and generosity of spirit I would not have been able to persist—my husband Charles. To these and any I have inadvertently omitted, my sincere thanks.

I would like to acknowledge the following for graciously granting permission to reprint previously published material:

Reprinted by permission of the publishers and the Trustees of Amherst College from *The Poems of Emily Dickinson*, edited by Thomas H. Johnson,

23

The House
without the Door

1

The Impression: "An Excess of Tension and an Abnormal Life"

It was with great curiosity and expectation that Thomas Wentworth Higginson, a visiting editor from Boston's prestigious *Atlantic Monthly*, arrived at the large brick country house of Emily Dickinson. As he waited in the "parlor dark and cool and stiffish"[1] on this August afternoon in 1870, he wondered about his enigmatic correspondent, a woman who described herself as "small, like the Wren" with "eyes like the Sherry in the Glass, that the Guest leaves."[2] During their eight year correspondence, she had sent him many examples of her poetry, which he read but never suggested she publish. In fact, he advised her to delay publication, to which she responded that the idea was as "foreign to my thought as Firmament to Fin."[3] Calling him her Preceptor and signing herself "Your Scholar," she asked simply to be taught. "I had no Monarch in my life and cannot rule myself" she confided, "and when I try to organize — my little Force explodes — and leaves me bare and charred — ."[4]

As Higginson waited, the stage was set for one of the most dramatic encounters in literary history. When the poet finally arrived, he was not disappointed. Let Higginson himself tell us what happened: "A step like a pattering child's in entry & in glided a little plain woman with two smooth bands of reddish hair & a face a little like Belle Dove's; not plainer — with no good feature — in a very plain & exquisitely clean white pique & a blue net worsted shawl. She came to me with two day lilies which she put in a sort of childlike way into my hand & said 'These are my introduction' in a soft frightened breathless childlike voice — & added under her breath Forgive me if I am frightened; I never see strangers & hardly know what I say — but she talked soon & thenceforward continuously — & deferentially — sometimes stopping to ask me to talk instead of her — but readily recommencing."[5]

The brief interview that follows does not disappoint contemporary onlookers. In an article published twenty-one years after the event, Higginson recalls how he sat back and listened to the poet whose "quaint and aphoristic" speech was studded with "phrases so emphasized as to seem the very wantonness of overstatement, as if she pleased herself with putting into words

27

what the most extravagant might possibly think without saying."[6]

The scene resonates in the reader's imagination, helping to construct the myth that towers over the life of Dickinson. Curiously Higginson does not narrate the second, more recent meeting only eighteen years earlier, but dismisses it by saying, "I have no express record of the visit." The reason may be inferred from his description of the poet to his sisters as my "eccentric poetess in Amherst" and to his wife's remark to him, "Oh why do the insane so cling to you?"[7]

Higginson undoubtedly believed that Dickinson was better kept at a distance. In a letter to his wife written the night of his first meeting with the poet, he admitted he had never been with anyone "who drained my nerve power so much. Without touching her, she drew from me. I am glad not to live near her."[8] In an article written six years after the poet's death, Higginson concludes that the poet was "too enigmatical a being for me to solve in an hour's interview" and that he felt if he tried to question her she would "withdraw into her shell."[9]

Higginson would never forget this meeting: his detailed memory of the poet, remarkably intact after twenty years, attests to the impact it had. His impression that Dickinson was suffering from "an excess of tension" created by "an abnormal life"[10] was partially correct. Indeed Dickinson's condition at the time of their meeting would be described today as an anxiety state or, more specifically, as a generalized anxiety disorder. All the signs were present: "These patients act as if they are continually prepared to run, and display marked motor tension, autonomic hyperactivity, apprehensive expectation, and constant vigilance."[11]

However, it was not the poet's seclusion that had caused this tension. Her chronic apprehension was part of a larger emotional disorder that in fact created Dickinson's abnormal life-style. Higginson could not have known at the time that what he was witnessing in the "tremulous, tense, and keyed up"[12] Miss Dickinson was the presence of an illness that would force her to restrict her activities more and more through the years until she became a virtual prisoner in her home. This chronic anxiety, coupled with the poet's fear of going beyond her father's house, would be diagnosed today as a severe agoraphobic syndrome. It is to this debilitating emotional disorder we must turn to explain Dickinson's abnormal life.

By the time Emily Dickinson had begun to write to Thomas Wentworth Higginson, she was almost completely housebound. In her letters, she had alluded to her seclusion and had written, " 'Of shunning Men and Women' — they talk of Hallowed things aloud — and embarrass my Dog."[13] Higginson's curiosity piqued, he was anxious to meet this unusual woman and wrote in June 1869, "I have the greatest desire to see you. I think if I could once see you and know that you are real, I might fare better."[14]

Several times during their correspondence Higginson had invited her to Boston. "All ladies do" he had written, suggesting it was a proper excursion for literary women.[15] But each time, his invitation was refused. "Father objects because he is in the habit of me."[16] In June 1869, Dickinson invited Higginson to Amherst because "I do not cross my Father's ground to any House or town."[17] Intrigued by her sequestered life-style and curious to know more, Higginson planned a visit. Just before his visit, he wrote: "It is hard (for me) to understand how you can live so alone, with thoughts of such quality coming up in you."[18] At this point, Dickinson was forty years old and had not left her house for five years. Her last trip had been to Boston in 1865 to consult a prominent physician, who had treated her for a recurrent eye problem. But since that time she had remained in her house enshrouded as Higginson described in a "fiery mist."[19]

If it were possible for Higginson to know about the illness of agoraphobia, he would have recognized that Dickinson's inability to leave home was a primary symptom of this complex and debilitating disease. When Dickinson first felt the effects of agoraphobia in the 1850s, it was still more than fifteen years before the illness would be clinically identified. It was not until 1872 that Dr. C. Westphal first published his monograph detailing the illness in the case histories of three male patients. He named it *Die Agoraphobie* and described the classic outlines of the disease: "the impossibility of walking through certain streets or squares, or possibility of doing so only with resultant dread of anxiety . . . no loss of consciousness . . . vertigo was excluded by all patients . . . no hallucinations or delusions to cause this strange fear . . . agony was much increased at those hours where the particular streets dreaded were deserted and the shops closed. The patients experienced great comfort from the companionship of men or even an inanimate object, such as a vehicle or a cane."[20]

Before Westphal, Dr. M. Benedikt had described the same illness calling it *Platzschwindel* or dizziness in public places after one of its physiological symptoms. Rather than emphasizing the physical manifestations of the illness, Westphal's term more clearly describes the activating mechanism of the disease—the fear that is "the primary element in the psychopathology" of the syndrome.[21]

Certainly fears and their avoidance were not new phenomena in the nineteenth century. Descriptions of fears can be traced back to "the morbid condition of Nicanor" who "as soon as he heard the first note of the flute at a banquet . . . would be beset by terror," or to Damocles, who "could not go near a precipice, or over a bridge, or beside even the shallowest ditch."[22] The term *phobia* itself was coined in the first century by Celsus, a Roman encyclopedist, who used the word in *hydrophobia*—a fear of water—to denote a symptom of rabies.[23]

Robert Burton's treatise *Anatomy of Melancholy* (1621) includes one of the most accurate descriptions of phobias. In it he distinguishes normal fears from such excessive conditions as agoraphobia and claustrophobia:[24]

"Montanus speaks of one that durst not walk alone from home, for fear he should swoon or die. ... If he be locked in a close room, he is afraid of being stifled for want of air, and still carries bisket, aquavitae, or some strong waters about him, for fear of deliquiums, or being sick, or if he be in a throng, middle of — church, multitude, where he may not well get out, though he sit at ease, he is so misaffected."[25]

If Dickinson read Burton, she might have recognized her own condition. But even though these nameless phobias were known to exist, there was no understanding of their extent or of the victim's disability. Burton realizes this and responds to the harsh criticism borne by phobics: "take away the cause; and otherwise counsel can do little good: you may as well bid him that is sick of an ague, not to be adry, or him that is wounded, not to feel pain."[26]

If Dickinson did recognize her condition, it would have brought her little relief, for it was not until the end of the nineteenth century that the term *agoraphobia* began to appear in psychiatric studies, and it was well into the twentieth century before research would provide greater understanding of the disorder and successful methods of treatment. Indeed if Dickinson had sought medical advice, it is improbable that she would have been correctly diagnosed, for even today the chances of misdiagnosis are great. Although "an estimated one million persons in the United States" have agoraphobia, the illness is "rarely diagnosed" because "many physicians, including psychiatrists, do not know what agoraphobia is."[27] "Unfortunately in American psychiatry such symptoms are frequently misdiagnosed as signs of incipient psychosis...."[28] Because the illness incorporates such a broad range of symptoms, it often produces a "diagnostic chaos" where "attempts to arrive at a consensus between dissenting diagnosticians would result in a fence-straddling label, e.g. severe mixed psychoneurosis or pseudoneurotic schizophrenia, a borderline state."[29]

This diagnostic confusion is reflected in the various names given to the disease. Through the years it has been called *peur d'espace* (fear of space), *horreur du vide* (dread of empty space), *locomotor anxiety*, *anxiety hysteria*, *street fear, anxiety syndrome*, or *phobic anxious state*. In 1871, it might have been known as *Da Costa's syndrome*, which included anxiety and panic attacks and was common after World War I; it was also termed *soldier's heart* or *cardiac neurosis*.[30] Most recently, it has been called *phobic anxiety depersonalization syndrome* and *endogenous phobic anxiety*.

In light of Cody's thesis that Dickinson suffered a psychosis, the following statement is particularly noteworthy: "It is not uncommon for these patients to be labelled schizophrenic. This diagnosis seems to rest on their pervasive anxiety (pan-anxiety) and their mixture of phobic, hypochondriacal, obsessive and addictive traits (pan-neurosis). The patient's fixed phobic refusal to travel alone may be interpreted as a delusional or paranoid mechanism."[31]

Psychologist Edoardo Weiss believes that agoraphobia is a neurosis rather than a psychosis. "Although some of the frightening inner experiences of agoraphobic patients, such as feelings of derealization, estrangement, and depression, are also found in some schizophrenic patients, we do not consider agoraphobia to be a psychotic affliction."[32] A recent article supports this point: "Agoraphobia is not due to a major depressive episode, obsessive-compulsive disorder, paranoid personality disorder, or schizophrenia."[33]

Despite authoritative medical testimony, there are documented cases of agoraphobics who are misdiagnosed and institutionalized for their symptoms. One agoraphobe complained, "I wasn't neurotic. I wasn't schizophrenic. I wasn't any of the things I had been labeled. I had panic disorder, which led to agoraphobia and a fear of a whole lot of things."[34] In another instance a patient was "referred" to the "psychiatric department of a local hospital" where he was asked if he heard voices. When the patient realized he was misunderstood, he told the physicians that he felt better. "This resulted in his being discharged as cured, despite the fact that a correct diagnosis was not made and his symptoms were unrelieved."[35] Dickinson herself suffered from the fear of madness, as is reflected in poems written in the early 1860s when she was undergoing a severe emotional disturbance. In a letter probably written in 1861, the poet makes light of losing her sanity: "Think Emily lost her wits — but she found 'em likely. Don't part with wits long at a time in this neighborhood."[36] Although she appears to be facetious, she may be saying that it is necessary to maintain the appearance of sanity for fear of censure or malicious gossip. It is to be remembered that in May 1859 Edward Dickinson was made "trustee of the lunatic hospital at Northhampton,"[37] and that earlier, in 1853, he had defended Mr. Eastman against divorce charges brought by his wife Prudence. In the case, lawyer Dickinson proposed that Mrs. Eastman was insane by "showing that the lady was at times greatly excited, and would talk rapidly and shed tears profusely...."[38]

Before the 1970s, agoraphobia was not easily identified as a "discrete syndrome"; when "patients did seek treatment, they were treated for other syndromes."[39] However since the late 1970s and early 1980s, a period of intensive research has yielded a more comprehensive and clearly delineated description of the illness. Today interest in anxiety disorders, especially panic attack, is "burgeoning."[40] A search of the files of *Psychology Abstracts* reveals that ninety-three articles appeared on the subject in the 1970s as compared to only eight in the last three years of the 1960s. Already in the first three years of the 1980s, there have been forty-four titles.[41] As a result of this increased research, the illness has been "more reliably diagnosed and successfully treated" and has received much attention from the media.[42] In 1981, agoraphobia earned its own heading in the American Psychiatric Association's *Diagnostic and Statistical Manual*. Known simply as the *DSM*

III, this handbook defines the illness and details its primary symptomatology to facilitate clinical diagnosis as well as to distinguish it from other disorders with which it may be confused.

What is agoraphobia and what are its symptoms? A description of agoraphobia is found under the general heading of "Anxiety Disorders." Categorized under phobic disorders, agoraphobia is distinguished from two other types of phobias: social phobias, in which the victim avoids situations, such as eating or speaking in public, where he or she "may be exposed to scrutiny by others"; and simple phobias where there is "a persistent, irrational fear of and compelling desire to avoid" an object, such as particular animal, or a situation, such as heights.[43] What distinguishes both a simple and social phobia from agoraphobia is that both involve a particular "circumscribed stimulus" and usually begin early in life, whereas agoraphobia, "the most severe and pervasive form" of phobic disorder, represents a complex of fears that begins at a later age.

In agoraphobia the "essential feature is a marked fear of being alone, or being in public places from which escape might be difficult or help not available in case of sudden incapacitation. Normal activities are increasingly constricted as fears or avoidance behavior dominate the individual's life. The most common situation avoided involves being in crowds, such as on a busy street or in crowded stores, or being in tunnels, or bridges, or elevators, or on public transportation. Often agoraphobes insist that family members or friends accompany them whenever they leave home."[44]

Although the *DSM* III distinguishes between two types of agoraphobia —one with panic attack and one without—agoraphobia with panics is more commonly found and as such has been called panic phobia.[45] The presence of panic attacks further complicates the disorder, making it one of the most difficult to treat, for each new panic episode sends its patient deeper into distress and renders him or her more fearful. In fact, the "principal" fear of sufferers is not the situation of being out of doors or in public places, but rather the fear of panic attack and its fantasized consequences.

While the term *agoraphobia* denotes a broad category of behaviors, Isaac Marks warns that the word falls short of a true description of the illness.[46] While at its most basic level the term can denote a patient's fear of leaving the house, it is overutilized in that it selects only one particular symptom to describe the illness. However, in more serious cases, the word describes "not only agoraphobia and the other phobias, but also panic attack, depression, depersonalization, obsession, and other symptoms."[47] In this case, the term is "underinclusive" and has limitations, only presenting part of the entire clinical picture.

Thus the label agoraphobia can be misleading, creating unnecessary "confusion about the syndrome." "While the literal translation would be fear of the marketplace and the dictionary definition is 'fear of open spaces,' these are only a fraction of situations agoraphobics fear."[48] It is more accurate to see the term as representing a "constellation of clinical events in a cluster of features which at the same time merges imperceptibly with anxiety states, affection disorders, even obsessive-neuroses."[49] Although the phobias center on going into public, they are accompanied by "non-phobic symptoms such as free-floating anxiety, mild depression, depersonalization, and mild obsessive-compulsion."[50]

Dr. Alan Goldstein of the Temple University Medical School warns that although the current *DSM* classifies various anxiety disorders of which agoraphobia is one, these "categories were never meant to be mutually exclusive." It is rare, Goldstein continues, that an agoraphobe "does not have other problems and characterological disorders," and "these attendant difficulties predispose to the development of agoraphobia and interact with the agoraphobic symptoms."[51]

2
"My Life Was Made a Victim"

Research into agoraphobia reveals that the disorder "begins in late adolescence or early adult life."[1] The age range is between eighteen and thirty-five, with the mean age of onset at twenty-four.[2] It occurs at this particular time because then the individual is moving from a state of dependence to one of independence and autonomy. During this transitional stage between late adolescence and adulthood those individuals who are untrained and inexperienced to cope with new adult demands may begin to show signs of agoraphobia and shrink back from responsibilities into a continued need for dependence.[3] While the illness rarely begins in childhood, some researchers believe that these subjects have suffered phobic symptoms earlier and that their agoraphobia may be related to childhood school phobia and separation anxiety. Some doctors see agoraphobia as another form of separation disorder.

But how does agoraphobia begin? According to the *DSM* III, "the initial phase consists of recurrent panic attacks."[4] In fact, since panic attacks are "almost always" present, some doctors see agoraphobia as "synonymous with acute and/or periodic panic attacks."[5] A recent study team concluded that "panic disorder and agoraphobia with panic attacks are not separate entities, but are slightly different presentations of a broader disorder."[6] The panic attack is described as "the sudden onset of intense apprehension, fear, or terror, often associated with feelings of impending doom. The most common symptoms experienced during an attack are dyspnea [shortness of breath], palpitations, chest pain or discomfort, choking or smothering sensations, dizziness, vertigo, or unsteady feelings, feelings of unreality, parenthesias [tingling sensation], hot and cold flashes, sweating, faintness, trembling or shaking, and fear of dying, going crazy, or doing something uncontrolled during the attack. Attacks usually last minutes, more rarely hours."[7]

In a recent article, Dr. David Sheehan, a research psychiatrist, traces the longitudinal progress of the illness. He outlines seven stages, which begin with subpanic symptoms, are followed by panic attack, and end with polyphobic behavior and depression.[8] Sheehan explains that in the beginning the patient will have "sudden episodes of isolated symptoms short of panic before the full-blown panic attack" occurs.

Turning to the life of Emily Dickinson, we see that as a young woman she was active and outgoing, involved in a life of social activities — "the last week has been a merry one in Amherst."[9] In her early twenties and before, Dickinson enjoyed visiting her friends. However, as early as February 1852 social anxieties begin to intrude. On this occasion, Dickinson leaves a note at Emily Fowler's door: "You will have read this quite, by the time I reach the office, and you can't think how fast I run."[10] This may not seem peculiar at first, but if we add another letter written a year later, we see that Dickinson's behavior was becoming unusual. Again to her friend Emily she writes, "I come and see you a great many times every day, though I don't bring my body." She continues "I love to come just as dearly, for nobody sees me then, and I sit and chat away, and look up in your face, and no matter who calls, if it's 'my Lord the King,' he doesn't interrupt me."[11]

By June 1853 a stronger social phobia takes hold, and we witness what Sheehan calls subpanic symptoms. In a letter to Austin, she tells of a memorable day in Amherst — the celebration of the inauguration of the Amherst and Belchertown Railroad. She speaks of the grand occasion and of her father who was "as usual, Chief Marshal of the day, and went marching around the town with New London at his heels like some Roman General, upon a Triumph Day."[12] In sharp contrast to her father's visibility, she describes herself: "I sat in Prof. Tyler's woods and saw the train move off, and then ran home again for fear somebody would see me, or ask me how I did." Dickinson is almost twenty-three at the time, not a young child, and yet she shrinks from social contact as well as from the fear of being seen.

The next sign of her developing agoraphobia is a dramatic one. The episode occurred six months after her flight from Professor Tyler's woods and shows that her social phobias were intensifying. In abundant detail Dickinson writes to Sue Gilbert to tell her that "my life was made a victim."[13] In the letter Dickinson documents her first terrifying panic attack:

> I'm just from meeting, Susie, and as I sorely feared, my 'life' was made a 'victim.' I walked — I ran — I turned precarious corners — One moment I was not — then soared aloft like Phoenix, soon as the foe was by — and then anticipating an enemy again, my soiled and drooping plumage might have been seen emerging from just behind a fence, vainly endeavoring to fly once more from hence. I reached the steps, dear Susie — and smiled to think of me, and my geometry, during the journey there — It would have puzzled Euclid, and it's doubtful result, have solemnized a Day. How big and broad the aisle seemed, full huge enough before, as I quaked slowly up — and reached my usual seat!
>
> In vain I sought to hide behind your feathers — Susie — feathers and Bird had flown, and there I sat, and sighed, and wondered I was scared so, for surely in the whole world was nothing I need to fear — Yet there the Phantom was, and though I kept resolving to be as brave as Turks, and bold as Polar Bears, it did'nt help me any. After the opening prayer I

ventured to turn around. Mr. Carter immediately looked at me—Mr. Sweetser attempted to do so, but I discovered nothing, up in the sky somewhere, and gazed intently at it, for quite a half an hour. During the exercises I became more calm, and got out of church quite comfortably. Several roared around me, and, sought to devour me, but I fell an easy prey to Miss Lovinia Dickinson, being too much exhausted to make any farther resistance.

    She entertained me with much sprightly remark, until our gate was reached, and I need'nt tell you Susie, just how I clutched the latch, and whirled the merry key, and fairly danced for joy, to find myself at home! How I did wish for you—how, for my own dear Vinnie—how for Goliah, or Samson—to pull the whole church down, requesting Mr. Dwight to step into Miss Kingsbury's, until the dust was past!

All the telltale signs are there: the sudden apprehension of fear, the overwhelming panic arising from no apparent cause, trembling, and an urgency to run and hide. The attack appears to last less than an hour, beginning on her way to church and continuing as she made her way to her seat, lessening during the services, only to impel her home to safety. The panic attack is horrifying to its victim. Since it appears suddenly and out of the blue—seemingly unrelated to the victim's life—the individual develops "an anticipatory fear of helplessness or loss of control during a panic attack."[14] Thus the patient develops what has been called "a fear of fear," which in reality is the fear of a recurrence of the attack with its attendant somatic and cognitive symptoms. Overwhelmed by the attack, the individual tries to insure that the attack will never occur again and avoids the setting in which the panic first occurred. Thus, a pattern of avoidance begins that is in actuality a secondary conditioning, since the primary conditioning is to the patient's reaction to his or her own fear.

    Current research suggests that a pattern of avoidant behavior is "tightly linked in time" to the panic attack and begins within six months of the episode.[15] Dickinson's behavior falls precisely into this range, for within a few months Dickinson goes to church five minutes early "so as not to have to go in after all the people get there."[16] On several occasions, she chooses not to go to church—for one reason or another. "I am sick today ... and have not been to church."[17] On one specific occasion Lavinia recalled that Emily "suddenly disappeared" when urged by her father to go to church. "No one could tell where she was. They hunted high and low, and went to church without her. Some hours after, Emily was discovered calmly rocking in a chair placed in the cellar bulk-head, where she had old Margaret lock her in before church."[18]

    Dickinson's avoidant behavior begins to generalize. Not only does she avoid crowded church services, but her fears extend to other places where she feels she will be "impeded from immediately returning to a 'safe' place."[19] When her family travels to Washington in April 1854, Emily refuses to go, and although her father wants her to go, he writes to Austin, "I will not insist upon her coming."[20] While the family is away, Susan Gilbert stays with Emily and writes to a friend, "I am keeping house with Emily while the family are in Washington. We frighten each other to death nearly every night."[21] We sense the timidity of the two lone ladies as well as the contagiousness of Dickinson's fears.

Dickinson's reluctance to leave the house continues to grow, even to the extent that she refuses invitations to visit friends. When in August 1854 her close friend Abby Root asks her to come, Dickinson reveals her growing limitations: "I thank you Abiah, but I don't go from home, unless emergency leads me by the hand, and then I do it obstinately, and draw back if I can. Should I ever leave home, which is improbable, I will with much delight, accept your invitation."[22] Dickinson, who is only twenty-three at the time, calls herself "old-fashioned" and says "that all your friends would stare," showing her fears of being looked at.

Already by the end of 1854, her friends are puzzled by her behavior and fearful that she is misunderstood. Eliza Coleman remarks to John Graves that "I know you appreciate her and I think few of her Amherst friends do. They wholly misinterpret her, I believe."[23]

The course of development of agoraphobia is known to "fluctuate markedly." "Within a given month, agoraphobes may vary from being totally housebound to being almost asymptomatic."[24] Thus while Dickinson was reluctant to leave home after the attack of January 1854, she visits the Hollands in September of that same year. In February 1855 she accompanies Lavinia on a trip to Washington but in a letter home admits her discomfort with people: "I have not been well since I came here, and that has excused me from some of the gaities, tho' at that, I'm gayer than I was before."[25] Her trip lasts five weeks and takes her from Washington to Philadelphia. One month after her return, Edward Dickinson buys the house that was once owned by his father, and plans are made for the move.

Jean Mudge suggests that this move was traumatic for Dickinson. In the first half of a letter sent to the Hollands immediately following the move, Dickinson paints a charming portrait of a state of disarray that prompts some verbal play: "They say that 'home is where the heart is.' I think it is where the house is."[26] However, the darker side of the move appears later in the letter: Mrs. Dickinson "has been an invalid since we came home ... I don't know what a sickness is, for I am a simple child, and frightened at myself."

The mother's illness places more responsibilities on Emily and leaves her excessively anxious. She tries to avoid the stressful situation by wishing she were "a grass, or a toddling daisy, whom all these problems of the dust might not terrify." She signs herself "your mad Emilie." Mrs. Dickinson's illness would last for four long years, giving the poet another reason for not leaving home. In 1858 Dickinson tells Mrs. Havens she would visit if she "could . . . leave home, or mother. I do not go out at all, lest father will come and miss me, or miss some little act, which I might forget, should I run away."[27]

This martyrdom to her family recalls a younger Dickinson who told friend Abby Root in 1850 that she refused a ride with a friend "I love so dearly" to stay home to care for a sick mother. "Oh I struggled with great temptation, and it cost me much of denial but I think in the end I conquered." However, when her mother went to sleep, she "cried with all my might."[28] Dickinson, in choosing to follow this path of dutiful obedience, feels much abused but later in life will begin to feel indispensable.

Her mother's prolonged illness after the move strained Dickinson's health. In a letter written in the summer of 1858, two years after the mother's illness began, Dickinson reveals that her worries have disorganized and depressed her. "Much has occurred, dear Uncle, since writing you—so much that I stagger as I write, in its sharp remembrance. . . . Today has been so glad without, and yet so grieved within—so jolly, shone the sun—and now the moon comes stealing, and yet it makes none glad. I cannot always see the light—please tell me if it shines . . . I hardly know what I have said—my words put all their feathers on—fluttered here and there."[29]

Not only is Dickinson fearful of leaving home, but she is also fearful of people coming into her home. In her letters, Dickinson refers to her habit of running from people. When she asks her cousin Louise Norcross to visit in June 1858, the poet reminds her that "you are one of the ones from whom I do not run away."[30] And in February 1859 she tells Mrs. Holland that when the bell rings she runs "as is my custom."[31]

In May 1862, a month after her correspondence with Higginson begins, Dickinson describes herself in a letter to her Norcross cousins: "I remember a tree . . . when you and we were a little girl, whose leaves went topsy-turvy as often as a wind, and showed an ashen side—that's fright, that's Emily."[32] "That's fright, that's Emily" epitomizes the poet who gradually, over a period of ten years, withdrew into a seclusion that would be total by the age of thirty-five.

But if Dickinson was agoraphobic, what other characteristics confirm this disorder? According to Goldstein "what professionals generally accept as agoraphobia is in fact only the tip of an iceberg. These symptoms—fear of and avoidance of being alone in public places—from which escape might be difficult or help unavoidable begin rather late in the total sequence of events."[33] This belief encouraged Goldstein and his colleague Dr. Dianne Chambless to investigate further. The result was their identification of four elements present in the severe agoraphobic syndrome they call *complex agoraphobia*.

3

"The World Looks Staringly"

The four elements present in the severe agoraphobic syndrome called complex agoraphobia are a certain personality type, a conflict situation, an inability to identify emotion, and a fear of fear. A good deal of investigation has gone into uncovering the personality type of the agoraphobe before the onset of illness, and for the most part, there is a consensus. Most studies confirm that these people are more dependent and less assertive and that, in general, they are more anxious. They also tend to be more neurotic and more depressed than the normal population.[1] One study suggests that they tend to be "soft, passive, anxious dependent people,"[2] most of whom are immature, timid, and clinging. It has also been found that many of them have suffered childhood fears and have "marked social phobias" making them prone to hypochondriasis."[3]

Due to their timidity and social anxieties, most agoraphobics have "significant interpersonal problems." Since they have a "need to please others" and "to court approval," they become dependent and submissive rather than let people know the truth about them.[4] When they do act assertively, they are troubled by their behavior.[5]

O. Diethelm believes that agoraphobics tend to be "dutiful, reserved, with high ideals and bottled up feelings,"[6] while R. P. Snaith in his study described agoraphobes as "highly suggestible, imaginative, and sensitive. They have considerable drive, high standards of conduct and exceedingly active intelligence." However, he continues, "they have been reared soft usually by neurotic parents on one of whom they are still emotionally dependent. They attempt to take part in a competitive world without adequate preparation for living."[7]

According to W. B. Terhune, these people come from financially secure families that were able to afford good educations. However, half of them fail "to take advantage of their opportunity, mainly becasue of homesickness when they were sent away to school."[8] The majority were "reared in overprivileged environments" where they were brought up protected and soft. The phobic syndrome thus makes its appearance when these "emotionally immature" people try to "realize ... ambitions and become independent successful members of society."[9] He believes that these people live under

39

circumstances that are "extremely unsatisfactory," considering their own "desires, ambitions, basic natures and personalities," and that when they come into "contact with the dangerous realities of existence, and suffer frustration ... they regress to a childish level of adjustment."[10]

It is also recognized that the personalities of the premorbid agoraphobes can also be "normally sociable and outgoing before the phobia begins."[11] However, once the phobia begins, their personalities change and they become more dependent and fearful. Dickinson was a sociable and outgoing person during her early years. According to Mrs. Ford's recollection of her, "There was nothing of the recluse about her. She was a free talker about what interested her."[12] At Mount Holyoke, she worked hard and was successful in her courses. She also appears to have been happy in the situation she found at school, remarking in a letter to her friend Abiah Root, six weeks after she left home, that although "this is my first trial in the way of absence for any length of time in my life," she is "contented." "Things seem much more like home than I anticipated and the teachers are all very kind and affectionate to us."[13]

However, a few months later in February 1848 there is mention of homesickness, especially after her visit home. The decision that she is "not to return another year" follows soon after.[14] She tells Austin that although "all are kind to me," they are "not like home faces"; only "twenty-two weeks more and home again."

In May 1848 she tells Abby that "Father has decided not to send me to Holyoke another year," and later, "Father wishes to have me home a year, and then he will probably send me away again, where I know not."[15] We realize very quickly that her father's word is law, something she jokes about in another letter to Abby when she describes that her brother came with "orders from headquarters to bring me home at all events" when she was sick.[16] Perhaps the incessant religious zeal of Mary Lyon (founder and teacher at Mount Holyoke) had worn her down, making her wish she were home with those she loved, but in any case, after her studies were completed in August 1848, she left, never to return.

After her return home, Dickinson's tone changes. In a note to Jane Humphrey, she compains that with "Vinnie away and my hands but two"[17] her family makes too many demands on her and that they offer her no understanding. She mimics her family's response to her complaints: "mind the house — and the food — sweep if the spirits were low." What need does she have for society when the neighborhood is full? She concludes that she loves to be "surly and muggy and cross" and that it is little wonder "good angels weep and bad ones sing songs."

At nineteen, Dickinson's recalcitrance is evident. In a letter to Abby written the last day of the year (1850), she confides that she loves "to buffet the sea" and "the danger." While her friend is "learning control and firmness," she is not and is thus risking God's love: "I'm afraid he don't love me any!"[18]

Dickinson's fearfulness is also evident. In a letter she writes to Austin in October 1851, she tells him she cannot go into his empty room because she is "half afraid, and if ever I have to go, I hurry with all my might and never look behind me for I know who I should see."[19] Without Austin and Vinnie to alleviate the sobriety of the Dickinson household, the poet grows depressed and lonely. Many times she admits she is "not in a merry case"[20] or is feeling "gray and grim"[21] or not feeling well.[22] A year later, her fears increase and begin to restrict her. In a letter to Jane Humphrey, she admits she cannot leave home because something might happen to her parents and Vinnie when she is gone.[23] In the same letter she writes: "I think of the grave very often," picturing herself dead with a "little white gown on, and a snowdrop on my breast, and ... the neighbors stealing in so softly."

By twenty-two, Dickinson feels old and describes a depression that she attributes to Austin's absence: "Somehow I am lonely lately—I feel very old every day, and when morning comes and the birds sing, they don't seem to make me so happy as they used to."[24]

Added to the agoraphobe's fearfulness is what Dr. Goldstein calls the "core problem" of the syndrome—the agoraphobic's "hypersensitivity to aloneness."[25] In order to deal with this sensitivity, which Goldstein says precedes the disorder, the agoraphobe forms relationships that are "permeated with anxiety about being adequately taken care of and about the possibility of being left."[26] Aloneness to the agoraphobic is frightening and indicates a vulnerability or lack of protection provided by some stronger other. Not having such an attachment, or more usually the threat of not having it, is frequently described as "floating in space, awareness of total helplessness, and no way of doing anything about it."[27]

Dickinson's contact with people throughout her life was achieved primarily through her letters. Reviewing her correspondence with family and friends, the reader detects Dickinson's need to form close attachments. Throughout her life, because of the fear of being left alone—a fear she may well have experienced when separated early in life from a primary figure such as her mother—she attempts to attach herself to protecting figures.

Dickinson's "hypersensitivity to aloneness" is evident not only during her "first trial" at college, but also after her return home when her sister Vinnie and her friend Jane Humphrey leave for school. It is clear from the letter's imagery that separation is like death to her: "Vinnie you know is away and that I'm very lonely is too plain for me to tell you—I am alone—all alone. ...When I knew Vinnie must go I clung to you as the dearer than ever friend—but when the grave opened—and swallowed you both—I murmured."[28]

During the early 1850s before Dickinson's first panic attack, her correspondence was dominated by letters to Austin. In just three years,

1851–53, she wrote to him sixty-six times. If we apply Goldstein's hypothesis that this hypersensitivity precedes the illness of agoraphobia and examine the letters to Austin before 1854—the year of her panic attack— we see ample evidence of her loneliness and fear of being without him. The word *lonely* is repeated many times during these months. In September 1851, after a visit to see him in Boston, Dickinson writes, "We have got home, dear Austin—it is very lonely here."[29] Again in October she exclaims in the middle of her letter, "Oh I am so lonely!"[30] and a few days later writes, "I find I miss you more 'when the lamps are lighted,' and when the winds blow high and the great angry raindrops clamor against the window."[31] In a curious note to Austin written the next month (November 1851), she tells him she is so lonely that she fancies she prefers death to being without him: "How lonely it was last night when the chilly wind went down, and the clear, cold moon was shining—it seemed to me I could pack this little earthly bundle, and bidding the world Goodbye, fly away . . . and never come back again to be so lonely here. . . ."[32]

The correspondence between Emily and Sue is also abundant between October 1851 and July 1852, for at this time Sue had accepted a teaching position in Baltimore, Maryland. A look at this exchange of letters offers some unique advantages, first because it is more clearly limited in time, and second because we can watch the relationship grow from an acquaintance to a more intense friendship. Lastly since Sue was not a member of the immediate family circle yet, we can see the correspondence as representative of others of its kind in which the poet's need for love and protection involves her in overdependent relationships.

The first letter to Sue is conventional enough, with Emily's simple request not to be forgotten.[33] In her next letter, however, Emily's purported mission to alleviate Sue's concern about her sister's health becomes instead an occasion for Dickinson to express her fear of being left alone: "when the 'bold Dragon' shall bear you both (Mat and Sue) away, to live in his high mountain—and leave me here alone."[34]

As the letters progress, Dickinson's appeal for attention grows more insistent. "Oh Susie, I would nestle close to your warm heart, and never hear the wind blow, or the storm beat again. Is there any room there for me, or shall I wander away all homeless and alone?"[35] In this letter, we see Dickinson's need to depend on and be protected by Sue—in this instance from the wind and the storm, frequent sources of anxiety for Dickinson.

Again in her next letters she returns to her theme that Sue is her protection, someone from whom she gets strength: "dear Susie . . . when the world is cold, and the storm sighs e'er so piteously, I am sure of one sweet shelter, one covert from the storm!"[36] Sue is someone she can run to "and hide away from them all; here in Susie's bosom, I know is love and rest, and I never will go away."[37] So, too, Emily worries that something will happen to her friend, that she will die and Emily will be left alone. As I have noted, these are common fears of preagoraphobics and may represent a reactivation of earlier separation anxieties. "Am I sad and lone, and cannot, cannot help it? Sometimes when I do feel so, I think it may be wrong, and that God will punish me by taking you away."[38]

As Sue's time to return comes nearer, Emily's passion is more pronounced. In a letter just a few weeks before Sue's arrival, the poet imagines them walking together as children hand in hand: "I would it were so Susie, and when I look around me and find myself alone, I sigh for you again."[39] And in a letter written just six days before Sue returns, Dickinson compares her joy and preparation for Sue to the return of a lover: "as if my absent Lover was coming home so soon—and my heart must be so busy, making ready for him."[40]

An important insight into the role Sue played in Dickinson's life may be gleaned after Sue returns from Baltimore and then again travels away from Amherst. Dickinson tells her in succeeding letters that she finds it lonely "to part with one of mine"[41] and that "it is harder to live alone than it was when you were in Baltimore."[42] The attachment is so intense that Dickinson tells Sue that "your absence insanes me so—I do not feel so peaceful, when you are gone from me—All life looks differently, and the faces of my fellows are not the same they wear when you are with me."[43] Then in an attempt to clarify exactly what she means, Dickinson writes, "I think it is this, dear Susie; you sketch my pictures for me, and 'tis at their sweet colorings, rather than this dim real that I am used, so you see when you go away, the world looks staringly, and I find I need more vail."[44]

The implication is clear. Sue is protection from the "dim real" world that "looks staringly." While she adds an excitement, a drama to Emily's duller life, Sue also protects her and gives Dickinson the strength she lacks. Thus, the poet needs "vail" or covering from the harsh outer world. In these few lines, Dickinson reveals her hypersensitivity to aloneness and her need for Sue. Without her, she is anxious, ill at ease, not "peaceful," to use her own word.

If we doubt that Sue's connection to Dickinson was life-giving, all we need do is read the aftereffects of their breakup. Sue, who had been away for a number of weeks, had not written to Emily, who details in a letter to Sue the impact of this neglect: "I do not miss you Susie—of course I do not miss you—I only sit and stare at nothing from my window, and know that all is gone–Dont feel it—no—any more than the stone feels, that it is very cold, or the block, that it is silent, where one 'twas warm and green, and birds danced in its branches."[45] What follows is a description of a numbed state of existence, a depression that transforms Dickinson into an automaton: "I rise, because the sun shines, and sleep has done with me, and I brush my hair, and dress me, and wonder what I am and who has made me so."

According to Dr. Goldstein, the fear of being deprived of their primary attachment has been described by agoraphobics as "death" or "nonexistence."[46] To Dickinson, therefore, life without Sue creates a state of nonexistence, a state of numbed being in which she walks without sense or meaning. Deprived of one of her "own," Dickinson experiences a death in life. Wolff underscores this trait, observing that the poet consistently treats the "themes of separation" as "mortal wounds that threaten death, disintegration, or even madness."[47]

4

"I Love So to Be a Child"

Agoraphobia begins at a stage of development when an independent action is called for. Since these individuals are overly dependent and have a low level of self-sufficiency, they feel incompetent to separate from their environment, even though this environment may be detrimental to their healthy development. Thus, the "situation generates considerable conflict."[1]

This conflict, the second of four elements present in complex agoraphobia, is generally interpersonal and places the individual in "an unhappy seemingly irresolvable relationship under the domination of a spouse or parent."[2] "The urge to leave and the fears of being on her/his own balance out, and the agoraphobic is trapped in this conflict, unable to move and lacking the skill to change the situation. The word 'trapped' is a key one here; recall that we noted that the agoraphobics feel fear any place in which they are trapped. Their definitions of what constitutes a trapped situation are extremely subjective, but what is important is that this is the way they label a given situation, not the validity of this label to an outsider. This may appear rather nebulous: it is helpful to view it as a semantic generalization on their trapped feeling in the conflict situation."[3] Thus such individuals are caught in a bind, in a situation that they want to move out of but feel they cannot.

When Dickinson returned home from Mount Holyoke, there was little opportunity for her to exercise autonomy. At a time when she should have been developing her own independence, she fit comfortably back into the family constellation. With Austin gone and Lavinia away at school, Dickinson fell under her father's strict control. Her mother's hypochondria also forged the links that bound her more closely to home. Instead of looking ahead to adulthood, the poet looked back fondly on childhood, telling her friend Abiah Root that "I love so to be a child."[4] Thus, Dickinson's life settled back into a familiar routine, into what Sewall calls the poet's "home-centeredness," a family trait she "carried to an extreme."[5] But although Sewall does not believe her behavior was indicative of "some deep neurotic fear or psychological compulsion," we can suggest that Dickinson, like a premorbid agoraphobic, was not equipped to be independent. Her "sense of self" was embedded in the intimate context of home life."[6] When she attempted to be independent, she became frustrated and "regressed to a childish level of adjustment."[7]

The third element — the inability to identify emotion — further complicates the conflict, for rather than understand and distinguish feelings such as hurt or anger, the individual focuses on the physical responses these emotions cause and labels them "inexplicable anxiety."[8] Because of this inability to accurately label emotions and respond accordingly, agoraphobics see the sources of anxiety as mysterious and unknown. For them, the panic attack comes "out of the blue" since the anxiety seems to have no connection to events in their lives. Thus, rather than understand or accept these emotional difficulties, the individual denies the triggering "interpersonal and intrapsychic events."[9] In this way, the agoraphobe does not connect the cause of conflict with his or her resulting physical responses and, therefore, cannot understand or correct them. The agoraphobe, thus, suffers under a cloud of darkness that further intensifies fears.

The last element — fear of fear — comes after the victim suffers the panic attack. Unlike someone with a specific phobia, like a fear of elevators or a fear of heights, that has a definite external trigger, agoraphobics fear the return of their own fears. That is, after the experience of panic attack with its horrifying physical symptoms, individuals try to avoid the situation that they believe engendered it. However, since the panic attack is brought on by "high levels of conflict, although physiological predisposition probably plays some role,"[10] the agoraphobic cannot escape. Thus begins a pattern of self-defeating behavior. In an attempt to avoid panic attacks, the agoraphobe "inevitably brings one on."[11] In this way, the fear of panic attack or "fear of fear" becomes the "phobic core in the syndrome."[12]

In a very interesting series of letters dating from the early 1850s, we see the young Dickinson struggling to assert herself within her father-dominated house. After an evening out visiting friends, Dickinson, who is already past twenty, arrives home at 9:00 P.M. to find "Father in great agitation at my protracted stay — and mother and Vinnie in tears, for fear that he would kill me."[13] In the same letter, Dickinson relates an episode that appears to be a desire to run away, to escape from the suffocating home environment. She writes: "I put on my bonnet tonight, opened the gate very desperately, and for a little while the suspense was terrible — I think I was held in check by some invisible agent, for I returned to the house without having done any harm!" Thus her desire to leave has been denied and she has done no "harm" — she has defied neither her father nor her culture, one that encouraged her state of dependence. The only "harm" was to herself. She continues to explain to her brother that she would reveal more about her feelings; however, since the "world is hollow ... I really do not think we had better expose our feelings." Either the poet cannot identify these feelings of independence or rebellion, or if she can, they are so terrible to her she cannot discuss them openly.

One situation that especially bothered Dickinson was her lack of privacy.

"No matter to whom addressed," Edward Dickinson read all the letters.[14] Then he had Emily read "them loud at the supper table again."[15] On 30 September 1851 she reports to her brother that "I reviewed the contents hastily — striking out all suspicious places and then very artlessly and unconsciously began. My heart went 'pit-pat' till I got safely by a remark concerning Martha, and my stout heart was not till the manuscript was over."[16]

Two years later she reveals her resentment to Austin: "I dont love to read your letters all out loud to father — it would be like opening the kitchen door when we get home from meeting Sunday, and are sitting down by the stove saying just what we're a mind to, and having father hear. I dont know why it is, but it gives me a dreadful feeling, and I skipped about the wild flowers, and one or two little things I loved the best, for I could'nt read them loud to anybody."[17]

Here the conflict between father and daughter has settled within Dickinson herself. Rather than refuse to read the letter, she reads it against her will. Rather than identify the conflict and connect it with her emotions, she says she doesn't know why she feels this way, but she gets a "dreadful feeling."

The extent of Edward Dickinson's invasion of his daughter's privacy is evident in a dream the poet has. "I waked up this morning thinking for all the world I had a letter from you (Austin) — just as the seal was breaking father rapped at my door. I was sadly disappointed not to go on and read."[18] Her father's domination extends even into her unconscious dream state.

The oppressive atmosphere of the house undoubtedly created in Dickinson a strong desire to leave. In a letter written shortly after her return home from visiting Austin, Dickinson wrote that home is "very lonely" without him and that "I have tried to make up my mind which was better — home, and parents, and country; or city, smoke, and dust, shared with the only being whom I can call my Brother." Her answer is "the balance is in your favor."[19] Dickinson clearly felt that away from home in the company of Austin she could be herself. But in the home, she was not allowed this luxury. There she must live by her father's rules. Dickinson wants to leave home; however, militating against this defiant and rebellious act were two factors: one, that Dickinson was living in a time when women were constricted by the "domestic sphere"[20] and rarely left home to live independently (although Sue could certainly have been a role model for her), and two, she was not self-sufficient enough (or so she had been convinced through years of overprotection) to cope on her own.

A letter to Emily Fowler in February 1852 reveals Dickinson's desire to leave. Although she does not go into her friend's house, she leaves a note saying, "Oh I want to come in, I have a great mind now to follow little Jane into your warm sitting room. . . . No, I resist temptation, and run away from the door just as fast as my feet will carry me, lest if I once come in, I shall grow so happy, happy that I shall stay there always, and never go home at all!"[21]

Then Dickinson runs as she will from Professor Tyler's woods and from church on the morning of her panic attack. "I have just shot past the corner, and now all the wayside houses, and the little gate flies open to see me coming home!" Her desire to leave and be free of her family is strong, yet she denies it because she does not feel adequately prepared to bring it about. Thus she runs literally and figuratively from this unidentified and frightening emotion, returning to the same home environment that gave rise to her discomfort.

In another letter that alludes to a conflict between father and daughter, Dickinson again confides in her brother: "We don't have any jokes tho' now, it is pretty much all sobriety, and we do not have much poetry, father having made up his mind that its pretty much all real life. Fathers real life and mine sometimes come in collison, but as yet, escape unhurt!"[22]

If we add to this father-daughter conflict the poet's own timidity and unwillingness to openly challenge her father, we see that we have the perfect breeding ground for panic attack and agoraphobia. Although Dickinson thought she was escaping collision with her father's world, the battle was already decided. Their worlds were definitely in conflict; she would not escape unharmed. The cost was personal. Dickinson's spirit of independence was eroded and her rebellious instincts driven further underground.

In a letter to Jane Humphrey, Dickinson reveals that she cannot leave her family because "what if they die when I'm gone."[23] She has submerged her desire to leave home; a choice of deliberate will becomes instead a physical incapacity — not that she won't, but she cannot because if she does she will be punished by the death of her family. Thus, she believes she is indispensable to her family's health and transforms a normal desire for independence into a dependent and neurotic subservience to others.

To sum up her fears of growing up and her inability to resolve conflicts, Dickinson confides in Austin, "I wish we were children now. I wish we were always children, how to grow up I dont know."[24] In a nostalgic letter she recalls their "long talks . . ., upon the kitchen stone hearth, when the just are fast asleep. I ask myself many times if they will come back again, and whether they will stay, but we dont know."[25] Perhaps she knew they could not return. The independent Dickinson, who at Mount Holyoke was rebellious and defiant, who was the "only one who did not rise" to be counted as a Christian in one of Mary Lyon's crusades,[26] was now weak and ineffectual. She had surrendered, given up the battle in which the victim would be herself. Her acts of rebellion would henceforth be confined to paper, where she could continue to be "wicked and evil" in the privacy of her thoughts.

5

"What If They Die When I'm Gone?"

What causes agoraphobia and triggers panic attacks with their frightening implications? Since Westphal's first description of the illness in 1872, many have attempted to explain its origins. Explanations range from psychoanalytic and behavioral causes to the currently popular theory that agoraphobia has a physiological basis. Although these theories appear to be distinct, evolving over years of study, they are not mutually exclusive and may, in fact, be interdependent. "The complementarity of these three approaches (the analytic, the behavioral, the biological) to anxiety in particular and to mental illness in general can perhaps best be seen in their application to a specific clinical syndrome — agoraphobia. . . . Clearly no single explanatory model is sufficient to supply an adequate explanation for all questions raised here; the full explanation can come only from a judicious combination of observations and concepts from a variety of approaches."[1] Thus, the entire picture must be considered before a conclusion can be reached.

One area that has received considerable attention from both the analytic and behavioral schools has been the role of parents. Studies examining the family constellation of the premorbid agoraphobic suggest that the family background is one marked by overprotection and insufficient care. John Bowlby, in his three-volume study *Separation and Loss*, shows that while the individual is nurtured in an overprotective environment, he or she suffers from a lack of maternal care, a finding supported by other researchers such as Terhune, A. S. Webster, and Gordon Parker. In 1956, W. I. Tucker "described a background of lack of parental affection, overprotection and overcriticism by parents in the majority of his one hundred phobic patients."[2] Thus there is a consensus that the family background is one marked by a history of "parental deprivation and poor parental relations."[3] This "deficiency of the parental relationship is such that children by being punished, criticized, or denied the opportunity to practice independent behavior grow up viewing themselves as basically incompetent and unable to cope with many situations. These early experiences serve as significant predisposing factors in the development of agoraphobia."[4]

One particular study should be singled out in relation to Emily Dickinson's home life. Willem A. Arrindell's 1983 study, "The Role of Perceived Parental Rearing Practices in the Aetiology of Phobic Disorders," concludes that "agoraphobics scored both their fathers and their mothers low on emotional warmth and their mothers high on rejection."[5] "As compared with the normals' ratings of their fathers, the agoraphobic subjects noted theirs as being less supportive emotionally."[6]

There is abundant evidence of Mr. Dickinson's lack of emotional warmth: from Austin who, after his father's death, kissed him and said, "There, father, I never dared do that while you were living,"[7] from Lavinia who did not marry after her father's death because, "like Emily I feared displeasing father even after he was gone,"[8] and from Emily who "feared" her father "as long as he lived."[9]

Dickinson's home life was not only devoid of warmth and affection, but of approval as well. On one occasion Dickinson writes that "Father was very severe to me; he thought I'd been trifling with you (Austin), so he gave me quite a trimming about 'Uncle Tom' and 'Charles Dickens' and these 'modern Literati.' "[10] Another time when the relations from Monson were visiting, Dickinson details that "They agree beautifully with Father on the 'present generation.' They decided that they hoped every young man who smoked would take fire. I respectfully intimated that I thought the result would be a vast conflagration, but was instantly put down."[11] Although she doesn't say by whom, we can be sure it was her father, since his was the imposing presence.

So, too, we do not need to be convinced of the overprotective atmosphere of the Homestead, where Edward Dickinson ruled with an autocratic hand. Overpowering and hypercritical, Edward Dickinson kept all his offspring in fearful submission. Even his son lacked the necessary strength to break his hold. After Austin joined a law partnership with his father in June 1855, his wife-to-be admitted that this decision was "a sacrifice for Austin's spirit and . . . a struggle with his preconceived ideas."[12] Lavinia speaks for all three children when she recalls that "I felt I had a right to freedom, but I was not strong enough to take it."[13]

If we judge the quality of Dickinson's relationship with her mother from the letters, we see it was clearly inadequate. The poet's barbs at her mother's lack of thought and "unobtrusive faculties"[14] are notorious, and her frequent allusions to her mother's emotional distance are revealing. Cody has carefully analyzed the relationship between Dickinson and her mother and has concluded that the mother's early rejection of the poet is at the root of the poet's hypothetical psychosis. After her sister Lavinia's birth, Dickinson was sent to stay with her Aunt Lavinia Norcross because, as Cody believes, the mother may have suffered a "postpartum depression."[15] It was this separation that adversely affected the two-year-old Dickinson and increased the emotional distance between the mother and the poet. "In sum, the strain and self-preoccupation attendant on Mrs. Dickinson following the birth of Lavinia widened the breach between herself and Emily, who may accordingly have felt rejected. This then followed for Emily a halcyon interval during which she became an affectionate and responsive child under the influence of her aunt's loving personality. But by so much as the visit fulfilled her emotional needs, the return home was a plunge into coldness again."[16]

This early separation from the mother and the lack of maternal care before and after the separation left Dickinson in the state of an "unsatisfied and love starved child."[17] Ironically it was not until Mrs. Dickinson herself suffered a debilitating stroke one year after her husband's death and became Dickinson's child that the poet first experienced the free flow of love between herself and her mother.

According to psychologist Nancy Roeske, the mother-daughter relationship is a difficult one and differs significantly from that of mothers and sons because of "shared identity issues."[18] "The withdrawal of a depressed mother"[19] at an early stage hampers the separation-individuation process and can lead to "painful ambivalence toward the mother," which is a common characteristic in the background of many agoraphobic women.[20] Since the mother-daughter relationship is such an important one and because the "intensity of agoraphobia has been related to maternal rather than paternal characteristics,"[21] it is an area that warrants closer attention.

Dickinson's most recent biographer, Wolff, traces that poet's fears of separation to a breakdown in the nonverbal dialogue between mother and daughter. During the early stages — beginning as soon as "the first hours of life"[22] — the child begins to learn about herself and her interaction with others. "When this stage of communication is skillful and loving, the infant learns to feel good both about her mother and about her own emergent self, acquiring a fundamental sense that the universe is on the whole benign. Little by little, the baby also begins to be able to tolerate separation from her mother, because she has discovered that the partner in this 'dialogue' is reliable — mother may leave, but she will always return."[23] When it is unsuccessful, however, as it was in Dickinson's case, "A sense of integrity of self, insufficiently confirmed in this initial phase, may always remain weak. Intimate relationships with others may be difficult to sustain; separation from loved ones may always be fearsome. The world may even seem a dangerous place, governed by an indifferent or hostile God."[24] Thus what Dickinson lacked in eye and face contact, she attempted to make up in language. However, while such communication is "better than failed nonverbal communication ... the move from nonverbal into verbal communication becomes, in this case, the acknowledgment of a loss that nothing can ever fully remedy. The 'magic time' of mother-infant intimacy ... has never properly occurred."[25]

There is not much known about Mrs. Dickinson, who is a shadowy, nonverbal figure in the background of the Dickinson home. However, from remarks made about her we can safely gather that in addition to not providing intellectual stimulation or adequate emotional support, she was a neurotic, suffering woman, given to living in the shadow of her dominant husband. According to Cody, "Poor Mrs. Dickinson was obsequious, self-abnegating, plaintive, fussy, uninterested in ideas or art, dependent and subject to profound spells of lassitude and discouragement."[26] Although Wolff is more generous with Mrs. Dickinson, describing her as "kindly and solicitous," she adds that she did not have "the capacity to comprehend the wants of those in her house."[27] Her emotional inaccessibility left the poet feeling "as if she 'never had a mother.' "[28] With the years, Mrs. Dickinson's inclination to withdraw grew more pronounced. "By the time her daughters had become young women, Mother tended increasingly to withdraw from the rest of the family with a series of illnesses, some identifiable and some vague and ephemeral."[29]

The reader of Dickinson's letters is made painfully aware of her mother's incapacitation through the years. As early as May 1850, Dickinson tells her friend Abiah Root that her mother "was taken" with an acute neuralgia that keeps her "on the lounge asleep suffering intensely."[30] Two years later, Dickinson writes to Austin that due to their mother's illness, she and Vinnie "have had to work pretty hard."[31] However, the illness that concerns us primarily is the one beginning after the family moved into the Dickinson Homestead; it was a major illness that frightened the occupants and lasted for four years. Dickinson refers to it in a letter to the Hollands in which she first details the amusing facts of their move and then turns to the more serious matter of her mother's illness. "Mother has been an invalid since we came home . . . and mother lies upon the lounge, or sits in her easy chair. I dont know what her sickness is, for I am a simple child and frightened at myself."[32]

Dickinson refers to the unidentified and unidentifiable illness numerous times in her letters, using the words *frightened* and *perplexed* to describe herself and her sister in this time of trouble. The cumulative effect of these years of worry can be seen in one dramatic letter written in the summer of 1858 to her Uncle Joseph Sweetser: "Summers of bloom and months of frost, and days of jingling bells, yet all the while this hand upon our fireside."[33] Thomas Johnson, editor of Dickinson's poems and letters, believes that this last phrase "alludes probably to the continued poor health of her mother."[34] But in 1860 Mrs. Dickinson appeared to be completely healthy and is mentioned as a guest at the home of Mary Shepherd: "as well as four years ago—when last she was here."[35]

The pattern that emerges is of a woman who is not physically strong, who when ill gives in completely to illness's domination rather than resist it, a submissive quality not unlike that shown in her relation with her husband. We do not know the exact nature of Mrs. Dickinson's long-lingering illness after her move to the Homestead, but it is possible that, as in the case of the emotional illness following the birth of Lavinia, Mrs. Dickinson succumbed to a depression brought on by the stress of the move. Wolff identifies this illness as a "deep despair" and admits that there is "no easy explanation," although it "sounds very much like depression."[36] Wolff suggests that what was a "victory" to Edward Dickinson—a return to his father's house—was a defeat for Mrs. Dickinson, a "fulfillment of all those elements in the marriage that had caused her emotional pain and had fostered her innate inclination to reticence and depression."[37] The fact that it lasted for four years indicates the type of brooding personality Mrs. Dickinson had.

In a recent study of the etiology of agoraphobia, Blake H. Tearnan notes that not only do agoraphobic subjects experience more depression and nightmares, but that their "mothers experience fears more often than normal subjects."[38] Certainly this is the case with Mrs. Dickinson, who appears from Dickinson's letters to be overly solicitous about Austin's health, clothing, and so forth, as well as of her daughters' safety. Although Dickinson is twenty-one and her sister nineteen, the poet tells Austin that Mother chooses not to visit him in Boston because "this mother thinks an objection, as should she go away too we should be quite alone, and the folks wouldn't think that safe."[39]

In addition to overprotection and lack of affection, a high rate of neurosis has been found in the homes of incipient agoraphobics. A definite correlation exists between the "chronic anxiety" of the mother with her resultant overprotective behavior and the fears of the preagoraphobic child.[40] As early as 1949, Terhune in his study of the phobic syndrome wrote that 75 percent of his patients reported at least one "seriously neurotic parent."[41] In fact it has recently been suggested that in the premorbid agoraphobic's home there are one or two phobic parents who themselves have poor anxiety tolerance.[42] Researchers note that in agoraphobic families there is a "greater number of psychiatric problems including neurosis, alcoholism, and depressive illness."[43] According to Terhune, "neurotic parents, especially if phobic, should realize that so far as their apprehensive children are concerned, they are psychologically infectious."[44] If we add this information to another study that reports that the "fathers of agoraphobics were absent" from home "with unusual frequency"[45]—definitely the case in Dickinson's home—then we see the enormous impact the mother's example had on the young Dickinson. Wolff corroborates this fact, observing that Mr. Dickinson's "habit of emotional withdrawal was lethally reinforced by his frequent absences from home."[46] Further, Mrs. Dickinson's response to "the almost palpable specter" of her husband's absence[47] "made things worse" since she equated it with death: "I felt quite like a widow."[48]

Thus, it is highly probable that Dickinson "learned" her phobic behavior, or at least her inability to cope with anxiety, by "modeling" her mother's inadequate coping skills. According to Marks, a leading behaviorist,

"Modeling or vicarious learning occasionally influences the production of phobias." He continues, observing that "agoraphobic patients not infrequently have close relations with the same disorder."[49] Mrs. Dickinson "never overcame her fears of separation, and she was surely the primary model for all three children."[50] Her granddaughter recalls that she was "anxious ... when any of her loved ones were even so briefly away from her care."[51] In *Emily Dickinson's Home*, Millicent Todd Bingham deflects the charge that the poet is "morbid" by observing that "From childhood her mother's anxieties had encouraged such an attitude."[52]

Studies of the families of agoraphobics reveal several "pathogenic interactions."

> These patterns include the following: a) an omnipresent family social network allowing the patient few, if any, experiences of autonomy; b) an illness during childhood/adolescence reminding the patient and the parents of his/her vulnerability and need for nurturance and support; c) a parent's illness, especially mother's, reminding the child of being unprepared to care for self. (This pattern has several permutations: in all, the patient feels or felt required to remain at home as the parent's caretaker or companion. The child is encouraged to believe that something dreadful might happen in her absence and if at home the child can save the parent. The patient's narcissistic omnipotence is reinforced within the home environment and the challenges of the outside world are easily avoided); and d) a psycho-pathologically dominant parent, mother or father, who may control all family members and demands an amoebic family structure for personal support."[53]

Dickinson's family fits these patterns. The first is clearly evident. From the beginning, Dickinson was not allowed to have control over her life's decisions. After a year's education at Mount Holyoke, Dickinson returned to a suffocating home situation and to a family insensitive to her needs: "... and my time of so little account — and my writing so very needless — and really I came to the conclusion that I should be a villain unparalleled if I took but an inch of time for so unholy a purpose as writing a friendly letter — for what need had I of sympathy — or very much less of affection — or less than they all — of friends."[54] The poet discovered that no matter how well educated and innately intelligent, a woman "would always be limited to the domestic realm."[55] Coupling the dearth of "acceptable roles for articulating an adult female identity" in her society with the poet's own "diffused sense of inner self,"[56] we can appreciate Dickinson's frustration.

The second pattern fits Dickinson's "bronchial ailment which enforced a long absence" from Holyoke.[57] Before the end of her first term, Austin came "with orders from headquarters" to bring her home.[58] Certainly in this era before antibiotics such precautions were warranted, since "a simple sore throat could have lethal consequences,"[59] but Dickinson's parents were overly solicitous. In a letter to Abby she recalls that during this illness she "was dosed for about a month . . . without any mercy, till at last out of mere pity my cough went away. . . . Thus I remained at home . . . comforting my parents by my presence. . . ."[60] In the same letter, Dickinson tells Abby that "Father has decided not to send me to Holyoke." Whether her health was an issue in this decision or not, it remains a subject of family concern. In October 1851 Lavinia tells Austin that Emily "is much improved. She has really grown fat."[61] Austin, in turn, tells Susan Gilbert that "Emily is better than for years."[62] These years of overprotection at this crucial adolescent stage undoubtedly convince Dickinson that she is unable to care for herself and is dependent upon her family's support.

The third pattern is directly related to Dickinson's caretaking of a sickly, long-suffering mother. This pattern begins six years prior to the mother's illness of 1856. In May 1850 Dickinson writes that she refused a ride with a "friend I love so dearly" to stay with her mother who was sick. Continuing, she adds that after her mother went to sleep, she "cried with all my might" and felt "much abused." She concludes, "Mother is still an invalid, tho' a partially restored one—Father and Austin still clamor for food, and I, like a martyr am feeding them."[63]

If we combine Dickinson's dutiful care of her mother and her martyrdom to her family with the evidence of another letter written two years later, we clearly see the emerging pattern of Dickinson's need to stay home. In this letter she fears leaving home, for "what if they die when I'm gone."[64] Any desire to leave home becomes impossible, because her family cannot live without her. Thus Dickinson replaces a natural instinct to leave home with a need to remain there as caretaker.

The last pattern needs no further annotation, since it is apparent that Edward Dickinson was tyrannical in all matters relating to his home. There he "was the undisputed sovereign,"[65] his rules covering all members of the household—wife, daughters, son, as well as animals. On one occasion Lavinia reports that he whipped the horse because "he didn't look quite 'umble' enough."[66]

One additional element in the transmission of the illness should be mentioned. Recent findings suggest that "panic disorder is familial and most likely genetic."[67] Thus, some specialists believe that "the incidence of fear between agoraphobics and their mothers" is most likely due to "genetic inheritability."[68] In a 1983 symposium exploring the neurobiology of panic disorder and agoraphobia, Dr. Thomas Uhde discussed the early medically based theory of William James (1890) who "introduced the concept that some individuals might be unusually sensitive to their own internal physiological cues."[69] This theory, according to Uhde, might help explain why individuals suffering from agoraphobia show a "vulnerability" to chemically induced panic attacks. The experiment, done in 1967 by F. N. Pitts and J. N. McClure, demonstrated that "agoraphobic individuals" experienced panic attacks when given infusions of sodium lactate, strongly suggesting that "panic disorder is a biological disease."[70]

Recent studies have focused on the area of genetics. There is strong evidence that the disorder has a "high familial prevalence."[71] Genetic transmission was "five times higher" in the case of monozygotic twins than for same-sex dizygotic twins, all of this suggesting that Dickinson may have been at risk genetically. In the *New England Journal of Medicine*, Sheehan, a proponent of the medical model of agoraphobia, writes that there is "increased evidence of the disorder among the relatives of affected persons."[72] In another article, he states that anxiety attacks and phobic symptoms are found especially "among female relatives."[73] However, Goldstein advises caution in designating biology as the single cause of agoraphobia: "Even if one accepts that panics are entirely the result of defective biology, it is a grand leap of logic to attempt to account for a full-blown agoraphobia as being entirely a biological flaw, particularly since many people who experience panics never become agoraphobic."[74] Dr. James Ballenger, editor of *The Biology of Agoraphobia*, agrees, defining agoraphobia as an "abnormal and progressive disorder with both biological and psychological aspects."[75] Current treatment of the disorder incorporates all three areas—biology, psychology, and sociology—into therapy.[76] One researcher sums up this approach by stating, "Rather than any one causal agent, it is more likely that a combination of biological, psychological and environmental elements contribute to the genesis of the disorder."[77]

Dickinson's home environment provided a rich and fertile ground for the growth of her phobic and neurotic ills. Her mother's behavior and influence as role model suggest that Dickinson learned to be neurotic and dependent rather than healthy and self-sufficient. Further, if the disorder has a genetic basis, Dickinson stood in the direct line of transmission, inheriting a biological vulnerability that predisposed her to the development of the disease.

6

"Newton Is Dead. The First of My Own Friends"

Before we take a closer look at Dickinson's panic attack of 1854, let us consider separation anxiety, which the *DSM* III lists as a predisposing factor to the development of agoraphobia.[1] Marks sees separation anxiety as a "common complication" of agoraphobia[2] but does not feel the two are necessarily related. On the other hand, some theorists believe that agoraphobia is another form of separation disorder.[3] It is generally agreed, however, that "persons with panic attack had a relatively high incidence of separation disorder in childhood."[4] Recent research supports this, one study reporting that among agoraphobic subjects, traumatic life events before the age of fifteen are common, one being separation from parents, especially the mother.[5]

In a three-volume study of separation anxiety, author John Bowlby parallels agoraphobia in adults with school phobia in children. In both, there are fears of leaving home, overdependency, and a family background of neurosis.[6] Bowlby recognizes that "an individual's susceptibility to respond with fear whenever he meets a potentially alarming situation is determined in very large part by the type of forecast he makes of the probable availability of attachment figures" and that this is based on the "types of experience he has had in his relationships with attachment figures" during his early years.[7] If these early attachment figures were undependable, disapproving, or rejecting, then the individual becomes insecure and when "faced with a potentially fear-arousing situation" is "more likely to respond with intense fear than an individual who feels secure and confident in his attachment figures."[8]

There are many theories suggesting that phobias are "reactivations of childhood fears," especially those which involve separation from primary figures. Freud, for example, equated the fear of separation from the mother as symbolically represented by the fear of leaving the house.[9] Researchers A. Frances and P. Dunn maintain that "space-related phobias symbolize . . . the attachment-autonomy conflict which in many families received its most dramatic formulation in the territorial language of the original infant-mother

57

phobic partnership."[10] "A given territory becomes safe because it becomes equated with and/or symbolizes mother and protection. The outside is feared for its inherent uncertainty but especially because entering it implies leaving the safety of mother, i.e. separation."[11]

Since physical separation is a "necessary precursor of psychological separation,"[12] individuals suffering from separation anxiety who believe that their "support figures were unreliable when needed" are incapable of taking such a step. In the "absence of consistent care-taking" their ability to "modulate anxiety and other effects" would also be decreased. Thus, in the event of a threat to their precarious sense of security, there would be understandable "episodes of panic anxiety and depressive response."[13]

Donald F. Klein, a proponent of the medical model of agoraphobia, notes that 50 percent of his severely impaired agoraphobics showed indications of separation anxiety in childhood[14] and theorizes that their panic attacks "have a close biological relationship to separation anxiety."[15] In "Anxiety Reconceptualized," he discusses his theory and acknowledges its debt to Bowlby's "stimulating work." "Bowlby had speculated that the child's tie to the mother did not depend on learning that she was a need gratifier . . . but . . . resembled more strongly the ethological notion of imprinting."[16] Thus, according to Klein, "separation anxiety is controlled by a biologically innate regulatory mechanism which automatically releases a distress signal (in the form of panic anxiety) under conditions of separation or the anticipation of separation."[17] If the individual inherited a low threshold of distress, then he or she has a biological vulnerability to panic attack and agoraphobia.

Recent study supports the biological basis of agoraphobia proposed by Klein and Charlotte M. Zitrin among others. It sees agoraphobia as "a maladaptive outbreak of separation anxiety, which . . . is an innate biological mechanism that controls attachment behavior."[18] Some researchers have compared agoraphobia with panics to the "acute separation anxiety shown by infants and toddlers" upon separation from their mothers.[19]

If we look into Dickinson's childhood years, we see evidence of rejection, parental insufficiency, and family disturbance. According to Cody's psychological portrait of Dickinson, the poet never felt "safely loved, she never felt safe at all. The entire course of her life reveals her exaggerated need for parental protection."[20] This need for parental protection encouraged her to form a variety of "anxious attachments" from which she tried to draw love, approval, and safety. Dickinson turned first to her brother and sister "for solace,"[21] the three forming "a bond that was of singular importance to them all."[22] However, she also looked outside of the family. We have traced the poet's attachment to Sue Gilbert, but there is another that demands particular attention, for it was this one that may have triggered Dickinson's panic attack of 1854. This was the poet's relationship with Benjamin Newton.

According to Bowlby, the acute symptoms of agoraphobia are "precipitated by bereavement, a serious illness, or some other major change in family circumstances."[23] Chambless and Goldstein have found a "high incidence of separation and bereavement as precipitating factors in the onset or worsening of symptoms."[24] Given the background of separation anxiety, it is understandable that when something threatens a source of security, an anxiety reaction like panic attack will result. Marjorie Raskin states that the anxiety comes in "response to loss, or threat of a loss, of an important other."[25] The *DSM* III also includes "sudden object loss" as a precipitator of agoraphobia.[26]

If we look at the events preceding Dickinson's first documented panic attack in January 1854, we realize that the death of Benjamin Newton occurred less than one year before on 24 March 1853. Dickinson's early subpanic episode—the fears that caused her to run from Professor Tyler's woods—occurred only three months after Newton's death in June 1853. The poet's first reaction to her friend's death is brief, appearing in a postscript to a letter she writes three days after the event, "Oh Austin, Newton is dead. The first of my own friends. Pace."[27] This is all. There is no mention of him again until 13 January 1854—two days before her panic attack.

Although the letters written between the time of Newton's death and 13 January 1854 contain no overt reference to Newton, their tone and content reveal a mounting despair. Less than one month after Newton's death, Dickinson complains that she misses Austin and that she wishes they were children still.[28] Two months later, she tells Austin how lonely and old she feels: "and when the morning comes and the birds sing, they dont seem to make me so happy as they used to. I guess it's because you're gone, and there are not so many of us as God gave for each other.'"[29] In this depressed state, which she "guesses" is the result of Austin's absence, she goes on to speak of death, "I feel very sure lately that the years we have had together are more than we shall have—I guess we shall journey separately, or reach the journey's end, some of us—but we don't know."

Is this a reaction to her shock at Newton's death?

In a later letter, separation is linked to her fear of death. Here her concern for her brother's safety escalates irrationally. She imagines he is "very sick," "delirious," or "killed." She concludes, "Thank God you are safe!"[30] Dickinson's separation fears are triggered even by happy events. In an unorthodox congratulatory letter sent to Emily Fowler Ford on the occasion of her marriage, Dickinson quotes a verse in the Bible, "I can go to her, but she cannot come back to me," and ends the letter with a hymn beginning, "How blest the righteous when he dies."[31] Dickinson's emotional difficulty with separation causes her to interpret marriage as the death of her friendship. "I begin to know that you will not come back again."[32] Wolff corroborates this, noting that to Dickinson "marriage, too (as an event that would separate Dickinson from the friends whom she had come to need), began to seem a 'type' of death."[33]

On 13 January 1854, Dickinson writes a letter to Edward Everett Hale, Benjamin Newton's minister. In it she reveals that Newton has lingered in her mind and troubled her for the ten months since his death. She describes his importance to her as "a gentle, yet grave Preceptor, teaching me what to read, what authors to admire, what was most grand or beautiful in nature, and that sublimer lesson, a faith in things unseen, and in life again, nobler, and much more blessed — Of all these things he spoke — he taught me of them all, earnestly, tenderly, and when he went from us, it was as an elder brother, loved indeed very much, and mourned, and remembered."[34]

She tells Hale that she and Newton corresponded "often" and that although she knew he was ill, "death ... surprised me." She asks him simply "if he (Newton) was willing to die, and if you think him at Home." *Home* is a loaded word meaning safety, protection, and peace.

Unfortunately we do not know what Hale told Dickinson if indeed he responded, but what is significant is that two days later, Dickinson's "life was made a victim." And although she wondered what she was afraid of and concluded "in the whole world was nothing I need to fear," she saw the "Phantom" and ran. This letter, followed in two days by the panic attack, is too strong a link to be considered coincidental. Indeed it was a trigger that set a wave of fear in motion which swept over the poet and overwhelmed her. The sudden death of Benjamin Newton reactivated Dickinson's early separation fears, and she reacted with panic. That is, the panic attack "followed the loss of someone important to her."[35]

It is significant that at the time of her panic attack none of her primary attachments were present. The importance of Dickinson's siblings cannot be overemphasized. Since the parents were "generally ... unavailable," the three children "learned early to band together."[36] As a result, they were close-knit and felt "personally wounded when one of the others was absent,"[37] Emily being the "most desolated by any separation from brother or sister."[38] Lavinia was in Boston with her father,[39] Austin was away at his job, and Sue was visiting relatives in Manchester, New Hampshire.[40] During the attack, Dickinson tells Sue, "In vain I sought to hide behind your feathers." In an earlier letter, as I have pointed out, the poet told Sue, "when you go away, the world looks staringly, and I find I need more vail."[41] Thus, in church without her family near and without her friend Sue to provide her protective "vail," Dickinson felt vulnerable. The poet's "hypersensitivity to aloneness" complicated by the sudden loss of Benjamin Newton, a withdrawn source of strength, left Dickinson open to attack. (Another contributing factor may be that no fewer than twenty-seven young people the poet knew died between February 1851 and January 1854.[42] In addition to Benjamin Newton, these included Abby Ann Haskell, aged nineteen, and Emily Lavinia Norcross, aged twenty-four, the latter being Dickinson's cousin and Holyoke roommate.)

In "The Topography of Agoraphobia," Dr. Wilfried De Moor characterizes the agoraphobe as a personality who denies problems. At the unconscious level, these unresolved problems create emotional turmoil that eventually results in anxiety. "The antecedent of the anxiety attacks," according to De Moor, is "one or another psychosocial background stresses that leads to psychological overload."[43] The death of Benjamin Newton falls into this category, representing for the poet an "unresolved bereavement" that may have brought on the "nameless anxiety attack."[44] Although the death of Newton deeply troubled the poet, she postponed dealing with the problem for almost a year before writing to the Reverend Mr. Hale.

With the onset of panic attack, the individual "becomes increasingly anxious and afraid of venturing outside, dependent on others for support, withdrawn, and retiring."[45] Thus after the attack of 1854, Dickinson begins a pattern of phobic avoidance, the anxiety attack conditioning her to fear the situation in which she first experienced panic. In the years that follow, the phobic fears fluctuate, receding at times, while at others growing stronger. Over time and without treatment, patients experience "a gradual worsening of the overall symptom picture":[46] "they become more socially phobic and finally polyphobic and agoraphobic. The final stage is depression."[47]

According to Sheehan, the progress of agoraphobia is longitudinal; the time scheme can be short, or it can be drawn out, the syndrome developing gradually over many years.[48] If the first stage occurred in June 1853, when Dickinson ran from Professor Tyler's woods, and reached a full-blown stage in the panic attack of January 1854, the entire course of Dickinson's illness comprises a period of twenty-seven years, fluctuating in intensity in the later 1850s and worsening in the early to mid-1860s. The final stage came after 1865 when the poet withdrew completely from the outside world, living in total seclusion for the last twenty years of her life. Biographer Wolff recognizes that the poet was "probably phobically" housebound and that her withdrawal was not a dramatic occurrence but "a slow process."[49]

In the spring of 1876, four years before her death, Dickinson wrote Higginson that "My earliest friend wrote me the week before he died 'If I live, I will go to Amherst,—if I die, I certainly will.' "[50] Thomas Johnson identifies this friend as Benjamin Newton. If he is right, then this is the last of only five references to Newton in a total of over a thousand letters. Yet despite this meager visible attention, Benjamin Newton, "the friend who taught ... Immortality,"[51] played a formative role in her life, influencing and guiding her from beyond the grave.[52]

7

"I Have Never Seen Anyone That I Cared for as Much as You"

After the panic attack, the agoraphobe is afraid not only of being in public places where he or she fears being "publicly humiliated" by a return of the panic episode, but also of being alone.[1] In fact, many agoraphobes avoid being alone and require a companion "when venturing beyond their 'safety zone.' "[2] Westphal, in his early discussion of *Die Agoraphobie*, described this aspect of the illness: "The patients experienced great comfort from the companionship of men or even inanimate objects, such as a vehicle or a cane."

In the twentieth century, this need for a trusted companion has been confirmed, along with the peace of mind it brings to the agoraphobe. This "demand for reassurance" is not a sign of helplessness but rather a desire for the "security of being protected by grownups."[3] Marks notes that the trusted companion can be "human, animal or inanimate."[4] Since such need for constant company "can strain relatives and friends," some resort to a dog.[5]

A pet can function as a "phobic partner," giving the individual a feeling of safety when in its presence, functioning as what L. Ovesey calls a "safe conduct pass."[6] With this companionship, the agoraphobe sets up an area in which he or she feels safe to travel. This "safety zone may be small or large," as the individual determines.[7]

It is easy to document Dickinson's love of and dependence on Carlo, the dog she described as "large as myself that my Father bought me."[8] We first hear of him in 1850 in a letter to George Gould in which she exclaims that "The Dog is the noblest work of Art, sir. I may safely say the noblest—his mistress's rights he doth defend—although it bring him to his end—although to death it doth him send!"[9]

In letters that follow we hear of Carlo's typical canine activities "terrifying man and beast" and his punishment of "being cuffed and hurled from piazza frequently." But we quickly realize that Carlo is more human than animal, more a companion than a pet. He has intelligence and is someone to whom the poet can turn: "I talk of all these things with Carlo," she tells Mrs. Bowles, "and his eyes grow meaning, and his shaggy feet keep a slower pace."[10] On another occasion she tells Samuel Bowles that Carlo doesn't understand his (Bowles's) long absence and so "the puzzled look—deepens Carlo's forehead."[11]

Carlo has feelings, too. When the Norcross cousins leave after a visit, he is lonely and "has asked for nothing to eat or drink, since you went away."[12] He also has an uncanny intuitive sense, for when Higginson calls Dickinson elusive she replies that she is "understood" by Carlo and thus "could not elude others."[13] So important is Carlo's high opinion of her that she prefers being unpublished and unknown lest "the approbation of my Dog, would forsake me."[14] Like the poet, Carlo is exclusive, not needing the companionship of many. Dickinson claims she shuns "Men and Women" because "they talk of Hallowed things, aloud—and embarrass my Dog."[15] But they both are tolerant: "He and I dont object . . . , if they'll exist their side."

It is clear from Dickinson's letters that with Carlo she feels safe to visit friends, to walk in the woods, and to be out of doors. In the second Master letter (letters addressed to Master whose identity is unknown), Dickinson invites the unidentified recipient to walk with her and Carlo "in the meadows an hour." [16] In various reminiscences, friends remember "Emily with her dog"[17] or that she went visiting "with her big dog who usually accompanied her."[18] Grace Smith writes that Dickinson's "companion out of doors was a large Newfoundland dog" who "stalked solemnly beside." She recalls that Dickinson once said, "I believe that the first to come to greet me when I go to heaven will be this dear, faithful old friend Carlo."[19]

When Dickinson went to Boston for her eye treatment, she told Higginson that "Carlo did not come because . . . he would die, in Jail."[20] Seven months later, Carlo did die, and in a short, poignant note the poet asks Higginson, "Would you instruct me now?"[21] After a companionship of sixteen years, Dickinson was deeply grieved by Carlo's death. Although Higginson attempts to comfort her, she responds that time will not be a "remedy" and that "Nature . . . plays without a friend."[22] Higginson sensed Carlo's importance to the poet. Five months after Carlo's death, Higginson writes: "it is hard to understand how you can live so . . . and even the companionship of your dog withdrawn."[23]

When Carlo died in January 1866, Dickinson had entered the most isolated period of her life. But years before her final withdrawal, Dickinson had learned to depend not only on her dog, but more directly on her sister Lavinia, who was "Emily's closest associate for more than fifty years" and who "became indispensable to her."[24] According to Dickinson, Lavinia was the more "practical sister," involving herself in the domestic world of the Homestead, cleaning and "dusting the stairs."[25] In contrast, Dickinson escaped the housekeeping routine to write a quick note to friends or to be alone with her thoughts. In her letters she complains that Lavinia and her mother "cleaned house all last week . . . I scolded, because they moved my things. I can't find much left anywhere, that I used to wear, or know of. You will easily conclude that I am surrounded by trial."[26]

Lavinia is more involved with affairs outside the home, going into the world to shop and to visit more frequently than her retiring sister. One of the aptest distinctions between the two comes from Dickinson herself: "Vinnie cruises about some to transact the commerce, but coming to anchor, is most that I can do."[27] Austin, too, notes the difference between the two, contrasting their dispositions during a visit to Boston in 1851: "Vinnie enjoyed herself, as she always does among strangers—Emily became confirmed in her opinion of the hollowness and awfulness of the world."[28] Vinnie was always more outgoing and given to fun. While she was away at school, her roommate described her ability to "take off" people and to write "funny letters," qualities that made her amusing and fun to be with.[29]

Another personality difference is seen in their dealings with other people. Dickinson, the more introverted of the two, suppressed her emotions, while Lavinia expressed them openly. In a letter to Austin, Lavinia notes that since Sue has not written Emily in a long time, Emily has been "very unhappy and me vexed."[30] In another instance, Lavinia tells Austin, "I shall first go to Mrs. Luke and give her a piece of mind, then Mrs. Fay another piece and see what effect will come of it. Mrs. Sweetser has interfered with my business long enough and now she'll get it, I tell you. . . . She has watched me long enough in meeting and her bonnet has bobbed long enough and now I'll have a stop put to such proceedings, I will indeed."[31] Lavinia is aggressive and fiery, dealing directly with interpersonal problems, whereas Dickinson, more introverted and shy, runs from emotions and conflict.

Although Emily is older, it is Lavinia who "mothers" Emily. In a postscript to Emily's letter, Lavinia tells Austin, "I think Emilie is very much improved. She has really grown fat . . . I am very strict with her and I shouldn't wonder if she should come out bright some time after all."[32] Lavinia clearly provided Emily with a "stable attachment figure in her environment,"[33] a role her parents did not fill.

In the letters the reader traces Dickinson's growing dependence on her younger sister. When Vinnie is away at school, Dickinson writes of her loneliness for her: "Vinnie you know is away—and that I'm very lonely is too plain for me to tell you—I am alone—all alone."[34] When Vinnie is away in January 1853, Emily again writes of her loneliness and her gratitude for having such a sister: "The day is long to me, because I have no Vinnie, and I think of those today who never had a Vinnie, and I'm afraid they are lone."[35] Dickinson treasures her sister's companionship. When Vinnie is ill, Dickinson tells the Hollands: "When she is well, time leaps. When she is ill, he lags, or stops entirely. . . . Sisters are brittle things. God was penurious with me, which makes me shrewd with Him."[36]

However, over time, the natural devotion and loneliness for Lavinia turns into an abnormal dependence. This is particularly apparent in 1859 when Vinnie is away from home. In a note to Mrs. Haven, Emily writes that "Vinnie has gone to enliven the house, and make the days shorter" for her aunt. "I would like more sisters, that the taking of one, might not leave such stillness. Vinnie has been all, so long, I feel the oddest fright at parting with her for an hour, lest a storm arrive, and I go unsheltered."[37] A month later, Dickinson reveals that Vinnie is still gone and "I am somewhat afraid at night."[38] Her admission of feeling "unsheltered and afraid" demonstrates Dickinson's need for the reassurance Vinnie could provide. Without Vinnie, Dickinson felt frightened and alone, vulnerable to fears that she symbolized in the sudden violence of a storm. Like the protective "vail" Sue offered, Lavinia shielded the poet from the outside world and calmed her timid nature. Writing to Joseph Lyman, Emily admits that "the tie" between Vinnie and herself "is quite vital."[39]

The most pronounced need for Vinnie came in the spring of 1863. In a letter to the Norcross cousins, Dickinson expresses an anguish so intense that we realize it is her own internalized anxiety that terrifies her. Lacking Vinnie on whom she depends totally, Dickinson is overwhelmed by imagined terrors. "The nights turned hot, when Vinnie had gone, and I must keep no window raised for fear of prowling 'booger,' and I must shut my door for fear front door slide open on me at the 'dead of night,' and I must keep 'gas' burning to light the danger up, so I will distinguish it — these gave me a snarl in the brain which don't unravel yet."[40]

This dramatic proof of Dickinson's dependence on Lavinia recalls the panic attack of 1854, ten years earlier, when Dickinson tried to run as fast as she could "to find myself at home" with "my own dear Vinnie."[41] This desire for home and Vinnie demonstrates how the trusted companion reassures the victim that no harm could come to her.

Immediately following the panic at church and Dickinson's decision not to go to Washington, Vinnie takes on the responsibility of her sister. In a letter to Austin, Lavinia writes, "Do you think it best for me to go to Washington? . . . I hate to leave Emily alone."[42] Later this responsibility demands even more than Vinnie's physical presence, for in a letter to Mrs. Holland, Dickinson reveals that Vinnie has become her conscience: "When Vinnie is here — I ask her; if she says I sin, I say 'Father, I have sinned' — If she sanctions me, I am not afraid."[43] In this instance the extreme dependence of the agoraphobe on the nonphobic companion is clear. Not only does the partner satisfy the practical demands of "daily living," but the individual's emotional needs as well.[44]

Although Lavinia was sensitive to her sister's needs, she did not always understand or approve her actions. For instance, Dickinson's weekly visits to the Dwights were "sunlight" to her, but the cause of her "sister's rage."[45] So, too, after Dickinson refuses to see Samuel Bowles upon his return from abroad, Dickinson writes to him, "Vinnie ... upbraided me."[46] When Dickinson is in Boston under the care of Dr. Williams, she writes to Lavinia about her condition and says, "You won't think it strange any more, will you?" indicating Vinnie's unsympathetic response to her eye ailment.[47] Yet when she returns from her treatment, Dickinson requests that "no one beside (Vinnie) come" to meet her. "You will get me at Palmer, yourself."[48] Although phobic relationships can lead to resentment, since "the call on service of others may degenerate into veiled tyranny,"[49] such was not the case between the sisters.

As the years advanced and Dickinson became more and more isolated, her dependence on Vinnie grew until Vinnie became all to her: protector, guardian, supporter, defender. Committed to her sister with an "uncritical devotion,"[50] Vinnie became a parent to Emily. Later in life with both parents still alive, Dickinson wrote that Vinnie "has no Father and Mother but me and I have no Parents but her."[51]

After the poet's death in 1886, a neighbor memorialized the sisters' dedication to each other: "Yesterday AM when I went over Vinnie said 'How can I live without her? Ever since we were little girls we have been wonderfully dear to each other — and many times when desirable offers of marriage have been made to Emily she has said — I have never seen anyone that I cared for as much as you Vinnie.' "[52] And in a letter to her parents, Mrs. Todd provides a fitting testimony to the two sisters' relationship: "Vinnie ... is well-nigh broken-hearted and utterly bereft. Those two sisters were everything to each other, and how Vinnie will ever survive it I cannot see."[53]

8

"I Had a Terror — Since September"

"I had a terror — since September — I could tell to none," Dickinson confides to Higginson in her second letter.[1] What was this terror and its cause? "Wadsworth's imminent departure? the first hint of trouble with her eyes? some frightening nervous or mental disturbance?"[2] The "terror" Dickinson alludes to could be a reactivation and intensification of panic attacks.

Researchers like Marks, Gelder, Klein, and Mendel agree that agoraphobia has a bimodal distribution of onset, with the first peak occurring in the late adolescent period and a second around the age of thirty. On the other hand, Sheehan believes that agoraphobia has a single age of onset, first appearing somewhere between the ages of seventeen and thirty-five. However, since the condition is "progressive, with increasing disability, and a chronic fluctuating course,"[3] a second series of panic attacks may represent an intensification of the preexisting illness. In either case — whether agoraphobia has a unimodal or bimodal age distribution — it is clear that agoraphobia fluctuates and is marked by periods of peak activity.

In Dickinson's case, there was a seven-year interval between her first panic attack at church and the unidentified terror of September 1861. Other case histories indicate similar time lapses. Ballenger cites one woman whose illness "began at age sixteen" and who was "unable ... to sit in the center section of the church"; she improved "until age twenty-three, when ... she experienced a severe panic attack."[4] In another instance, a thirty-seven-year-old woman, whose "anxiety and phobic avoidance waxed and waned for years," told the attending doctor how her symptoms had begun nearly "twelve years earlier when she experienced a panic attack" and had only recently, within the six months before she sought treatment, "intensified again."[5] A recent journal article suggests that there may be as much as a "nine year latency period between the onset of panic attack and the development of the severe handicaps characteristic of agoraphobia."[6] Recent evidence corroborates that panic attack and agoraphobia are time-linked. It also suggests that the disorder can appear, abate, and be latent for a number of years before reappearing. Within months of her first attack, Dickinson reacted with avoidant behavior. Possibly she experienced few attacks after 1854, perhaps none at all, until 1861 when it is likely that some "major life-stress event"[7] triggered a second series of panic attacks.

Dickinson had been under a nervous strain several years before 1861. After the move back to the Homestead in November 1855, Mrs. Dickinson's health deteriorated, leaving the responsibility of her well-being and the care of the home in Emily's and Lavinia's hands. In 1856, Austin's marriage to Sue Gilbert increased family conflict. As early as August 1854, there had been a falling out between Sue and Emily. However, "when Austin married Sue, the break in Emily's life was real."[8] The birth of Austin and Sue's first child, which followed in 1861, further severed ties. In a note to Mrs. Samuel Bowles, Richard Sewall detects the tone of "symbolic finality": "As for Austin," Dickinson wrote, "he dont live here — now — He married and went East."[9]

When Vinnie goes to care for her Aunt Lavinia in March 1860, Dickinson admits to Louise Norcross she has had "a curious winter" and that she hasn't "felt well, much."[10] After her aunt's death, the poet is distraught: "I sob and cry till I can hardly see my way 'round the house again."[11] In the same year, she sends Samuel Bowles the poem "Two swimmers wrestled on the spar," preceded by the line "I cant explain it, Mr. Bowles."[12]

Critic Ruth Miller speculates that the article written by Mr. Bowles that appeared in the *Springfield Republican* on 7 July 1860 dealt the poet "a staggering blow."[13] This article, "When Should We Write," dismissed the "literature of misery" written mainly "by women who may be gifted, full of thought and feeling and fancy, but poor, lonely, and unhappy" and represented "the ultimate rejection of all Emily Dickinson stood for." According to Miller, it caused the poet great pain as well as destroyed any hopes she might have had of finding a receptive audience in Bowles.

It should also be remembered that three years before the "terror," Dickinson had begun to write the Master letters. Examining these letters and the poems written then, we realize that both their content and language record Dickinson's anxiety. In 1860 Dickinson spoke of a "drop of Anguish" (poem 193), but by 1862 this anguish became the inundating maelstrom of poem 414. Whatever created her turmoil threatened her mental and physical state, for in a letter to her Norcross cousins, she wrote, "Think Emily lost her wits — but she found 'em, likely. Don't part with wits long at a time in this neighborhood."[14]

Panic attack victims often use the word "terror" to describe their situation. William Leonard, a former professor at the University of Wisconsin, spoke of the "terror of the seizure of terror,"[15] and writer Ruth Vose titled the third chapter of *Agoraphobia*, in which she details the horror of an attack, "The Terror."

Part of this horror is the victim's fear of insanity, of losing his or her mind. Thus the need for privacy, for silence — what Dickinson admits to Higginson, "I could tell to none." Ruth Vose writes that she "shared the all-enveloping desire for no-one to find out about my agoraphobia, a desire which was born of fear that people could not understand, would think me strange or even insane. I suspected that my symptoms did show some form of severe mental illness, so there was no reason that I could see why the rest of the world should disagree with me."[16] It is common for sufferers not to tell anyone—even their doctors, for fear of being misunderstood or judged insane. "The latent fear of going insane can give enormous impetus to the agoraphobe's fear of loss of control. The secret belief that you must be, a 'head case', with all the weird frights and illnesses you are experiencing, makes it paramount that tight control is maintained at all possible times."[17] In *Plaintext*, Nancy Mairs describes her own painful experience as an agoraphobic, how she was misdiagnosed as a schizophrenic and "drugged with powerful antipsychotics." Later she was diagnosed as "suffering from 'severe depression and anxiety' and given antidepressants with tranquilizers and electroconvulsive therapy." When "years afterward" she heard the term *agoraphobia*, she recognized it as her own disorder, although she never spoke of her symptoms out of "shame at my own weakness."[18]

To solve the mystery of their illness, many agoraphobics seek help, usually "in their mid-thirties,"[19] and generally for a physical rather than a psychological cause. Since the illness has such a wide range of symptoms, it has been called "one of the great imposters in medical practice."[20] When patients go for treatment, they may single out one disturbing symptom, such as chest pain, choking, dyspnea, or dizziness. Since they do not know the cause of their panic, they choose the doctor according to their most prominent symptom. Thus, if heart palpitations are troublesome, the victims may go to a cardiologist; if nausea and stomach pain predominate, they see a gastrointestinal specialist. Such an array of symptoms confuses the doctor who treats the symptom rather than the disease.

This confusion is reflected in the various names given to the syndrome. If the presenting symptom is tachycardia, it might be called *cardiac neurosis*; if the symptom is dizziness, then it is *vertigo hysterique*; if the symptom is loss of bowel control, then it is known as *spastic-colon syndrome*. The diagnosis becomes a "nightmare." One study notes that 70 percent of the subjects "had consulted more than ten physicians." Their doctors' inability to correctly diagnose their illness intensified the patients' feelings of fear and isolation.[21]

Da Costa's syndrome is an interesting case in point. First described in 1871, it includes "chronic anxiety and panic attacks."[22] However, its most prominent symptom involves the heart—palpitations, breathlessness, and pain. Two famous patients of the syndrome, Florence Nightingale and Charles Darwin, were diagnosed as suffering from heart disease and became chronic invalids as a result of the prescribed treatment of bed rest. In each instance, symptoms were diagnosed rather than the disease.[23]

According to Marks, agoraphobic patients begin to seek help seventeen months to five years after their attacks. The mean age at Maudsley Hospital

(England) was thirty-four years.[24] This information corresponds with Dickinson's situation. For if her terror in September 1861 was a recurrence of panic attack, then it is approximately two and a half years later, in February 1864, when the poet first goes to Cambridge to consult Dr. Henry Williams about an eye disorder.

Much has been said about the romantic implications of Dickinson's "terror." However, modern scholars believe that Dickinson suffered from an inherited eye disorder that her mother, sister, and brother had. This would explain Dickinson's seclusion, her complaint about bright light, and her sprawling handwriting later in life. But although they all suffered from eye problems, "Emily panicked" — according to Wolff — when she thought her eyes were in jeopardy, and the "terror" reflected her fears of impending blindness.[25] It was "in the fall of 1861" that the poet experienced "the most severe symptoms," although her eye problems "persisted for several years."[26]

This explanation makes more sense than some hazy romantic entanglements, yet questions still remain. Why would the poet hesitate to tell anyone, especially if her eye problem was shared by other family members? There would be no shame or disgrace attached to it. Furthermore, if this is the reason Dickinson chose this time to bind her fascicles together, as Wolff suggests — "Thus the extraordinary number of poems in the handwriting of 1862 probably has a simple, if horrifying, explanation: Emily Dickinson feared (with cogent reason) that she was beginning to go blind"[27] — we have to ask whether someone with "severely impaired vision"[28] would be able or even willing to overtax and strain her eyes in such a prodigious undertaking.

Answers elude us until we turn to the literature of agoraphobia. There is ample evidence that the agoraphobic syndrome includes a sensitivity of the eyes. Thus Dickinson's eye problem may have been a physical symptom of agoraphobia. In a list of symptoms of anxiety neurosis, an earlier category for agoraphobia with panic attack, Dr. Henry Laughlin describes headaches, tinnitus, and blurring of vision as symptoms.[29] He goes on to detail that some patients describe the symptomatic headache as being pressure "behind the eyes."[30]

Further evidence comes from agoraphobic victims themselves. Vose lists one of her symptoms as blindness. "Apart from a tiny area on the periphery of my vision I was totally without sight, a symptom which I now know was a negative scotoma, usually associated with migraine."[31] Leonard's case history is particularly revealing. In his autobiographical account, he writes that in the beginning he felt like "a somatic freak — no doctor seems even to be able to explain my pains."[32] He records a problem with his eyes — "aching and aching, month after month for two years of unrelieved pain."[33] He relates that he had been to many oculists, had many pairs of new glasses, and yet the pain, which caused him many sleepless nights, persisted. One oculist concluded that the cause of this ache—"an actual physical ache—the sudden heavy twinge, half ache, half shooting pain" was "certainly neurotic,"[34] since the examination revealed nothing but astigmatism. The pain "hung on during long months when I scarcely used my eyes at all" and lasted for more than three years. Then one day it left —just as mysteriously as it had come.

This vivid account parallels Dickinson's eye disorder, which she also describes as an ache. Despite her treatments and protracted rest, her eyes do not improve: "This makes me think I am long sick, and this takes the ache to my eyes."[35] Then, just as mysteriously, after her second and final visit to the doctor in May 1865, her eye trouble disappears and "is never alluded to again."[36]

According to Cody, Dickinson's eye trouble is more than somatic. In "Watchers upon the East: the Ocular Complaints of Emily Dickinson," Cody argues that the poet's "photophobia" was "essentially a psychosomatic affliction" brought on by "a grave psychological upheaval" that had begun years before her eye trouble. Since this upheaval Dickinson had an "intense emotional investment" in her eyes that aggravated any organic basis of the disorder and caused her to have "irrational expectations of blindness."[37]

He speculates further that the treatments may have included psychological counseling. The fact that Dickinson saw the doctor on Sunday suggests that she was "a special patient seen during off hours."[38] The poet's "eye disorder was part of an overall depressive picture," and the doctor's role and the poet's emotional reliance on him was more "psychotherapeutic" than medical.[39] Cody concludes that Dickinson's "two year illness ... was an expression of her emotional life."[40]

The treatments appear to have had little effect on Dickinson's condition: "The eyes are as with you, sometimes easy, sometimes sad ... I think them better than when I came home. The snow-light offends them, and the house is bright; notwithstanding, they hope some. ... They say I am a 'help'. Partly because it is true, I suppose, and the rest applause. Mother and Margaret are so kind, father as gentle as he knows how, and Vinnie good to me, but 'cannot see why I don't get well.' This makes me think I am long sick, and this takes the ache to my eyes."[41]

Dickinson's remark that her sister "cannot see why I don't get well" suggests that Vinnie may suspect an underlying emotional cause. Earlier letters allude to Vinnie's reluctance to take the ailment seriously. "You wont think it strange any more will you?" she asks Vinnie in May 1864. In that same letter Dickinson writes that the doctor "wrote to Father, himelf, because He thought it not best for me."[42] The illness now has the authority of the physician, who may have had more to say to Father than the poet guessed.

In the late 1970s, a new theory identifies the root of agoraphobia as an organic brain dysfunction, or OBD. This dysfunction, which manifests itself in visual-perceptual problems, is thought to acccount for up to 75 percent of all agoraphobics. The treatment, developed by Drs. Peter Blythe and David McGlown, has been successful and has brought a new understanding to the illness. Since Emily Dickinson's primary presenting symptom was an eye disorder, the theory bears a closer examination.

As early as 1870 when Benedikt first described the illness later known as agoraphobia, he singled out giddiness as the primary symptom. He named the disorder *Platzschwindel*, meaning "a public place where you get giddy," and traced the cause of this dizziness or giddiness to a "dysfunction of the eye muscles."[43] Today proponents of OBD as the cause of agoraphobia base their work on the same principles, believing that the visual-perceptual dysfunction leaves the individual "stimulus bound" or incapable of ignoring "irrelevant movement within the visual field." This dysfunction gives "rise to a threatened loss of balance," which triggers the agoraphobic's symptoms of dizziness, nausea, inability to judge distance, weakness in the legs, and derealization.[44]

Blythe distinguishes two types of organic brain dysfunction: "one where the gross muscle coordination and balance difficulties are predominant and the other where visual-perceptual problems and occulomotor dysfunction are the most significant."[45] The latter has nothing to do with eyesight, "which can be corrected by optician's lens," but "everything to do with how the eye muscles work and whether the eyes work in concert sending signals back to the visual cortex of the brain."[46] One visual-perceptual problem involves "defective eye movements which result in eyes not yoking together" and "latent strabismus, both divergent when the eye turns out, and convergent when the eye turns in."[47]

This same visual problem has been identified in Emily Dickinson. In 1979, eye specialist Dr. Martin Wand suggested that the poet "probably suffered from extropia,"[48] an eye disorder caused by faulty eye muscle coordination. He diagnosed her condition as strabismus, the inability to direct both eyes to the same object, and based his findings on a deviation in Dickinson's right eye that he detected in the poet's daguerreotype.[49] (Mary Elizabeth Bernhard questions Dr. Wand's use of the daguerreotype as a "sufficient basis for a 'definitive' analysis" of Dickinson's eye problem and suggests that until more substantial evidence is found, i.e., "medical records," that the diagnosis be considered "speculative and uncertain.")[50]

The combination of Wand's hypothesis and Blythe's research suggests that Dickinson's eye disorder can be explained by OBD. In an interesting letter to Mrs. Holland in March 1859, Dickinson writes that she is "afraid at night" and attributes her fear to the movement of her furniture in the room. "Of course one cant expect one's furniture to sit still all night, and if the Chairs do prance—and the Lounge polka a little, and the shovel give it's arm to the tongs, one dont mind such things! From fearing them at first, I've grown to quite admire them, and now we understand each other, it is most enlivening!"[51] This account of "dancing" furniture correlates with the perceptions of individuals suffering from OBD, who "see things moving which . . . cannot move."[52] Since these people are unable to distinguish actual from imagined movement around them, they become frightened.

In her first documented panic attack, Dickinson writes that in an attempt to calm herself she "discovered nothing up in the sky somewhere, and gazed intently at it, for quite a half an hour." After the service she reports, "several roared around, and, sought to devour me."[53] In her discussion of OBD, Vose compares the anxiety attack to motion sickness and seasickness, in which holding the head still helps to control the dizziness and nausea.[54] Like Dickinson during an attack, she rested her eyes on "anything to keep the other feelings from overwhelming" her. "The common factor in all the things I chose to look at is that none of them moved, so causing less stress to the eyes, and keeping the tension level stable."[55]

Clinical studies done by Blythe and McGlown confirm that 82 percent of the patients suffering from OBD have "a latent convergence in one or both eyes."[56] Because these individuals are "stimulus bound" and have "poor scanning ability,"[57] they pick up all movement around them and cannot tolerate a lot of activity or people around them. "They become overwhelmed by the barrage of stimuli to the eyes."[58] Thus it is possible that when Dickinson was out in open fields—as she was when she watched the train festivities from Professor Tyler's woods—or in public places like church, she experienced the characteristic dizziness or vertigo caused by this visual dysfunction and was inundated. "Patients are often emotionally upset after an episode of vertigo, and particularly when it develops without warning; they may become extremely frightened."[59]

The research into organic brain dysfunction suggests further that those people who suffer from OBD are more prone to neurosis due to their "lower stress tolerance" and, therefore, are "more likely to be affected by emotional and physical stress."[60] They can cope with their disability as long as their stress level is tolerable. But when stresses exceed a healthy level of control, the dysfunction reveals itself in a frightening episode of panic. When Dickinson faced "the Phantom" in her attack of 1854 and the terror "she could tell to none" in 1861, she experienced panic that today could logically be explained by those who believe in the impact of OBD: "When there is a concentration of irregular movement, noise and bright light, the stimulus can get too much and the nervous system will 'blow a fuse.' "[61] (New theories into the biological bases of phobias appear daily. One recent book, *Phobia Free*, relates the causes of phobias and panic attack to inner ear problems. Chapter 5 connects malfunctions of the inner ear with visual problems such as "fear of bright lights, fear of crowds" and suggests that they produce anxiety. "The inner ear system guides the movement of our eyes, enabling us to track the movement of visual information in our environment. If this tracking process is impaired, the eyes may be incapable of keeping pace with this visual information and anxiety may surface." Further, this "visual tracking problem" may be aggravated by "underlying balance and/or compass and/or motion related problems," which can also provoke anxiety.)[62]

9

"I Told My Soul to Sing"

Victims of agoraphobia seek relief in a number of ways. One way is by being active at night, when they can move about "more freely ... than in the daytime."[1] Some wear dark glasses that shield them from bright light. (Recall Dickinson's complaint that "the snow-light offends them [her eyes], and the house is bright.")[2] One patient writes of feeling "better in the evening than in the morning, partly because the darkness seems to have a quieting effect on me."[3]

In an account of her long-standing agoraphobia, Mrs. F. H. details her fear of light. She writes that "walking alone in broad daylight was my worst hazard."[4] "... at night I could go about more freely than in daylight without the dread fear that I couldn't get home, because darkness to a considerable degree, hid my fears from me; in the dark I couldn't see the things that prevented me from going home."[5] So, too, other agoraphobes find the night comforting because "they cannot see where they are in space and the brain is less confused."[6]

As early as January 1850, Dickinson documents her preference for the night and its privacy. Telling Jane Humphrey about the letters that are not written but are thought, she writes, "I have written those at night—when the rest of the world were at sleep—when only God came between us—and no one else might hear. No need of shutting the door—nor of whispering timidly—nor of fearing the ear of listeners—for night held them fast in his arms that they could not interfere—and his arms are brawny and strong."[7]

In December 1850, Dickinson claims the night as her own: "I write Abiah tonight because it is cool and quiet, and I can forget the toil and care of the feverish day, and then I am selfish, too, because I am feeling lonely."[8] In another note she records a visit to Abiah's friend: "Yet I went in the dusk, and it was Saturday evening, so even then, Abiah, you see how cares pursued me."[9] This was July 1854 when Dickinson had begun her pattern of avoidance. Six months later, she writes to Sue in Grand Haven, Michigan, "I miss you, mourn for you and walk the Streets alone—often at night ..."[10]

Not only does she walk alone at night, but she writes and plays the piano "after honest hours."[11] In 1858, Dickinson dedicates a poem to her father, "to whose untiring efforts in my behalf, I am indebted for my morning-hours viz-3 AM to 12 PM."[12]

Dickinson chose the night for its cloak of invisibility and for the privacy it gave her to express her thoughts. Although the evidence of agoraphobia is apparent in the poet's restrictive life-style and ultimate seclusion, it is in the poetry that we fully sense its impact. For as Dickinson experienced the mental anguish of this terrifying and unknown illness, she turned to poetry and learned how to survive. Writing poetry while the "souls of sanity" slept was her primary way of coping with her situation.

In June 1869, when Dickinson told Higginson she could not come to Boston, she included this cryptic remark: "Of our greatest acts we are ignorant — You were not aware that you saved my Life. To thank you in person has been since then one of my few requests."[13] Curious to know how he had saved her life, Higginson went to Amherst. However, if he had reread her letters, he would have found the answer in her third letter to him. Written 7 June 1862, the letter refers to the death of Benjamin Newton: "My dying Tutor told me that he would like to live till I had been a poet, but Death was much of a Mob as I could master — then — And when far afterward — a sudden light on Orchards, or a new fashion in the wind troubled my attention — I felt a palsy, here — the Verses just relieve — "[14]

The letter reveals how the poet felt when her friend died in 1853. Although his death did not find expression in the letters of the period, it was at work subterraneanly, undermining her sense of purpose as a poet and her belief in a long life — a life she had seen was uncertain. In this short paragraph, the fear of death is objectified in the image of death as a crowd, which to the agoraphobic is terrifying. "Death was much of a Mob as I could master — then." Newton's death had caught her off guard. She was over-whelmed, which she images in "a sudden light, a new fashion in the wind" — objective realities that create fear and induce a "palsy" or uncontrollable bodily shaking present in panic attack. She alleviates this fear by writing poetry.

This brief letter explains the reason she writes, one similar to her admission in her second letter when she writes of the "Terror" that causes her to "sing, as the Boy does by the Burying Ground because I am afraid."[15] Dickinson identifies the generator of her poetry — the fears that fuel her creativity and find relief in expression. Poetry is therapeutic, allowing her to live within her circumscribed world.

To begin the study of the poems, we must go to the end of the poet's life, to her death in 1886 and the discovery of her 1,775 poems. We can only imagine Lavinia Dickinson's surprise when she opened her sister's cherry bureau drawer and beheld the production of her sister's lifetime: the forty bound fascicles, the unbound fascicle sheets, the miscellaneous worksheets, drafts, and copies, the "scraps" of poetry collected in her sister's bottom drawer. Recently these fascicles, along with other fascicle pages, worksheets, and "scraps" — the term used by Mabel Loomis Todd — were reassembled by Ralph W. Franklin in *The Manuscript Books of Emily Dickinson*, an edition that brings together for the first time the manuscripts of the poet "restored as closely as possible to their original order."[16] The fascicles are the booklets of poems recopied by Dickinson onto standard stationery and tied together by hand. These were private acts of publication in a world in which she said that publication was as foreign to her "as Firmament to Fin."[17]

It was Mabel Loomis Todd who named these booklets *fascicules* and her daughter Millicent Todd Bingham who used the word *fascicles* — a corrupted form of the word — to refer to them. Lavinia Dickinson had called them simply "gatherings" of poems. In 1955, when the variorum edition of Dickinson's poems was published, its editor Thomas Johnson called these collections of poems *packets*. However, in each instance, whether the word *gatherings*, *packets*, or *fascicles* is used, it refers to the forty books assembled by Dickinson in which she attempted to preserve her poems.[18]

Franklin identifies the fascicles as Dickinson's "own form of bookmaking" and describes the process this way: first the poet selected the poems to be copied and transferred them from worksheets "onto uniform sheets of stationery." She then destroyed the worksheets and stacked the "copied sheets on top of one another," binding them together by hand with needle and twine. She began this practice in 1858–59 and "stopped binding fascicle sheets about 1864." This, according to Franklin, was "a conscious change rather than an action deferred and then forgotten." Franklin theorizes that Dickinson may have stopped this practice because "once she had survived the crisis and drive of 1861–1863, her need for self-publication declined, and with it the desire to leave an organized legacy for the world."[19]

Before Franklin, most critics chose to organize the poet's enormous production via a thematic arrangement. Editors Mabel Loomis Todd and Thomas Wentworth Higginson used four subject categories to introduce the poems: life, love, nature, time, and eternity. Charles Anderson divided the work into four areas — poetics, mind, nature, and death. However since Franklin's work — beginning with *The Editing of Emily Dickinson*, in which he suggested a reordering of the variorum edition — closer attention has been focused on the forty bound fascicles and their arrangement. In *The Poetry of Emily Dickinson*, Ruth Miller argued that the poems in the fascicles are one "long-linked poem" and that they follow a narrative structure of quest through resolution. Comparing Dickinson's fascicles with Francis Quarles's *Emblems, Divine and Moral*, Miller suggests that Dickinson borrowed this pattern from Quarles in order to develop her own themes and images in poems that are "discrete but intricately related."[20]

Most recently William Shurr, in *The Marriage of Emily Dickinson*, used the fascicle arrangement to explain another narrative structure. To him, "the narrative core of Emily Dickinson's fascicle poetry is the classic love triangle involving the married couple and the outsider."[21] In this scenario Dickinson is the outsider who loves an already married man and pledges "herself in a spiritual marriage." The relationship is consummated, and the result is "pregnancy or the deep fear of pregnancy," which, according to Shurr, explains the "terror since September." Shurr finds this tragic story unfolded within the scope of the fascicles and believes it reveals "a portrait of Dickinson as the American poet of romantic love par excellence."[22]

Another recent study by M. L. Rosenthal and Sally Gall investigates two of the forty fascicles as examples of the "multiple sequence" later developed by Yeats, Pound, and Williams in the twentieth century. The authors focus their attention on fascicles 15 and 16 because taken together they "make an epic of subjective life ... pressing in its pursuit of the inmost depths of feeling."[23] They believe other fascicles also show clear relationships.

What these fascicles mean in terms of sequence and arrangement has become an area fraught with controversy. Sewall admits that "it is possible that the gatherings were not haphazard and that the editorial freedom so far taken with them may have violated Emily Dickinson's profoundest intentions."[24] To be sure "the fascicles ... are central to understanding Dickinson's habits of composition and organization. Their implications for biography and criticism are pervasive."[25] Several studies have already explored the meaning of Dickinson's arrangement and undoubtedly there will be more. Rosenthal predicts that "a thorough study of all forty fascicles" will "be one of the great voyages of discovery in modern criticism."[26]

Franklin addresses the question of fascicle arrangement directly. While the "possibility" of finding some artistic arrangement at the core of Dickinson's fascicles is "attractive," it "is not supported by the developmental history of the fascicles."[27] Instead he sees them as an attempt by the poet "to reduce disorder in her manuscripts"[28]: "they served Dickinson as her workshop put in order and, for the years they cover, are a comprehensive record almost complete, of the poems in her possession—a condition at variance with their being forty careful selections for artistic purposes."[29]

If this is so, what can be said of the fascicle reconstruction and its advantages to the student of Dickinson? First, the bound fascicles, which cover a period of six years from 1858 to 1864, provide a lens through which a more focused angle of vision is possible. The boundary years—1858 and 1864—limit the number of poems under consideration and permit a more incisive look at the poet's work. Secondly, since the poems were gathered within approximately the same time frame, they provide an enduring record of the poet during the crisis years. When the poems are related to the life of Dickinson, they open up the events of those troubled years and yield a deeper insight and clearer meaning.

10

"A Prison Gets to Be a Friend"

According to Allen Tate, "There is none of whom it is truer to say that the poet is the poetry."[1] Wolff agrees, noting that the "real Emily Dickinson resides in the poetry. Life has been supplanted by art."[2] Indeed Dickinson is the poetry. She lived the experience of her poems rather than imagined it. The speaker of the poems was not some supposed or representative person as she claimed, but herself. In her creative work, Dickinson reacted to the same pressures and torments she experienced in life. Forced to hide behind her poetry out of a need for privacy and an embarrassment at the poems' "bald" truth, Dickinson explored the landscape of her world and charted its terrain. Poetry was her way out, a way to deal with a life that otherwise would have been impossible to bear.

As we look through the fascicle poems, we recognize the pattern of an agoraphobic life-style: the flight from fears, the need for protection within her father's house, the atmosphere of family conflict, and the desire for release from tormenting inner pressures. Without an understanding of agoraphobia, Dickinson's life appears erratic and eccentric without any direction or design. However, once we locate evidence of the syndrome within the fascicles, we are struck by the clarification it brings. "Dickinson's pattern is in her poems, and they are a more reliable map to her life than the abstract psychological theories frequently and ruthlessly applied to her."[3] With the facts of her life as a background and an understanding of the illness as a guide, we can carve a path through the external details of Dickinson's life and enter into the terrors of the crisis years.

Although agoraphobia is not a rare illness but "the most common of all phobias,"[4] afflicting eight to ten people in every thousand,[5] it is only in the twentieth century that it appears to be common. This is not only because it has been more reported, but because more research has been done in recent years. Much has been suggested about the root causes of the illness, from psychological and emotional causes to biologic and genetic factors. However, even those who believe that agoraphobia springs from a physical dysfunction use psychotherapy since the physical and the psychological are interrelated in this complex syndrome. The event that sets the phobia in motion can be any one of several, including such occurrences as a serious illness, a major

79

operation, a sudden shock, or the death of a loved one. While this triggers the phobia, it is not the primary cause, which often hides beneath a network of emotional and psychological anxieties. A phobia by its very definition is "a defense against a still deeper fear—a basic insecurity ..." that began earlier in life when the individual was "utterly helpless and quite unable to cope with ... [the] terror."[6] At that time fears were repressed and later projected onto a newer fear like going out of the house. This fear is dealt with by avoidance, by remaining indoors. Thus while the individual may believe he or she is imprisoned in the house, he or she feels secure and safe on "familiar ground."[7]

> Some keep the Sabbath going to Church—
> I keep it, staying at Home—
> With a Bobolink for a Chorister—
> And an Orchard, for a Dome—
>
> Some keep the Sabbath in Surplice—
> I just wear my Wings—
> And instead of tolling the Bell, for Church,
> Our little Sexton—sings.
>
> God preaches, a noted Clergyman—
> And the sermon is never long,
> So instead of getting to Heaven, at last—
> I'm going, all along.[8]

When we read poem 324 (fasc. 9), which was written about 1860, we enjoy the sparkling wit of the speaker who goes to church in her garden where "a Bobolink" is "Chorister" and "God"—"a noted Clergyman"—"preaches." However, when we place this poem within the context of Dickinson's life, its pantheistic suggestions fade to reveal Dickinson's fear of crowds and public gatherings. If we recall her panic attack in January 1854, her decision to arrive early at church to avoid the eyes of the congregation, we realize that this poem—as pleasant as it appears—poetically documents Dickinson's decision to "stay Home" from church, a common reaction to the agoraphobic's fear of experiencing panic in front of onlookers. Witness this remark from Martha K., a housewife who lives within a large house that "she seldom leaves except to work in the garden." "I don't even like to go to church anymore, unless I can sit in the back row, on the aisle, in case something happens. One day we went and the aisle seats were taken, so I couldn't stay. I mean, I'd feel so awful having to run out of the church in front of everybody, or passing out where they'd all see me!"[9] This corresponds with Dickinson's experience that January day when "the aisles seemed, full huge enough before, as I quaked slowly up—and reached my usual seat!"[10] As uncomfortable and frightening as her terror was, Dickinson could deal with it by staying away from church.

In the late 1860s, Dickinson's phobia became more pervasive until she was not able to go "out of the house at all."[11] Another agoraphobe's account emphasizes this complete restriction. "Finding myself in the midst of a large gathering would inspire a feeling of terror on my part. This could be relieved in but one way—by getting away from the spot as soon as possible. Acting on this impulse I have not been to church, theatres, even funerals, simply because of an utter inability to control myself to stay. For ten years I have not been to church, to the theatre ... or any form of popular gathering, except where I could remain in the background, with means of egress convenient. Even at my mother's funeral, when it would be supposed that everything else would be subordinated to the impulse of natural affection, I was utterly unable to bring myself to sit with the other members of the family in the front of the church."[12] Dickinson, too, did not attend her father's funeral but "stayed upstairs in her own room with the door open just a crack, where she could hear without being seen."[13]

Poem 325 (fasc. 13) encapsulates Dickinson's pattern of flight and the meaning of home. The protection the poet felt within her home is typical of agoraphobes who are "defending themselves against deep rooted feelings 'of unsafety' " and who equate safety with their home and parents.[14] In "Of Tribulation these are They" the reader can perceive how Dickinson's home functioned as her safety zone.

> Of Tribulation—these are They,
> Denoted by the White.
> The Spangled Gowns, a lesser Rank
> Of Victors, designate—
>
> All these—did conquer—
> But the Ones who overcame most times—
> Wear nothing commoner than Snow—
> No Ornament—but Palms—
>
> "Surrender"—is a sort unknown
> On this Superior soil—
> "Defeat", an Outgrown Anguish,
> Remembered—as the Mile
>
> Our panting Ancle barely passed,
> When Night devoured the Road—
> But we—stood—whispering in the House—
> And all we said—was
>   SAVED!

While the poem seems to describe Dickinson herself in her wearing of the "White" and in her endurance of "Defeat"—"an outgrown Anguish"— the poem is a "paraphrase of Revelation 7."[15] In Revelation, we recognize the source of the word *tribulation* along with the identification of those dressed in white — "out of great tribulation, and have washed their robes, and made them white in the blood of the Lamb." However, the second half of the poem grows directly out of Dickinson's own fear and her escape home. Here we see the imagery of flight in the "panting Ancle" [*sic*] as it runs desperately home to be "saved," a word "spelled out in large letters."[16] When the poem was first collected in *Poems* (1891), it was titled "Saved!"[17] drawing attention to the poem's dramatic conclusion, a climax that underscores the speaker's fearful impulses. While this poem was written no later than 1861, as its placement in fascicle 13 suggests, it is conceivable that it refers to the experience in January 1854. If so, then it reinforces the horror of that day since it demonstrates that the experience is graphically preserved in her memory, "Remembered — as the Mile" becoming part of her storehouse of images. Doctors report that "most subjects recall vividly the onset of panic attack and cite it as a significant life event. Sometimes they identify the hour, day, and precise location, even many years later."[18] Since this poem was sent to Higginson in July 1862, it might also indicate that Dickinson was still experiencing panic attacks.

The image of the house as safety emerges from Dickinson's own life-style, not from the text of Revelation 7. *House* and *home* were important words to Dickinson, representing equally important concepts. Mudge, in *Emily Dickinson and the Image of Home*, estimates that these words plus cognates of each appear in 210 poems or "about twelve percent of her known poems."[19] To Dickinson, the word *home* is especially significant since it "reflects her inner landscape, which may be called her 'spatial inscape,' a sensitivity to space dependent on both personal and social factors."[20] Thus in poem 325 we are witnessing the poet's limitation of space, her withdrawal into the house in which she felt "SAVED!" In this poem there is a unique blending of materials: biblical sources with Dickinson's own personal experience. Dickinson may have envisioned herself saved in a religious sense through the suffering she endured, but the actual basis for her "salvation" was the literal sense of protection she experienced staying within her father's house. While following the metaphorical line of the poem, the reader risks overlooking its literal foundation, an experience that springs from the life of the poet.

It is not uncommon for the agoraphobic victim to be ashamed of fears and to try to hide them from outsiders. In fact, "embarrassment about having agoraphobia" is cited in a recent study as one of the reasons the disorder is so difficult to diagnose.[21] In poem 412 (fasc. 15) the speaker's sentence is reviewed and she is made aware of "The Date, and manner, of the shame," a shame that is unidentified. Agoraphobes do not know the cause or reason for their fear. In an attempt to cover up this shame and in fear that someone might think him or her "mentally disturbed," the victim "suffers in silence."[22]

Interestingly, many agoraphobes write of their illness anonymously.[23] "The urgent need for anonymity must hide many thousands of agoraphobes from the eye of the public."[24] One agoraphobe admits that she had an "all enveloping desire for no one to find out about my agoraphobia—a desire which was born of fear that people would not understand, would think me strange or even insane." She continues "Initially I suspected that my symptoms did show some form of mental illness, so there was no reason that I could see why the rest of the world should disagree with me."[25] Dickinson might well be addressing her own secret shame of agoraphobia and her need for silence when, in poem 381, she declines to share "A Secret." It is better to be afraid of the secret itself, "A Secret—kept— / That—can appal but One—" than to be afraid of the secret "And Whom you told it to—beside."

The idea of hiding is most tellingly dealt with in an early poem from fascicle 9. This poem reveals the speaker's life-style, one that matches Dickinson's own habits of hiding from people. In stanza 1, the "I" speaker and her companion Tim "bolt the door tight / To prevent a friend" and then "hide our brave face / Deep in our hand" (poem 196). Poem 903 (fasc. 3) also speaks of hiding. Dickinson often sent flowers and verses to people as a token of her friendship. In this instance the speaker announces, "I hide myself within my flower" and concludes with the desire that the recipient will feel "Almost a loneliness" for her.

Another poem that deals with hiding refers to the agoraphobic fear of being a public spectacle or being stared at. "The fear of being 'seen' or drawing excessive attention to oneself in a public place is a common theme in agoraphobia," one victim stating she did not "feel 'strong enough' to absorb all the attention."[26] "One group of fears centers around doing something 'embarrassing' that will draw public attention, such as trembling, blushing, vomiting. Others are centered on doing something unremarkable (such as eating, drinking, or writing) in front of other people."[27] One agoraphobic woman went outside only when streets were empty because "Then nobody would see me, no matter what I did."[28] In poem 891, the speaker is especially sensitive to "Nature's sentinels" and complains that she cannot find "Privacy." In the second stanza, she states: "In Cave if I presumed to hide / The Walls—began to tell— / Creation seemed—a mighty Crack — / To make me visible—."

The speaker's discomfort with visibility recalls poem 413, in which even Heaven is distrusted because God "Himself—a Telescope / Perennial beholds us— / Myself would run away / From Him—and Holy Ghost— and All—." Thus the speaker in both poems desires anonymity rather than visibility and is prepared to run and hide. In her account of agoraphobia, Mrs. F. H. describes the feeling of being watched and judged: "the many windows in the tall buildings weren't windows, but eyes that watched me with a malign intent."[29]

It is significant that in poem 413 God's vision and judgment of the speaker are the most painful. Not only does the poet fear places, but people who criticize her as well. In one case study it was determined that the patient "was afraid to reveal her vulnerable, anxiety-ridden self for fear she would be ridiculed." In another, an agoraphobe had parents who were "monolithic authority figures during her childhood; indeed they had criticized and jeered at her when she demonstrated shyness and anxiety in social situations."[30] In Dickinson's letters, we hear how her father was critical of her and made her feel foolish at times. She reserves her rebellion against her father and her home for poems in which the speaker challenges God and defies authority, for example, poem 61 (fasc. 7), "Papa Above!" This defiance was hidden, like the poems "in Lady's Drawer," and undoubtedly informed the battlefield imagery found in Dickinson's poems.

In poem 594 (fasc. 29), the conflict is set in the province of one's own soul: "The Battle fought between the Soul / And No Man — is the One / Of all the Battles prevalent / By far the Greater One — ." It is a battle endless to "endure." In this scene, Dickinson envisions herself in need of aid. In poem 42 (fasc. 2), she cries out for help at the onslaught of "Another Day!" The speaker in extremis calls for prayers from the "Passerby" because the "issues" of this war are crucial: "Steady — my soul: What issues / Upon thine arrow hang!" This battle of the soul, enacted over and over as visualized in poem 594, brought defeat rather than victory, Dickinson consciously identifying with the victim. In poem 67 (fasc. 5), the speaker knows the sweet taste of success only because it is not hers: "As he defeated — dying — / On whose forbidden ear / The distant strains of triumph / Burst agonized and clear!" and in poem 639 (fasc. 33) she recognizes "My Portion is Defeat — today / A paler luck than Victory." The poem's ending is telling. To have victory, the loser would have been "Contenteder — to die." Losing means living on in the pain and remembrance of one's defeat.

What Dickinson could not deal with were her normal desires to be independent and free of her dominating family life. These brought overwhelming anxieties as well as guilt. Recall the letter when her rage at her father took her outside where she "opened the gate very desperately, and for a little while the suspense was terrible."[31] According to Wolff, the poet's anger toward her father was "a veritable time bomb!"[32] Her rebellion was "held in check" at a great personal cost, for Dickinson's inability to assert herself and to be independent kept her at home in an environment that alternately poisoned and sustained her.

However, her problem was also her solution, for "one of the undoubted advantages of agoraphobia" is that "it can provide unconsciously a most convenient escape from life's problems."[33] Thus Dickinson found escape in the prison of her home — "There is a certain security in your present position — you know when you are in prison — it is familiar ground. Your emotional lifestyle gives you a 'safe' feeling—as an invalid feels more at home with illness."[34]

The poet reaped certain rewards from her imprisonment. In poem 652 (fasc. 22) Dickinson admits that "A Prison gets to be a friend." Here is the pattern of the agoraphobic as he or she flees the terrors of the outside world to a home that is a "guarantee of security and protection."[35] One agoraphobe's greatest fear was that if she left home she would never get back: "As I went on, the words, 'Home is where love is. You will never get back home,' came with insistence."[36] An investigator argues that the "need to find security in 'staying home' is distinct and not merely reactive to the fear of going out." "The home is often chosen as the inanimate environment . . . one that calms and reassures," one "experienced as an extension of the self or self-object." He names this distinctive element *hestiaphilia* for the agoraphobic love of hearth and home.[37]

In poem 652, Dickinson depicts this hestiaphilia; the speaker, tallying the gains against the losses, looks on the prison of her home "with gratitude":

> A Prison gets to be a friend—
> Between it's Ponderous face
> And Our's—a Kinsmanship express-
> And in it's narrow Eyes—
>
> We come to look with gratitude
> For the appointed Beam
> It deal us—stated as our food—
> And hungered for—the same—
>
> We learn to know the Planks—
> That answer to Our feet—
> So miserable a sound—at first—
> Nor even now—so sweet—
>
> As plashing in the Pools—
> When Memory was a Boy—
> But a Demurer Circuit—
> A Geometric Joy—
>
> The Posture of the Key
> That interrupt the Day
> To Our Endeavor—Not so real
> The Cheek of Liberty
>
> As this Phantasm Steel—
> Whose features—Day and Night—
> Are present to us—as Our Own—
> And as escapeless—quite—

> The narrow Round—the Stint—
> The slow exchange of Hope—
> For something passiver—Content
> Too steep for looking up—
>
> The Liberty we knew
> Avoided—like a Dream—
> Too wide for any Night but Heaven—
> If That—indeed—redeem—

We recognize Dickinson's large country home, "its ponderous face" in its beams and planks. Between herself and the prison, a kinship has grown, despite its "narrow Eyes"—that is, the restricted and limited life it allows her. The gratitude she finds in stanza 2 is that of the anxious person who finds comfort in the safety and protection the house grants, its "appointed Beam" like the food she needs and "hungered for." Thus safety to her —which seclusion within the house brings—is essential in her life. Never leaving the house, she gets to "know the Planks" and is familiar with their "sweet" sound, even though their narrowness made them "miserable" at first. But the planks are not as sweet as the memories of younger, freer days, when she could enjoy the "plashing in the Pools." By contrast the confinement within the house provides "a Demurer Circuit—A Geometric Joy" and makes the idea of being set free—the "Key" to freedom—not as real as the "Phantasm Steel" of her prison.

It is interesting to note her use of the word *Phantasm*, a choice over a variant *Companion*, which reveals that the prison is figurative—within her own mind. Yet well she knows its features, both "Day and Night," and realizes that they are "escapeless—quite." The "quite" at the end of the line reinforces the fact that although Dickinson knew her prison was insubstantial—figurative rather than literal—she was still incapable of leaving its confines. In the last two stanzas we witness the course of her life as an agoraphobic, the "narrow Round," the growing restrictions, the daily inroads on her outside social life that slowly change her "Hope" of ever leaving to something "passiver."

Doctors treating agoraphobia would identify the speaker's "narrow Round" as a "circle of safety." It is a "most common pattern" in agoraphobes "where there is a 'circle of safety' around their homes within which they can freely travel unaccompanied. The circle may have a radius of a few blocks or a few miles and is generally marked by boundaries of broad or heavily trafficked streets the agoraphobic is particularly hesitant to cross."[38] This circle has also been called a "locus of control"[39] and can easily be translated into Dickinson's "narrow Round" or "Circumference."

The placement of "Content" at the end of the line allows the word to be read in two ways: one, that she became content within this narrow life, or two, that the emotion she exchanged hope for was something else, something nameless, and "Content" was "too steep for looking up," something she could never achieve.

The last stanza is painful because although the whole poem implies an acceptance of the imprisoned life, the last stanza recalls the terrors of agoraphobia, the "Liberty" she knew—but "Avoided" because it was "like a Dream"—not possible for her to achieve in this life. This dream of liberty, this prospect of a fuller life was "too wide for any Night but Heaven." It is not possible in real life, but perhaps in Heaven, "If That—indeed—redeem." There is doubt of ever reaching fulfillment, not in this world and perhaps not in the next. Instead of resignation, there is a painful despair.

Agoraphobics also suffer from claustrophobia, the fear of being closed in or trapped. "Most agoraphobics have extensive symptoms, and it is exceptional to find a discrete fear of open spaces without other fears."[40] Since the disease is complex, the term *agoraphobia* is underinclusive: "these patients have fears not only of going into open spaces but also of shopping, crowds, travelling, closed spaces, to name but a few."[41] "The term is chosen because the commonest and most constricting elements of this condition are fears of going out into public places of various kinds. But simply knowing that a patient has fears of going out into the street and crowded places enables one to predict that many other features of the syndrome will be present, including the fact that he may also be claustrophobic, be afraid of fainting, dying or going mad or losing control."[42] This is more easily understood if one realizes that what patients actually fear are their own reactions to fear. These fears are internal rather than external. Dickinson was unable to escape her fears because they were within her. Thus it can be seen that since agoraphobia comes on from within, it is quite comprehensive and incorporates a wide range of fears.

It is not difficult to see this element of claustrophobia in Dickinson's poetry. Ruth Miller lists eleven poems that have the metaphor of the cage or prison in them.[43] Linda Huf, in *A Portrait of the Artist as a Young Woman*, finds the imagery of entrapment balanced by the imagery of flight as "the female artist sees herself as caught in a trap" and "conceives of her escape from prison in Icarian terms."[44] This imagery, although not exclusively feminine, is particularly revealing in the poetry of Dickinson where entrapment appears alternately self-willed and involuntary. This paradox is explained at a deeper psychological level by Alexandra Symonds, who maintains that "all these fears which the patients described, the fear of being closed in, trapped, helpless, and without control, are symbolic expressions of how the individual closes herself in, keeps down her impulses and imprisons herself." "These women are actually afraid to be in control. They feared the consequences of taking their life into their own hands."[45]

In poems 538 (fasc. 30) and 613 (fasc. 21), Dickinson defines her entrapment as being enforced by outside agents—"They shut me in the Cold." Literally closed in—"in the Closet" in poem 613—she is symbolically cut off from the warmth of their attention—"Themselves were warm." Accompanying this entrapment was an emotional void, a cessation of love that she doesn't directly name but describes vaguely: they "could not know the feeling 'twas." In poem 613, she turns to a vision of flight, the impounded bird who "has but to will / And . . . Abolish his captivity" (variant reading). Unfortunately the speaker does not share this ability—"No more have I." Mudge believes that perhaps these poems represent a childhood punishment, that Dickinson may have been locked in her closet as a form of discipline "proscribed by the Reverend Mr. Abbott in *The Mother at Home.*"[46]

Poem 612, a poem related to 613 in content and position, depicts the gnat's power as superior to the speaker's: "How mightier He—than I." Like the bird in 613 who could will an end to his captivity, the gnat can find release in death, an option the speaker envies: "Upon the Window Pane / To gad my little Being out— / And not begin—again." The anguish of entrapment leads to such a need for escape that even suicide becomes appealing. The speaker's need for escape, however, is doomed to failure, as seen in poem 77 (fasc. 6) where the "I" tugs "childish at my bars / Only to fail again!"

Other images of claustrophobia are found in 128 (fasc. 6) and 475 (fasc. 33). Poem 128 asks questions that are not answered: "Who built this little Alban House / And shut the windows down so close / My spirit cannot see?—Who'll let me out some gala day / With implements to fly away, / Passing Pomposity?" Here the idea of being shut in is accompanied by the desire to be let out, "to fly away." Poem 475 is perhaps more hopeless since not even a dream of liberty is possible—"Because Escape—is done—" The condition or state of "Doom" is identified with a "House," but this one is "without the Door." In its finality, it is death; in its symbolic power it is being locked in with no hope of exit. After one enters "from the Sun," "the Ladder's thrown away" and the only sustainer is "the Dream / Of what they do outside." "They" is anonymous, referring perhaps to the creatures of nature, or to the "they," who earlier, in poems 538 and 613, shut her in.

Dickinson desired to be free from the family who dominated her, from the home that became her prison. In letter after letter to Austin, she rehearses an independence she is never able to achieve, choosing to be with her brother rather than with her parents, wishing to tell him things she could never speak aloud at home. Her desire for freedom is imaged in the poems, where the gravity of her situation is evident in the desperateness of the act. Suicide or violent release was a definite poetic option. "Suicide poems and obliquely suggestive ones make a considerable list."[47] "Indeed, she thought about suicide in a crucial cluster of powerful poems, well aware that it was given to her to be done with life. . . . Life astonished her with its denials."[48] Cody cites several poems that "deal with the suicide theme" which accompanied Dickinson's "personality disintegration."[49]

Embedded in fascicle 14, the gathering immediately preceding the most tormented fascicles, poems 277 and 423 address suicide, the first confronting the issue directly while the second does so in a more oblique way. Both are included in the same fascicle with poems 272 and 584, which deal with the numbing aftereffects of some shock, making the idea of release from emotional anxieties more appealing.

In poem 277, Dickinson uses imagery contained in her letter to Austin.[50] Here Dickinson reveals an emotional duress at its height. Rather than openly express rage at a father who treats her like a child, she represses it. She tells Austin that she ran out of the house, "opened the gate very desperately" and "was held in check by some invisible agent." Within the context of poem 277, she is at another gate—the fleshly gate—which she imagines bursting and escaping. She longs to "step in Liberty." Once past the barrier and away from the anonymous "them" who hold her back, she is safe: "They cannot take me—any more!" The thought that follows is significant. It is not the force that she recalls which holds her, but "Dungeons," the feeling of being trapped or locked in. After this act of defiance and the achievement of freedom, all else pales in importance—"Unmeaning—now to me."

The other "slant" reference to suicide in poem 423 (fasc. 14) is more desperate, although less violent. Instead of the imagery of breaking through, the poet uses the imagery of sewing. In its final stanza, there is a striking analogy to children at play. In this poem, we visualize the poet threading her way through the fascicles, tying the packets together and placing them in "her mysterious Drawers." Although this interpretation lies within the subtext, it is instructive as to the poem's total meaning. We see Dickinson trying to control her fate, as she arranged and stitched her work together, ordering her life. It is precisely this lack of control that is at the heart of the poem, for the speaker notes there are ends to periods of time, a knot or finality that cannot be "untied" by any power. She turns to the earth, who "lays back their tired lives" in "her mysterious Drawers," putting them to rest "tenderly." However, in the last stanza there is a shift of imagery to children who, "weary of the Day," "cannot put" themselves "away." Although tired of activity, they are unable to control their lives. By extension, the poem speaks about power and powerlessness, Dickinson recognizing that, like a child, she is powerless to end or "knot" the years and put herself away.

11

"A Thing So Terrible"

Franklin's reconstruction of the forty original fascicles offers a new route for Dickinson studies, inviting readers to enter the frame of specific fascicles and find gatherings that are linked, if not aesthetically, then chronologically. Although the time frames are approximate, Franklin's statement that Dickinson's "copying was systematic and may have kept up fairly well with her poetic production"[1] suggests that the poems were copied close to their composition date. If so, then the date of the fascicle should afford the reader a closer look into the life circumstances of that period. Franklin's study also confirms that Dickinson's production during the year 1862 was "extraordinary": "Twenty of the forty fascicles may be assigned to that year alone." While this reflects the poet's "new resolve in 1862 to organize her poetry,"[2] it also emphasizes the enormous creative energy she poured into her work at this time. Although these twenty fascicles warrant a complete examination, the total of over three hundred poems makes a comprehensive consideration impossible for this present study. Rather, two fascicles, 15 and 16, will serve as entries into the year 1862. In their study of the modern poetic sequence, Rosenthal and Gall recognize "the violent psychological and artistic upheaval" reflected in these two fascicles and focus on the "sheer power" they contain.[3] They describe these groups of poems as "extraordinarily adventurous psychologically" and see them as "representative," with an "internal coherence" working within.[4]

Fascicles 15 and 16 are especially significant not only because of their proximity to the "crucial event" of 1861, the "terror since September," but also because they identify the emotional and mental anguish of that period. If, as Porter writes, Dickinson "claimed the aftermath as her special territory,"[5] then what we witness in these two fascicles is the psychic event itself—the "crucial experience" that inaugurated her "preoccupation...of aftermath."[6] Through their imagery and thematic structure, these two fascicles penetrate the heart of Dickinson's fears and terrors. Beginning with the tense control of the "First Day's Night" through "I Felt a Funeral in my Brain," the reader is plunged into nightmare and experiences the physiological changes of agoraphobic victims and the mental and emotional torments they endure.

Dickinson's confusion and anxiety as a victim of an unknown and terrifying disease is vividly apparent. Once we place the illness of agoraphobia at the heart of specific poems written during those anguished years of 1858–64, they open to us with a renewed meaning. For although Dickinson could not master her terror, she could describe it. Applying her sharp analytical skills and her gift of observation, she succeeded in making her emotional and mental states more understandable.

> The first Day's Night had come—
> And grateful that a thing
> So terrible—had been endured—
> I told my Soul to sing—
>
> She said her Strings were snapt—
> Her Bow—to Atoms blown—
> And so to mend her—gave me work
> Until another Morn—
>
> And then—a Day as huge
> As Yesterdays in pairs,
> Unrolled it's horror in my face—
> Until it blocked my eyes—
>
> My Brain—begun to laugh—
> I mumbled—like a fool—
> And tho' 'tis Years ago—that Day—
> My Brain keeps giggling—still.
>
> And Something's odd—within—
> That person that I was—
> And this One—do not feel the same—
> Could it be Madness—this?

Cody identifies poem 410, the first in fascicle 15, as a metaphorical redaction of a "prodomal depressive reaction"[7] brought on by the altered reality of psychosis. In his analysis he details the speaker's progression from prepsychotic terrors to the disintegration of self and finally insanity. Clark Griffith sees the experience as "undefined" yet believes that it is "the power of time" that is the "deliverer of the poet's 'other' self."[8] Rosenthal analyzes the poem as the first in a poetic sequence that begins "in medias res"—that is, at the height of "intensity." The poem, which presents "a monotonous tidal wave of obliterating horror," moves through a "succession of tenses—past perfect to past to present—showing us the "phases" of "psychic trauma that changes but does not cease." Like Griffith, Rosenthal agrees that the cause of the trauma is undefined: "We are never told what the 'thing so terrible' was."[9]

The poem appears to be directly related to the poet's terror of September, not only because of the poem's date of composition (1862), but because its imagery echoes the language of Dickinson's letter to Higginson, where she admits that she sings "as the Boy does by the Burying Ground—because I am afraid."[10] There is a clear parallel between this "terrible" thing and her experience of terror. However, in this instance, her ability to calm herself through the music of words is damaged. Her strings are "snapt" and, like a stringed instrument, she must mend herself. However, before that is possible she records the arrival of another terror more horrible than the first. It so overwhelms her that it blocks her "eyes," causes her brain "to laugh," and makes her mumble "like a fool." She is changed from within, not the same as she was before, but someone who does not "feel the same."

Adding up the verbs—*snapt, blown*—we sense the destructive power of this terrible thing. In its size—"a Day as huge / as Yesterdays in pairs"— its dramatic growth, its ability to block her eyes and not allow her to see beyond, its power to change her behavior to a totally inappropriate one, we recognize the force it exerts on her very fiber. Whatever "it" is, it has the power to stop life without killing, the ability to alter its victim mentally and to make her question her sanity.

In this poem, Dickinson records her reaction to a complete, full-blown panic attack, something that left "her Strings snapt" and "Her Bow—to Atoms blown." Dickinson had probably experienced these attacks since 1861 and perhaps in "stuttering" sequence,[11] so that her anticipation of another attack was overwhelmingly frightening to her. What she is describing here are two major effects of panic attack: the first is the fear of recurrence and the second is the fear of personality disintegration. Her question at the end of the poem "Could it be Madness—this?" shows us her confusion and her fear, a fear she was probably reluctant to admit: "Something's odd— within— / That person that I was— / And this One—do not feel the same—."

There is a commonality in the experience of agoraphobia victims. They describe their attacks in similar ways with similar words. The word *terror* and the word *it* often appear, demonstrating that the victim is at a loss trying to understand what is happening. Compare Dickinson's use of the verb *snapt* with one agoraphobe's description of an attack: "something inside me snapped."[12] The line "I mumbled—like a fool" parallels another patient's fear that "I am going to babble or talk funny."[13] In account after account, the victim writes of the same nameless horror: "When panic struck me, all common sense, reasoning and normality were blown to the winds in a blinding sheet of terror, which deprived me of the ability or will to think, move or breathe properly. I felt (and was) white as a sheet, with every drop of blood appearing to have drained out of my body; mouth dry, and hands and body clammy with cold sweat."[14] "It is as scientific a fact as any I know that my phobic seizures at their worse approach any limits of terror that the human mind is capable of in the actual presence of death in its most horrible form."[15]

Like the speaker of poem 410, the victim is terrified of the next panic attack. The anticipation of the event becomes more unbearable than the event itself. After an initial episode, one victim stated that his "fear of the Fear" increased dramatically.[16] According to Fraser Kent, the "most painful part" of the agoraphobic's problem is "the endless anticipation of disaster."[17] A recent article describes the "anticipatory anxiety" victims feel. "They are haunted by the thought that 'it' might happen. The general strategy that determines their lives is that of avoidance behavior. The anxiety is actually 'a chain of events' from the decision to go somewhere to the anticipation of the attack to the expected horror of the experience to finally deciding not to go and an abatement of their anxiety. Depending on the subjectively perceived seriousness of the anticipated effects one will, sometimes days or weeks in advance, experience stress at the prospect."[18]

There is much variation in the frequency and distribution of panic attack "within and between individuals." The attacks can occur "in waves" or in "random patterns with intervals between . . . ranging from hours to months to years."[19] It is apparent in poem 410 that the speaker is experiencing episodes of attack with only hours in between.

In "The Treatment of Agoraphobia," Chambless and Goldstein address "the anticipatory anxiety," which they describe as remaining "long after the client no longer experiences anxiety in the actual situation. This is related to the fact that she can never feel completely sure that an event that she interpreted as catastrophic, that is anxiety, will not occur again."[20] One agoraphobe clearly expressed the phenomenon of anticipation: "After it was over, I would dwell on the symptoms, and I was so terrified that whatever I did, it would happen again. That's the greatest fear, I think, is anticipation [*sic*]. When am I going to get it?"[21]

Agoraphobic victims especially fear insanity since there is no apparent cause for their panic. "Health care professionals tend to reinforce fear that they are 'crazy,' since extensive laboratory tests and medication often fail to bring any relief."[22] In a discussion of agoraphobia, Klein recognizes that the panic attack is a very "threatening, upsetting situation " and leaves its victims "extremely insecure." Klein describes how patients, in their search for the cause or meaning of the attack, explain "that something horrible and external is happening to them, which is that they are dying or they are going crazy."[23]

However, despite the victim's fear of the panic and his or her phobic reaction to the place where it occurred, in reality nothing has changed. The only thing that has changed is internal: "Actually, nothing has been altered around that person; the change has occurred within."[24] Thus, the speaker's remark in "The first Day's Night" — "Something's odd within" — is accurate, since there is no real outer change, only that felt within.

In addition to the victim's fear of madness and the threat of personality disintegration, there are also "feelings of unreality."[25] These feelings, also called *depersonalization* (when the individual refers to a change within the self) or *derealization* (when there is a change in the environment), have been described by one phobic as "looking through the wrong end of a telescope," as being "outside things," as if the individual were cut off and "watching herself react."[26] Nothing the victim touches or hears or sees feels real. This sense of unreality, this break in contact with the real world, leads the patient to ask, "Am I going crazy?"

In poem 410 that is exactly the speaker's experience. The final question is the same. But before the question comes the awareness of being and feeling different. The speaker looks at herself from outside: "That person that I was / And this One"—the words "this One" clearly differentiating the former self from the one she has become now—"do not feel the same." This conclusion parallels the experience of one agoraphobe who "looked in the mirror" and was frightened. "I didn't know who I was and what I wanted. That scared me."[27] In this frightening experience of depersonalization, the individual is alienated from herself; there is also a loss of feeling that appears unnatural.

Perhaps we can best understand this lack of feeling in poem 411, the one immediately following 410 in fascicle 15. In this poem, the speaker discusses the colors of the grave—green in the summer, white in the winter. However, the reader's attention is drawn to the last two stanzas, where an attempt to describe the color of another grave is made. This "Duplicate" is not a literal grave found in the field or cemetery but is "within." Its color is one we've seen "upon a Bonnet bound," the color of mourning and of loss. This description, coming between poems 410 and 414, relates it to the loss or lack of feeling that is experienced in the two enveloping poems. It is a psychic and an emotional loss, comparable to one agoraphobic's description of how "she seemed to recede into her own mind toward 'a black nothingness.' " If this sensation were to continue, she feared "she would 'never come back' (become insane)."[28]

In his study of agoraphobia, Klein explains that "one outstanding characteristic" of victims of panic attack is "that they are intensely puzzled." "They are shocked by the experience. It is a bizarre external thing to them. And, therefore, they are faced with the necessity for explanation."[29] In poem 414, the speaker experiences panic attack and tries through a series of "as if" statements to explain what is happening. Held steady in the powerful grip of the poem, the reader watches as the speaker struggles for survival.

> 'Twas like a Maelstrom, with a notch,
> That nearer, every Day,
> Kept narrowing it's boiling Wheel
> Until the Agony

Toyed coolly with the final inch
Of your delirious Hem—
And you dropt, lost,
When something broke—
And let you from a Dream—

As if a Goblin with a Guage—
Kept measuring the Hours—
Until you felt your Second
Weigh, helpless, in his Paws—

And not a Sinew—stirred—could help,
And sense was setting numb—
When God—remembered—and the Fiend
Let go, then, Overcome—

As if your Sentence stood—pronounced—
And you were frozen led
From Dungeon's luxury of Doubt
To Gibbets, and the Dead—

And when the film had stitched your eyes
A Creature gasped "Repreive"!
Which Anguish was the utterest—then—
To perish, or to live?

An unidentified experience is described figuratively: it is a maelstrom, a goblin, a sentence of hanging. In each situation, the speaker faces certain death, either by drowning, by being devoured, or by being hanged. In each instance, the speaker is helpless and out of control, suffering the anticipation of certain death. The speaker undergoes physical, emotional, and mental changes. First, anticipation of the terror, suggesting he or she has lived through it before. Secondly, although it is terrifying, it is not terminal and does not kill the speaker. Thirdly, it creates such fear that its victim goes beyond fear to the point of numbness. Fourth, in each case the victim feels sure this is the end, that the horrible event has mastered him or her; however, in each instance, the terrible force is "Overcome."

The mental, emotional, and physical states described here are identical with panic attack—the "hallmark of the agoraphobic syndrome."[30] The panic attack is defined as "the sudden onset of intense apprehension, fear, or terror, often associated with feelings of impending doom" and is characterized by sweating, dizziness, shaking, pounding heart, and feelings of unreality. Often it is accompanied by "an anticipatory fear of helplessness or loss of control."[31]

In a description of the phenomenon from a recent article, the authors describe panic attack as "dramatic as seizures which begin with a distressing presentiment of imminent danger in which the patient feels as if 'I am dying. This is the end. Oh my God, I'm going.' "[32] So severe is the attack that it is "indistinguishable from the reaction to overwhelming threat — being threatened with death."[33] While the fear may appear ridiculous to both the doctor and the patient since there is no apparent cause, its results are devastating. In a passage startling for its dramatic imagery, one agoraphobe writes that the seizure is like "a red-hot iron ... run down the throat."[34]

Compare the speaker of the poem (414) with other victims' descriptions of panic attack: "Before I experienced any of the symptoms of agoraphobia, I recall that ... I was taken suddenly with 'spells' which lasted about thirty minutes. During these attacks I was entirely conscious and rational — a sort of 'coldness' that produced a very unusual sensation, or perhaps lack of sensation. I tried to master these fears by the elementary device of 'try and try again' to no purpose. ... Terror would drag me back."[35]

"... fears which continually kept me in a state of anxiety so severe as often to practically paralyze me for hours and I lay wracked and tortured on my couch."[36]

"Always exhausted, always cold. My hands were clammy with sweat. I cried weakly and easily. I was afraid to go to sleep. But I did sleep to wake with a constricting headache, dizziness and tachycardia. To these were added waves of panic fear followed by depression. The panics almost overwhelmed me."[37]

"I am convinced this is my last hour ... perhaps my last minute ... I suffer the intensest seizure of terror yet. The feel of onrush is so fiercely authentic that my very reason spontaneously omits the rational explanation. The feeling is inexplicable and ominous."[38]

"I feel a sinking loneliness, an uneasy, a weird isolation. Sinking ... isolation ... diffused premonition of horror. I am alone, in the universe. Oh, to be home ... home. I shake with terror. I guess I am dying."[39]

"... scared stiff," my "muscles frozen by terror," I am "feeling so weak" that I have to "hang on to something or someone for support." "The first time I literally froze to the spot. I could not move, talk or even think, but just stood against a barn door, dumb with terror, with every cell in my body screaming to go home."[40]

These direct statements of panic attack victims match Dickinson's poem: the overwhelming fear, the sense of doom and isolation, of being beyond fear and out of physical control. We also see that the fear of fear dominates: as Leonard puts it, "I am in terror of the seizure of terror; and I fear the seizure at a given distance."[41] There is also a similarity in language. Like Dickinson, who uses the word *it* to describe her unidentifiable terror, phobic victims also refer to their fear as *it*: "It's like a fear of something, but I can't name it. I don't know what it is, and I feel afraid."[42]

It is a typical agoraphobic's word. The agoraphobe thinks, "What if it was to come back? Since 'it' is fear — stress itself — as long as she is afraid of 'it' returning, it is already on its way."[43] In a discussion of agoraphobia, one researcher speaks of panic attack almost as if he had Dickinson's poem in mind: "It is the experience of being taken by surprise by a nameless anxiety attack and the resulting bewilderment, that leads to panic and its mental symptoms. It is precisely these effects, experienced as catastrophic, that are so anxiously anticipated by agoraphobes."[44] Critic Jay Leyda suggests that Dickinson deliberately left the situation unidentified, a technique he calls "the omitted center,"[45] to enhance the symbolic value of the poem and enlarge its possibilities. Yet in this particular instance, Dickinson faced an unknown disease that no one, least of all herself, could comprehend. Thus, she used the most appropriate word to describe her inexplicable fear.

The images of the poem are especially revealing if we note the physiological symptoms of agoraphobia. These "most frequently include heart palpitations, dizziness, a sense of inability to breathe, and for some people a heaving stomach and an urge to urinate and defecate."[46] A list of symptoms of panic attack shows how varied they may be:

1. Breathing difficulty, air hunger
2. Sudden increase in heart rate
3. Choking or smothering sensation
4. Dizziness, faintness, disorientation or "rubbery legs" feelings, unsteady gait
5. Sudden sinking feeling in abdomen or chest
6. Paresthesias or sudden rushing wavelike sensations running through the body (hot or cold spells)
7. Sudden breaking into sweats
8. Sudden impulse to flight
9. Sudden feeling of intense fear without knowing why
10. Sudden sense that death is at hand or that something very serious will happen to one's health
11. Sudden feeling of having lost control over part of body or mind (sensations, power, proprioception, special senses, consciousness)
12. Chest pain, discomfort or pressure.

Of these twelve symptoms, "eleven of them could be symptoms of an organic disorder"; however, the "tip-off to panic attacks" is the fear of dying, going crazy, or losing control.[47] According to Sheehan, from whose writings this list was taken, anxiety attacks include "at least three" of the above "for a major anxiety attack and / or one to two for a minor anxiety attack."[48] In a recent study the presence of fear of "imminent death, going crazy, becoming immobilized, or losing control" qualified the panic attack as "severe."[49] By all accounts, the speaker's attack is both major and severe.

The striking maelstrom image with its violent wheellike whirling corresponds with the panic victim's dizziness, as she feels herself pulled deeper into its terrifying vortex. So, too, the "Dream" that is broken, from which the victim emerges, parallels the feelings of unreality, the trancelike state induced by the sheer terror and suddenness of the attack. The "sense was setting numb" corresponds to the fainting, the loss of control that the victim fears but feels coming on. The muscular paralysis—alluded to in stanza four, "And not a Sinew stirred could help," and in stanza five, "And you were frozen led"—indicates how helpless these people feel as panic overcomes them and they cannot break its hold. The feeling of "impending doom, such as death"[50] is particularly vivid in the last two stanzas when the victim comes through and lives, even though she thought this was the end.

Looking more closely at the poem, the reader notices several significant aspects of agoraphobia at work. For one, we see how depersonalization works. It is, as Marks described it, "a switch or cut-off mechanism which is triggered when anxiety reaches a given level."[51] It comes as a release to its victim, "a haven," one victim called it, allowing the speaker to short-circuit feelings that are too terrifying to deal with. Although depersonalization acts as a safety valve, it is still frightening. One sufferer compared it to the out-of-body sensation of people who experience clinical death: they "see their own bodies from a few feet above before returning to live in their 'corpses' once more."[52]

Another aspect of the poem that draws our attention is the use of the word *goblin*, which appears in six of Dickinson's poems. In 414, the goblin is a bestial creature, also called a "Fiend," who holds the victim "helpless in his Paws." The horror is implicit in its complete control of the speaker and in the state of fear its presence brings. Claire Weekes notes that one trait of agoraphobics is obsessive thinking that includes grotesque thoughts.[53] In a discussion of her symptoms, Mrs. F. H. speaks of the "strange spectral actors that come from the phantasmagoric chambers" of her mind. These were the "horrid old witch-woman," "the Big Red Devil," and the "ghouls," among others, who terrified and haunted her.[54]

One of the major problems of agoraphobics is their inability to recognize the situation or conflict that creates their anxiety. Because they cannot label the emotions that trigger their distress—the anger and frustration that often result from interpersonal relationships—they feel as if these panic attacks come "out of the blue" with no connection to their lives. Often these victims will deny their feelings and will also externalize or objectify them. Thus in this poem, the anger or hostility the speaker feels is projected into the goblin creature who controls the victim's last moments until "God-remembered—

and the Fiend / Let go." In a study of depersonalization, M. Roth records that victims complain of "a dread of faces" with "a sinister, evil aspect sometimes associated with an illusion of distortion of mouth, nose or eyes."[55] Interestingly, Roth also reports that patients experience "disturbances in the sense of passage of time,"[56] a fact that may relate to the "Guage" [sic] the goblin carries to measure the period of the victim's distress.

Griffith also addresses the goblins Dickinson creates, interpreting them as her vision "of all that is ugliest and least knowable in human experience."[57] We see this ugly and mysterious quality in a narrative written by an agoraphobe whose description of panic attack uses imagery strikingly similar to that in poem 414:

> After about a week of peace, I suddenly ran into a veritable whirlwind of panic. I was walking in a nearby square, when all at once I felt I was in imminent danger. So poignant was this feeling which gathered force by the second that I almost cried out "save me! save me!" I glanced at the passers-by, at some boys bowling, and felt that I would have to get protection from someone. Protection from what, I knew not, but I was sure that it was something awful, something catastrophic and inescapable. Thinking to run to cover like some hunted thing, I had a wild impulse to dash into one of the houses that lined the square and ask for sanctuary. After my fear had reached its crescendo, I got the vague impression of two shadowy persons not far from me. They weren't ordinary persons, but magnified non-natural beings more like elemental forces. One was in the semblance of a man. He, it was, who was about to attack me. He became clearer. But, the other one, a woman, remained in shadow, an aloof shadow looking on at what was about to happen to me. When I saw her, I turned to her as if to beg her to intercede for me against the anger of the man. But she remained impassive, a spectator to whatever was about to take place.[58]

In this long passage we recognize the terror, the swirling whirlpool of panic, and the creation of goblin assailants who look on without compassion or pity. For Dickinson's speaker, as for Mrs. F. H., the experience was horrible to endure and impossible to forget.

In his treatment of agoraphobia, Dr. Manual Zane developed a technique known as "contextual therapy," which he based on observations of phobic behavior. Zane describes the mental and emotional changes the victim undergoes during the panic attack: "Phobic behavior can become overwhelmingly painful and disorganized as the person involuntarily focuses on and reacts more and more to increasing and accelerating numbers of unmanageable realities." This accelerating loss of bodily and mental control and increasing feelings of fear and panic result from what has been called the "phobogenic process."[59]

According to Zane, the process is divided into three stages: the initial, the rising, and the spiraling. The initial stage occurs when the person reacts to an actual phobic situation such as a crowded place or the thought of such a place. The patient begins to experience symptoms like a quickened heartbeat, dizziness, or nausea. In the next or rising stage, the person's somatic symptoms become the springboard for more threatening thoughts. The patient's focus switches from external dangers to "future-oriented imagined dangers."[60] The fears increase rapidly, creating more physical distress. In the last stage, the "phobic person is rapidly spiralling toward outright panic."

In the poem "'Twas like a Maelstrom" the phobogenic process is at work. The initial phase, the situation to which the speaker reacts, is unidentified, although the terror it produces is explained in three analogous situations — each of which is life-threatening. In each, the speaker reacts with mounting fear and tension. The speaker is already in the second or rising stage of the phobogenic process, for the somatic symptoms, such as weakness in the limbs and loss of physical control, have given way to the more frightening possibility of imminent death.

In the last or spiraling stage, the speaker is in a state of panic, "overwhelmed and cut off from external reality."[61] Thus the speaker experiences depersonalization or derealization, becoming insensible to the external world and behaving like an automaton. In this final stage the speaker experiences what Zane calls "the dread of all dreads — the fear that recovery will never begin and this awful experience will become an endless, unbearable nightmare."[62] "Which Anguish was the utterest — then — / To perish, or to live?" This concluding question reveals the intense suffering of the speaker who feels dead already. Vose, in her depiction of agoraphobia, writes of the "loneliness of depersonalization," of the feeling of isolation and being cut off from "everyone including yourself." "Physically, I could not move, my blood flowed so slowly that my limbs were icy cold and my face quite white, and I could only see about a square inch in the centre of my normal range of vision. Everything around me became totally unreal, and I neither knew nor cared who or what anything was."[63] To someone experiencing this pain, death is not too high a price to pay for its cessation.

The panic attack is so horrifying that the victim asks if life is worth living. The answer from actual victims has often been no. The cost is so devastating and they are left so vulnerable after each attack that it might be better, they think, to die. One agoraphobe said, "I can only die once and it probably won't be as bad as this."[64] Another victim recalled, "I used to tell my parents, 'If you care about me, pray that I won't wake up in the morning.' I was afraid of dying, but I wasn't afraid of being dead."[65]

In her study, Vose notes that agoraphobia "can and does kill people."[66] She documents two instances where desperate agoraphobes chose suicide rather than live with their fears of recurrent panic attacks. A current journal article confirms this, stating that panic victims have "a significantly higher mortality rate from ... suicide."[67] Home is not a "haven" to agoraphobics, Vose continues, but a prison in which the victim, like the speaker of another Dickinson poem, is doomed to stay "Wrecked, solitary, here" (poem 280).

Finally, here is the testimony of another victim of agoraphobia, who comments on poem 414:

> I cannot think of anything else it could be describing except a panic attack. It is a perfect description. Release from the ordeal comes suddenly, on entering one's own home. ... One never knows how severe an attack will be or even if there will be one at all. One prepares for it, expecting it, and yet it may not happen. You may not even have to go out after all, "Dungeon's luxury of doubt," from which one is "frozen led" — frozen with dread, "To gibbets and the dead" — the worst thing she can think of, or at least the worst thing which people who read the poem can think of, and she is trying to communicate with people to whom this would be the most terrifying experience — people who cannot conceive of what she has to face. ... Nowadays, we know we are not going to die. How could she know that? She would have nothing with which to compare her symptoms, and no-one would understand them if she described them. Agoraphobia cannot be comprehended by anyone who has not suffered some degree of it.[68]

Poem 419, coming in the same fascicle as poems 410 and 414, and immediately after the unnatural reversal of 415 — "Sunset on the Dawn" and "Midnight's at Noon" — suggests an adjustment to an abnormal situation. Perhaps the speaker, who must "grow accustomed to the Dark," is depicting a period of respite between the violence of panic attacks, when the reeling victim tries to adjust to those "larger — Darknesses —." Dickinson wrote to Higginson, after the death of his wife, that "Danger is not at first,...but in the after-slower-Days."[69] "Those Evenings of the Brain" may reflect those "after-slower-Days" when the poet tried to acclimate herself to what remained.

> We grow accustomed to the Dark —
> When Light is put away —
> As when the Neighbor holds the Lamp
> To witness her Goodbye —
>
> A Moment — We uncertain step
> For newness of the night —
> Then — fit our Vision to the Dark —
> And meet the Road — erect —
>
> And so of large — Darknesses —
> Those Evenings of the Brain —
> When not a Moon disclose a sign —
> Or Star — come out — within —

The B[r]avest—grope a little—
And sometimes hit a Tree
Directly in the Forehead—
But as they learn to see—

Either the Darkness alters—
Or something in the sight
Adjusts itself to Midnight—
And Life steps almost straight.

The intervals between attacks can "vary considerably, sometimes from day to day."[70] According to Marks, "Episodes of panic can be followed by periods of normal activity," and "agoraphobia fluctuates not only over time, but also with changes in the sufferers and in their environment."[71] It is unclear what causes these fluctuations, but they may be related to "increasing and decreasing stress experience, which influences self-confidence."[72] Is poem 419 a reaction to life lived on the edge of terror that now between attacks "adjusts itself to Midnight / And Life steps almost straight"? The phrase "almost straight" suggests that the situation is still unresolved.

12

"I Dropped Down and Down"

Fascicle 16 opens dramatically, with the speaker recalling the time "Before
I got my eye put out." Startling in its imagery, the poem suggests that
Dickinson may have had a problem with her eyes prior to 1864, a sensitivity
to light that might also be deduced from poem 419 where the speaker must
accustom herself to the dark. The theme of these two poems is the same:
the speaker must learn to see differently in response to some major change
in her life.

> Before I got my eye put out
> I liked as well to see—
> As other Creatures, that have Eyes
> And know no other way—
>
> But were it told to me—Today—
> That I might have the sky
> For mine—I tell you that my Heart
> Would split, for size of me—
>
> The Meadows—mine—
> The Mountains—mine—
> All Forests—Stintless Stars—
> As much of Noon as I could take
> Between my finite eyes—
>
> The Motions of The Dipping Birds—
> The Morning's Amber Road—
> For mine—to look at when I liked—
> The News would strike me dead—
>
> So safer Guess—with just my soul
> Upon the Window pane—
> Where other Creatures put their eyes—
> Incautious—of the Sun—

In poem 327 the speaker, like the giant Polyphemus, got his "eye put out."
We want to ask by whom? for what reason? In contrast to the "other
Creatures" who are "Incautious—of the Sun," the speaker can only put her
"soul / Upon the Window pane" for the light is too strong for her "finite

eyes." Might this change reflect the phobia that kept her hidden within her house, "safe" from the outside world? The poem, sent to Higginson in August 1862, may directly relate to the "terror—since September" mentioned in her April 1862 letter and the aftermath of that nameless experience. Although Dickinson describes a photophobia or fear of light in letters written during and after her eye treatment in 1864–65,[1] it appears probable that she suffered from an eye problem at least two years prior to that date. Since poem 327 was written before August 1862 (when it was sent to Higginson), Dickinson may have had an earlier eye problem. Biographer Sewall supports this hypothesis. In *The Lyman Letters*, the excerpt "An Exile and A Return" refers "unmistakably and in much the same idiom to the trouble with her eyes." Thus the "terror—since September" may refer to Dickinson's eye trouble. To Sewall, this explanation is more "plausible" than the popular notion that Wadsworth's departure for California caused her fear. Dickinson's fear of blindness, of "the threatened loss of her power to read," is in her own words "the only [woe] that ever made me tremble."[2]

Eye problems are common complications of the agoraphobic syndrome. Blurred vision, headaches, and dimness of vision[3] are often cited as symptoms of anxiety. The recent theory of OBD singles out eye dysfunction as a precipitator of fears that set off panic attack. One victim experienced "double vision" that led to "dizziness and headache" and eventually to panic attack.[4] Vose complained of temporary blindness,[5] and Leonard endured two years of unrelenting eye pain.[6] More specifically, victims of agoraphobia have listed the fear of "going blind" as part of their disorder, a finding aligning their fears with Dickinson's.

One of the most dramatic records comes from Mrs. F. H., who identifies her primary symptom as "a long standing fear of light." In "Recovery from a Long Neurosis," she writes about her phobias, which "were concerned with a good many things, but the central one, the core of them, was an abject fear of light. The fear was so overpowering that I darted out into the daylight only to be driven back, as if by an Unseen Force, into the darkened room where I could find a comparative peace and feeling of safety, although even there I had to fight off periods of intense fear."[7] It was only during the night—"the gentle night"[8]—that Mrs. F. H. could do anything. In time, she understands that her fear of light was symbolic of "the fear of what was hiding in the corners of my mind,"[9] the result of a deeply rooted familial conflict.

Victims of agoraphobia often shun daylight as a consequence of their phobia of light: "thirty-seven percent reported their fears were better in the dark, and twenty-three percent felt their phobias were aggravated by daylight."[10] Sunlight and warm weather also intensify agoraphobic fear.[11] One patient writes, "I preferred to move around at night, under cover of darkness. During the day sunglasses were a boon, since besides shielding me from the bright sunlight, they helped to hide my face and fears."[12] Thus, many agoraphobics stay indoors away from the sunlight and move about "more freely at night."[13] According to Todd, Emily Dickinson had not been outside her home in fifteen years "except once to see a new church when she crept out at night and viewed it by moonlight."[14] Although Todd thought this romantic, it is more accurately understood as a reflection of Dickinson's phobias.

On the surface, poem 279, the next in fascicle 16, appears to be about death. However, it may be a death to a way of life, rather than an actual death. In agoraphobia, the last stages of withdrawal are complete when the patient is "housebound, immobilized and restricted to a point where there are few new stimuli to which conditioning may occur. It is 'the end of the line' of phobic acquisition."[15] Thus, the victim may be bidding "Goodbye to the Life I used to live / And the World I used to know" since she is unable to participate in a full life. Entitled "Farewell" when it first appeared in *Poems* (1896), the poem could have been the poet's farewell to a normal life-style.

Following a figurative death in "Tie the Strings to my Life," poem 280 depicts a figurative funeral—"a Funeral in my brain"—setting up a metaphor for a vivid exploration of agoraphobia with panic attack.

> I felt a Funeral, in my Brain,
> And Mourners to and fro
> Kept treading—treading—till it seemed
> That Sense was breaking through—
>
> And when they all were seated,
> A Service, like a Drum—
> Kept beating—beating—till I thought
> My Mind was going numb—
>
> And then I heard them lift a Box
> And Creak across my Soul
> With those same Boots of Lead, again,
> Then Space—began to toll,
>
> As all the Heavens were a Bell,
> And Being, but an Ear,
> And I, and Silence, some strange Race
> Wrecked, solitary, here—
>
> And then a Plank in Reason, broke,
> And I dropped down, and down—
> And hit a World, at every plunge,
> And Finished knowing—then—

The speaker envisions a death within herself and uses the "concrete details of a funeral service . . . to function like players in a psychological drama."[16]

The dramatic repetitions of sound perceptions, especially treading and beating, sharpen our awareness of the speaker's sensations during this metaphorical burial of self. The speaker's sensitivity to sound, to the drumbeat of the service, the creaking of "Boots of Lead," and the tolling of the bell, recalls Leonard's description of panic attack: his "swirling attacks of consciousness" were "accompanied ... mysteriously by incipient rush of sound." He refers to his "phobias of bells"[17] and later to the fact that "sounds tortured" him.[18] Victims of panic attack often suffer tinnitus or ringing in the ears, as well as "migraine-like headaches" with "various degrees of unilateral throttling pain."[19]

Here, too, are the earmarks of depersonalization and derealization as the mind goes numb and space begins to toll. Poem 280 recalls poem 414 as the speaker's mind goes numb and the self disintegrates. In a real life parallel, Weekes writes that because the tension is so frightening and it builds so suddenly and intensely, victims see themselves as "collapsing." "Their fear is so acute and their imaginations so active that at the peak of panic they feel that their minds go numb, that they can neither think nor act clearly."[20]

In poem 280, the speaker experiences both "spatial disorientation" and a sense of "the surroundings as strange, unreal and detached."[21] In stanzas 3 and 4, the speaker hears the tolling of space and feels cut off and isolated from the rest of humanity. The drumlike beating of the funeral service suggests the heart palpitations panic victims experience. "The heart compensates for an unusually quick beat by taking a restful pause, so that the beat following the long pause is therefore actually forceful, so the heart seems to thump. To a sensitized person each extra systole can feel as disconcerting as the jerk of a sudden descent in an elevator — uncomfortable indeed when he is subjected to long runs of extra systoles."[22]

The comparison of the thumping heart to "the jerk of a sudden descent of an elevator" leads us to Dickinson's final image, the sharp sense of falling through space, breaking a "Plank in reason" "at every plunge." This last stanza repeats the dizzying spin of the maelstrom (poem 414) as the speaker drops down and down, pulled into the interior vortex from which there is no escape. One panic victim described her feelings as "she seemed to recede into her own mind toward 'a black nothingness.' This sensation was accompanied by a gripping pain in her head and ringing in the ears. She was sure that if this feeling were to continue further" she would go insane.[23]

The image of the "Plank" reflects Dickinson's use of house imagery to represent the mind. Griffith comments on Dickinson's "instinctive awareness of what, since she wrote, has become the most melancholy findings of modern psychology" — her "sense that the mind is not a unity, but a broken wholeness." In this instance, the mind or brain, constructed of planks, breaks — "a Plank in Reason, broke" — and the victim falls down into the other realms of the house, perhaps into the cellars where "the 'seething excitations' exist below and are hidden."[24]

The end of the poem suggests to scholar-psychiatrist Cody a psychotic breakdown, "a reason-disrupting prostrating psychosis."[25] However, victims of panic attack experience similar symptomatology and fear that their minds may "be going to pieces."[26] In *The Locomotive-God*, Leonard describes a split between the "rational self-directive intelligence, on the one hand" and the "subconsciously conditioned torture and confusion on the other" where "intelligence was shut off to the task of controlling and managing the self in its terror, but powerless to control and manage the terror, as such."[27] This description dramatically echoes the "split" in the brain in poem 937, a possible variant of 280,[28] and the speaker's inability to make the two parts "fit."

This sense of mental disorder is typical of the panic attack victim. Dr. C. Branch, author of *Aspects of Anxiety*, writes that these attacks usually begin with fear as a "sense of imminent dissolution or loss of mind."[29] Other instances of the fear of mental illness lead the victim to feel that if he or she loses control "people will find out what I am like, and I will be taken to a mental home where I really know I belong."[30]

Some agoraphobics have been institutionalized as insane. In *The Autobiography of David*, the anonymous David dedicates his book to "my friends, the insane; to all those who are seeking to understand the mysterious forces which control human behavior; to those who believe in a divine purpose behind apparent chaos."[31]

In a current medical journal, Dr. David Diamond explains that agoraphobia is a clinical syndrome in which "states of self-fragmentation" are "at the psychopathologic core."[32] In poems 280 and 937 Dickinson graphically depicts the brain "coming apart," its disintegration amply reflecting Diamond's analysis of agoraphobic fears: "The physical sensation becomes the center of hypochondriacal concern because it carries with it the dread of life-threatening illness. The threat and the dread are, in actuality, related to self-fragmentation—that 'coming apart' which reduces the person to the state of overwhelmed helplessness and complete vulnerability."[33]

Poem 280 ends with a dash, a powerful lack of finality and a sense of uncertainty. Does the last line mean that the speaker "Finished knowing"— that is, passed into not knowing or madness—or that after the experience the speaker finished knowing where he or she was? The sense of doubt, although not directly stated, parallels the uncertainty at the end of poems 410 and 414: "Could it be Madness—this" and "Which Anguish was the utterest—."

Since poem 281 immediately follows poem 280, it is possible that it addresses itself to the aftermath of a similar attack, an episode that is "so appalling—it exhilirates / So over Horror, it half Captivates."

> 'Tis so appalling—it exhilirates—
> So over Horror, it half Captivates—
> The Soul stares after it, secure—
> To know the worst, leaves no dread more—

> To scan a Ghost, is faint—
> But grappling, conquers it—
> How easy, Torment, now—
> Suspense kept sawing so—
>
> The Truth, is Bald, and Cold—
> But that will hold—
> If any are not sure—
> We show them—prayer—
> But we, who know,
> Stop hoping, now—
>
> Looking at Death, is Dying—
> Just let go the Breath—
> And not the pillow at your Cheek
> So Slumbereth—
>
> Others, Can wrestle—
> Your's, is done—
> And so of Wo, bleak dreaded—come,
> It sets the Fright at liberty—
> And Terror's free—
> Gay, Ghastly, Holiday!

Although "it" has been survived—"Overcome" in the language of poem 414—and "The Soul stares after it, secure," the ordeal is recorded in the present tense, presumably because it is an ongoing experience with still more to come. The speaker offers examples of how once achieved or mastered, there is a respite from one's fear. For instance, the "Ghost" can be grappled with and conquered and the "Truth" can be dealt with through prayer. That is, by some, for the speaker, who uses the first person plural "we," has given up "hoping—now."

In the last three stanzas, the message is clear although disheartening. The experience of death is final: the breath is gone and the soul sleeps. While "Others, Can wrestle," the fight of the dead is over. The speaker compares this state to woe that is anticipated and "dreaded" until it "come." When it does, it sets the "Fright at liberty / And Terror's Free—." However, the last line indicates that this is only a temporary break—a "Holiday"—not a permanent solution. The conclusion takes us back to the unnamed "it" referred to four times in the first stanza that is synonymous with "Horror" and "Torment."

Poem 445, coming after the speaker's readiness for death in 279 and the metaphorical funeral of the self in 280, marks a continuity in time. It is the anniversary of the death of the speaker. One year ago "I died," the speaker announces, recalling the sense impressions of her death: the sight of the corn—"how yellow it would look"—and the red of the apples. It was the fall of the year when she died—before Thanksgiving, around harvest time.

(One wonders if this timing relates to the "terror since September"?) The speaker thinks about the celebrations of Thanksgiving and Christmas without her. Who would miss her? This thought, which "grieved" her, is replaced by the prospects of a reunion when "some perfect year" the family should "come to me."

Predicated on a metaphorical death, it is a poem of wondering—what if—revealing that the death may have been some event similar to the experiences of poems 410, 414, and 280 which changed the course of her life, some event she had to "grow accustomed to" in poem 419, or some death as in poem 411 where the "Grave" was "within." Whatever it was, it was beyond her control, since she writes "I wanted to get out, / But something held my will."

Finally, poem 608, the next to last in fascicle 16, asks a question the poet may have asked herself as she became more phobic and housebound. "Afraid! Of whom am I afraid?" It was a question she had asked herself in 1854 during her first panic attack. At that time she concluded, "In the whole world was nothing I need to fear."[34] In poem 680, the speaker negates any fears she may have. In each stanza, the speaker asks the question—first of death, then of life, and finally of resurrection—and in each instance she denies her fears. Perhaps in 1862 the poet realized that the source of her fears was not in broad concepts such as these, but that it was within, in the deep unknowable regions of herself.

To summarize, fascicles 15 and 16 are knit together by a series of interrelated images as well as by a sequence of events. In both fascicles, the poems reflect the physiological and psychological experience of the agoraphobic as she lives through the state of panic and beyond. The full-blown panic attack overtakes its victim before she can do anything to prevent it. She experiences various physical discomforts and fears that the worst is happening: she is dying or going insane. In poems 410, 414, and 280 especially, the speaker describes the devastation of the attack, the pain and despair faced as she imagines the worst—being "out of control, trapped with no exit, becoming psychotic."[35] In these poems, all the symptoms of agoraphobia are present, the dizziness, the loss of sensation and consciousness, the pounding heart, the feeling of intense fear, the loss of control, the fear of dying or going crazy, the desire for flight, all of which attest to the presence of a major anxiety attack.

In both fascicles there is a consistency of imagery as well as of time. Although Franklin denies that there is sequence building in the fascicles—that they are "careful constructs governed by theme, imagery, narrative and dramatic movement"[36]—he admits that "arrangements" have been found and that "even to the skeptical" "there are suggestions" of artistic design.[37] Sewall proposes that the poems appear to have "coherence" because of the "recurrent" nature of the poet's "major themes, images, and symbolic structures."[38] Since the poems emerge from a particularly troubled period of Dickinson's life, it is possible that they not only share the same subject matter but incorporate a particular thematic and imagistic structure as well.

In fascicles 15 and 16 there is a movement away from light and seeing to darkness, night, and adjustment. In the first poem, the speaker describes the night of the first day and the horror that "blocked my eyes." In 411, there is the black color of "the Grave within." In poem 414 the speaker complains of a "Film" that "stitched" her eyes causing her not to see. In 415, there is a reversal of nature—"Midnight's—due—at Noon"—when the blackness of night occurred at the height of day. These poems are followed by 419, "Those Evenings of the Brain," the "larger Darknesses" to which the speaker must adjust. In poem 421, the speaker refers to a "Vail" that the lady wears and "dare not lift." It is a poem directly alluding to Dickinson's own life-style, her habit of hiding away from people and not seeing them; although, like the speaker of 421, she "wishes" to, she dares not. The poem uses the same language Dickinson used in her letter to Sue when she wrote: "I need more vail." The vail is a metaphor for the life-style that the poet finds herself entering more completely as she begins to accustom herself "to Midnight." Weekes uses this same veil image to describe the agoraphobic feeling of unreality as the sufferer withdraws "from the outside world—as if there is a veil between it and him, a veil he can neither lift aside nor break through."[39] What follows are two poems about death, about dead objects, unnamed and referred to by the word "it." "It" is lifeless, inanimate, insensate. Are these herself—dead to life, corpselike and unable to participate in life?

In fascicle 16, the emphasis on darkness continues in the dramatic imagery of poem 327. Here the speaker states that her "eye" was put out and then recounts the joys of those "Creatures that have Eyes"—the sky, the meadows, the forests, the stars. Here the reference to a withdrawn life is apparent; these ordinary pleasures of nature are not hers "to look at when I liked." Although she is "safer," in contrast to those who are "Incautious—of the Sun," she must watch life through "the Window pane." What follows is a clear progression from this enforced blindness or restricted vision of poem 327 (notice that the speaker says, "I got my eye put out," suggesting that it was not voluntary but something inflicted on her) to a death in poem 279, through a funeral in poem 280, to the anniversary of that death in poem 445. Thus there is a chronology of events: the experience begins in the first poem of fascicle 15, there are adjustments to it, and then life as she knows it comes to an end.

Interestingly, this chronology and structure follow the progression of stages in agoraphobia, beginning with the early signs of the disorder—perhaps for Dickinson a visual problem or photosensitivity—to the full-blown panic stage (in poems 410 and 414) where the victim becomes obsessed with her mental well-being (poem 410) and experiences episodes of derealization and depersonalization (poems 414 and 280). The patient progresses from a single phobic stage to a social phobic stage, as seen in poem 421 when she wears a "vail" between herself and people, to a polyphobic stage where the patient is "severely disabled" and stays away from the world outside, as in poem 327. Finally there is the last stage, when the victim, unable "to control the disorder psychologically," looks ahead to a bleak future, is "depressed, downhearted or blue episodically,"[40] an emotion expressed in the third stanza of poem 281: "The Truth, is Bald, and Cold— / But that will hold / If any are not sure— / We show them—prayer— / But we, who know, / Stop hoping, now—."

There is clearly an order here, a sequence of events that cannot be overlooked. Rosenthal suggests that the fascicles "present" an "inner, associative voyage of discovery"[41] and that they "cohere as a system of tensions, modulations, and reciprocal tonal forces."[42] There is a continuity of time as well as dramatic structure. We watch the speaker struggle for survival over a period of time. Although at the start of fascicle 15 the speaker complains that "her Strings were snapt," she is able to gather together her poetic powers and write of the harrowing experience. By the end of fascicle 16, she has passed through the crucial experience and looks back at it from a distance: "When we stand on the top of Things / And like the Trees, look down— / The smoke all cleared away from it / And Mirrors on the scene—" (poem 242).

13

"Blank—and Steady Wilderness"

Agoraphobia with panic attack is vividly seen in fascicles 15 and 16; however, it is present in other fascicles as well. Given the fluctuating nature of agoraphobia, its pattern of waxing and waning,[1] it is likely the poet experienced its symptoms and addressed them throughout the fascicle years—1858–64—in varying pitches. Like poem 414, poems 510 and 512 recreate panic attack.

> It was not Death, for I stood up,
> And all the Dead, lie down—
> It was not Night, for all the Bells
> Put out their Tongues, for Noon.
>
> It was not Frost, for on my Flesh
> I felt Siroccos—crawl—
> Nor Fire—for just my Marble feet
> Could keep a Chancel, cool—
>
> And yet, it tasted, like them all,
> The Figures I have seen
> Set orderly, for Burial,
> Reminded me, of mine—
>
> As if my life were shaven,
> And fitted to a frame,
> And could not breathe without a key,
> And 'twas like Midnight, some—
>
> When everything that ticked—has stopped—
> And Space stares all around—
> Or Grisly frosts—first Autumn morns,
> Repeal the Beating Ground—
>
> But, most, like Chaos—Stopless—cool—
> Without a Chance, or Spar—
> Or even a Report of Land—
> To justify—Despair.

In 510, the poet dramatically tells the reader, "I stood up." Whatever the horror of the feeling, it made her feel dead when she was alive. It also

112

confused the time of day, making it appear to be night although it was noon. The suggestion of physiological symptoms are here too: the speaker, perhaps feeling faint, is blacking out. In the next stanza, the speaker feels hot and cold, alternately perspiring and shivering as she feels her flesh "crawl" with heat and her extremities cool as "Marble." She is ready for burial, a living corpse. Her breathing, too, is affected as she recalls she "could not breathe without a key." The silence of the event made it appear to be Midnight— "When everything that ticked—has stopped— / And Space stares all around." The gripping cold of the experience stops or repeals "the Beating Ground," which may refer to the beating of the speaker's heart. But the most outstanding quality of the experience was its endlessness—its "Stopless" character—making the speaker feel hopeless, lost "Without a Chance, or Spar / Or even a Report of Land— / To justify—Despair." The despair at the end of the poem is the natural outcome of agoraphobia, since the victim feels there is no solution.

This experience parallels the panic attack in its physiological symptoms and its episodes of depersonalization where the victim is numb from extreme fear. The speaker, who has no "cognitive structure within which to understand what" is happening,[2] describes it through her senses. Once again we have no named event, only an enigmatic "it." In the designation of panic, Sheehan identifies "a major anxiety attack" as one in which at least three of the twelve symptoms are present. In the attack described in poem 510, there are six of the twelve symptoms present, including breathing difficulty; dizziness, faintness; parenthesias or sudden rushing wavelike sensations running through the body (hot or cold spells); sudden feeling of intense fear without knowing why; sudden sense that death is at hand; and a sudden feeling of having lost control over part of the body or mind.

The image of the spar recalls poem 201 (fasc. 9) where "Two swimmers wrestled on the spar." Dickinson often used sea or drowning imagery to depict her troubled mental state. There are many references to being at sea in her letters. For instance in May 1860, she wrote to Mary Bowles to say, "We don't know how dark it is, but if you are at sea, perhaps when we say we are there you won't be afraid."[3] Earlier in 1858, the first Master letter finds the speaker ill and at sea—"Each Sabbath on the Sea."[4] In 1860, Dickinson sent Samuel Bowles poem 201 and preceded it with the line "I cant explain it, Mr. Bowles."[5] Johnson notes, "It is clear that about this time she was undergoing a turbulent emotional disturbance."[6] The poet, undoubtedly over-whelmed by the illness that persisted and intensified during these years, felt defeated. Her despair is apparent in this even more hopeless image in 510, where there is no spar for rescue.

> The Soul has Bandaged moments—
> When too appalled to stir—

She feels some ghastly Fright come up
And stop to look at her —

Salute her — with long fingers —
Caress her freezing hair —
Sip, Goblin, from the very lips
The Lover — hovered — o'er —
Unworthy, that a thought so mean
Accost a Theme — so — fair —

The soul has moments of Escape —
When bursting all the doors —
She dances like a Bomb, abroad,
And swings upon the Hours,

As do the Bee — delirious borne —
Long Dungeoned from his Rose —
Touch Liberty — then know no more,
But Noon, and Paradise —

The Soul's retaken moments —
When, Felon led along,
With shackles on the plumed feet,
And staples, in the Song,

The Horror welcomes her, again.
These, are not brayed of Tongue —

Poem 512 also recalls poem 414 in its image of the goblin in stanza 2 and
its condemned felon in stanza 5. The soul is the scene of the experience. It
has been wounded and is "Bandaged." In a perceptive study, Diamond uses
the word *bandage* as the poet does in this poem. The word *bandaged*, used
only three times by Dickinson, implies that the soul is hurt and in need of
repair. In his article, Diamond describes agoraphobia as a disorder that involves "self-fragmentation," and he states that "metaphorically speaking"
the patient "seeks a secure calming environment that...will bandage the
wound to the self opened by the panic state." It is at these moments in her
hurt and damaged state that she is vulnerable to attack. "Some ghastly Fright"
comes up "to look at her." In stanza 1, the enfeebled soul is too appalled
to stir. Feeling the terror of panic, she is immobilized, unable to escape. The
state of fear is externalized in the goblin who will " — with long fingers —
/ Caress her freezing hair — ."
   Sometimes, the poem continues, the soul escapes and behaves wildly —
dancing "like a Bomb" — tasting a liberty like that of the bee as he leaves
his "Rose" dungeon. However, these moments are fleeting. The soul is
"retaken" and like a "Felon" is shackled and "led along." The nameless
horror reclaims its victim. The poem focuses on the fluctuating course of
panic attack, its suddenness, its diminishment, and then its reappearance.
It is a chronicle, too, of the alternate states of fear, release from fear, and

the return of fear, a subject that is "not brayed of Tongue"—a personal matter of which only she is aware.

Kent finds "a remarkable similarity in the terms agoraphobics use to describe their 'attacks'—weakness, nausea, palpitations, breathing difficulties. There is a helpless certainty that they will faint, have a heart attack, or die." In describing the duration of the attacks, he writes that they "usually last only a few moments, but some people report that the symptoms persist for hours." "In those cases," he continues, "the phobia has a slow, insidious onset, the first attacks are widely separated in time, but then they begin to accelerate."[8] In this instance, we have little reference to time or to the duration of the attack. However, the escaped soul "swings upon the Hours," enjoying her freedom, but in the same stanza the speaker refers to "moments of Escape." There is an alternation between the release and the renewal of the "Horror." Research indicates that there is "great variation in the frequency and distribution of panic attacks within and between individuals" and suggests that it is this "lack of predictability" which increases the overall stress of its victims.[9]

In what could be a psychological addendum to poem 512, Diamond relates "the varying degrees of self-cohesiveness" of the agoraphobe to "the frequency and intensity of the symptoms": "When the complex interaction of forces that bear on the sense of the self yield a more cohesive configuration, symptoms are lessened. When the compensatory or defensive structures are under more stress, the threat of self-fragmentation is greater and is defended in part through agoraphobic behaviors. The forces and stresses, both internal and external, which impinge and interact with the sense of self, although continual, are ever-changing in direction and magnitude. In the complexity and individual variability of this interaction the kaleidoscopic character of clinical agoraphobia is generated."[10] Thus, when the speaker feels safe and relatively stress free, she has "moments of Escape." But when the "defensive structures" are stressed, the self is under attack and is "retaken"—"The Horror welcomes her, again."

> The Sun kept setting—setting—still
> No Hue of Afternoon—
> Upon the Village I perceived—
> From House to House 'twas Noon—
>
> The Dusk kept dropping—dropping—still
> No Dew upon the Grass—
> But only on my Forehead stopped—
> And wandered in my Face—
>
> My Feet kept drowsing—drowsing—still
> My fingers were awake—
> Yet why so little sound—Myself
> Unto my Seeming—make?

> How well I knew the Light before—
> I could not see it now—
> 'Tis Dying—I am doing—but
> I'm not afraid to know—

Poem 692 (fasc. 35) recapitulates the classic physiological symptoms of panic attack: the speaker grows faint in the first stanza where "The Sun kept setting—setting—still" even though it was afternoon. In stanza 2, there is perspiration as the speaker senses "Dew" on her "Forehead" and on her "Face" but "No Dew upon the Grass." In stanza 3, there is the numbness of fear, a muscular paralysis as her "Feet kept drowsing—drowsing—still." In the final stanza, the speaker blacks out; she says of the light, "I could not see it now," and in her limited knowledge of what is happening, she believes she is at the brink of death. "During such attacks there is a strange feeling of loss of control and impending doom, such as death by a heart attack or stroke, or madness."[11] Compare the speaker's reaction in this poem to actual comments from victims of agoraphobia: "I felt like I was going to faint, dizzy and shaky in the legs."[12] "I thought, Oh, no! here it comes again, and I had this feeling that something awful was going to happen to me."[13]

The panic attack is "the central feature in patients suffering from agoraphobia with panic attack."[14] After a series of such attacks, the individual begins to avoid the situation or place where the attack occurred and eventually becomes phobophobic, that is, fearful of the panic attack itself, of "having another spontaneous panic attack."[15] It is at this stage that the sufferer lives in the state of ever-present fear, worrying about what will happen when he or she goes out. The victim feels "at the mercy of some thing" (recall the goblins in poems 414 and 512) and is always on guard against the panic that "comes so quickly I can't do anything about it." The "nerve trigger" is "well-oiled" and reacts quickly to events, people, things, sensations that previously would not have provoked fear.[16] Thus the panic watch becomes more intense and the horror more appalling in anticipation. This "anticipatory thinking"[17] accounts for much of the chronic tension in which the individual lives. Vose states that "the actual event is often easier to tolerate than the anticipation of it. Towards the end of my agoraphobe experience, I found that my only real problem was the fear of fear."[18]

Such "anticipatory" fear is found in poem 362 where the poet compares the lightning to the sudden "out of the blue" experience of fear that torments her.

> It struck me—every Day—
> The Lightning was as new
> As if the Cloud that instant slit
> And let the Fire through—

It burned Me—in the Night—
It Blistered to My Dream—
It sickened fresh upon my sight—
With every Morn that came—

I thought that Storm—was brief—
The Maddest—quickest by—
But Nature lost the Date of This—
And left it in the Sky—

It is no coincidence that the image of lightning is used. It is one chosen by agoraphobic victims, who often liken the attack to "being struck by lightning."[19] It is something, the speaker says, that "struck" her "every Day" and was always "new"; it was never finished, but an ever-present "Lightning" that "burned" her in the night, even into her dreams, which were "Blistered" by it. Clinical studies have established that since agoraphobes are unconscious of the problem triggering their attacks "a great many patients . . . experience their first panic attacks in their sleep."[20] The fear carries over into the day when "it sickened fresh upon my sight." The poem concludes with a sense of the endlessness of this "Storm." Since "Nature lost the Date of This," it would be a continuous assault.

Poem 471 might be paired with this. In this poem the speaker refers to a night that feels interminable, that is measured by the "Days between," the reverse of normal calculations.

A Night—there lay the Days between—
The Day that was Before—
And Day that was Behind—were one—
And now—'twas Night—was here—

Slow—Night—that must be watched away—
As Grains upon a shore—
Too imperceptible to note—
Till it be night—no more—

Here the night's duration, marked off by "The Day that was Before" and the "Day that was Behind," suggests a night of pain, similar to that in poem 362, where the "Fire" "burned" the speaker "in the Night." This poem also echoes poem 410 where the speaker emphasizes the first day's night as a temporary end to "a thing / So terrible." In this poem, however, it is this "Slow Night—that must be watched away / As Grains upon a shore / Too imperceptible—to note" until that time when "it be night—no more." Dickinson has used night before to refer to the experience of panic attack. Especially in 510, she described the experience as "like Midnight, some— / When everything that ticked—has stopped— / And Space stares all around." So, too, her adjustment to the aftermath of the experience is referred to as "Those Evenings of the Brain" when the sight "Adjusts itself to Midnight / And Life steps almost straight" (poem 419). These references to night, to dealing with the pain of some overwhelming problem, recall the "nights . . . when Vinnie had gone" and the "snarl in the brain which don't unravel yet" and "that old nail in my breast" that "pricked me."[21]

In poem 770 (fasc. 23), the speaker admits, "I lived on Dread," a state that knows "Danger" and "Fear," qualities the victim of panic attack knows well.

> I lived on Dread —
> To Those who know
> The Stimulus there is
> In Danger — Other impetus
> Is numb — and Vitalless —
>
> As 'twere a Spur — upon the Soul —
> A Fear will urge it where
> To go without the Spectre's aid
> Were Challenging Despair.

In the poem, the speaker compares this "Stimulus" to a "Spur — upon the Soul" that prompts it to act or react in a vital way. If the spur were the fear of panic attack, the speaker would accommodate her life to this fact, avoiding any situation in which the anxiety was triggered. However, this reaction to external circumstances is in reality not the solution. Although the individual tries to avoid the external place she believes triggers an attack, she can never avoid that attack since the phobia is actually a "portable" one, one that resides within herself.[22]

So, too, in poem 705 (fasc. 37), the speaker compares suspense, or the anticipation of something to come, with the fact of death:

> Suspense — is Hostiler than Death —
> Death — thosoever Broad,
> Is just Death, and cannot increase —
> Suspense — does not conclude —
>
> But perishes — to live anew —
> But just anew to die —
> Annihilation — plated fresh
> With Immortality —

Here is a possible reference to the threat of panic attack. We witness the same emotion at the heart of poem 414. After the nameless horror accosts her, the victim asks, "Which Anguish was the utterest — then — / To perish, or to live?" Which is better — living with the sense of disaster over and over again, or dying once? In poem 705, the speaker admits that "Suspense—is Hostiler than Death." Thus, death, which "concludes" its task, is preferred to suspense, or the anticipation of something horrible to come, which "perishes—to live anew."

The idea of numbness during and after panic attack appears repeatedly in the poems. In poem 272 (fasc. 14), for instance, the speaker refers to the tight chest muscles, the constricted breathing of the agoraphobic under a state of tension. Although the victim tries to breathe, it is only "Pantomine" because "the Lungs are stirless" and the "Bellows" is "numb."

> I breathed enough to take the Trick—
> And now, removed from Air—
> I simulate the Breath, so well—
> That One, to be quite sure—
>
> The Lungs are stirless—must descend
> Among the Cunning Cells—
> And touch the Pantomine—Himself,
> How numb, the Bellows feels!

The physiology of the individual is abnormally altered due to the stress of panic. This breathing difficulty parallels the situation of the speaker in poem 510 who "could not breathe without a key." The panic victim's "inability to take a deep breath" is caused by the extreme tension he or she feels in the chest muscles. The victims do not understand this feeling and "gasp and gulp" for breath, "half believing that unless they succeed, they will suffocate."[23]

Griffith complains that poem 272 is "too cryptic to be anything more than a tease and a curiosity. . . . we cannot visualize and hence can never hope to explain . . . the motivating circumstances, the experiences that have brought the body to its present straits." He dismisses this poem and those that deal with "the physical self" as having "no real capacity for dramatic actions" and, consequently, sees them as "the least interesting part of the total self" that Dickinson explores.[24] However, if we place the agoraphobic syndrome at the center of these poems, we gain a deeper insight into the physical discomforts the poet documents, as well as into the nature of the psychic disturbance that fueled them.

This state of numbness more specifically refers to the phenomenon of depersonalization, which causes the victim's mind to shut off. Thus, the individual feels nothing but instead experiences changes in the sense of self. According to Roth, depersonalization results in "a compelling self-scrutiny" and a "loss of spontaneity," which leads patients to complain "that activities no longer flowed from them unawares, as it were; they were compelled to scrutinize each thought, act and emotion in its detailed development. There was an associated subjective experience of...being a passive spectator of the activities in which the self was engaged."[25]

The most dramatic result of depersonalization is its impact on the minds of victims. They see themselves as different, strange, altered in some way. Sometimes they are frightened by themselves, especially by the feeling that they are going crazy or losing their mind. They fear for their sanity and feel on the edge of madness. One victim, in response to the therapist's asking what "the worst possible consequence" of an attack would be, answered, "I'm really afraid of being insane!"[26] In poem 556 (fasc. 27), Dickinson recognizes the harmony of the working brain and the enormity of a change, even a slight one: "The Brain, within it's [sic] Groove / Runs evenly—and true— / But let a Splinter swerve— / 'Twere easier for you— / To put a Current back." Once altered, the brain is not easily mended. Like poem 937, this poem dramatically reveals the sense of mental disorder and disintegration experienced by victims of panic attack. Too often, the symptoms are misinterpreted. Chambless recognizes this danger and states that "Depersonalization is a symptom of high anxiety not necessarily associated with psychosis. Too frequently, therapists, like agoraphobics, err in viewing this as a sign of 'craziness.'"[27]

Roth concurs and writes that "the great majority of cases of depersonalization seen in everyday psychiatric practice are neither caused by a gross cerebral lesion nor found in the setting of any constitution as specific as that of the schizophrenic or manic depressive." Instead he shows that "prominent depersonalization occurred in cases of chronic neurosis."[28] While in depersonalization patients feel detached from themselves, derealization, which is the "more common of the two," "is characterized by a temporary feeling of spatial disorientation, a feeling that the surroundings are strange, unreal and detached. Distance perception may be altered and the ground may seem to move or be unsteady underfoot."[29]

> I saw no Way—The Heavens were stitched—
> I felt the Columns close—
> The Earth reversed her Hemispheres—
> I touched the Universe—
>
> And back it slid—and I alone—
> A Speck upon a Ball—
> Went out upon Circumference—
> Beyond the Dip of Bell—

In poem 378 (fasc. 38), the speaker experiences both derealization and depersonalization. After the extreme claustrophobia of the two opening lines, the speaker apprehends the world in a disoriented way, seeing the hemispheres reversed and the universe a "Ball" sliding into space where the "I" goes out "upon Circumference / Beyond the Dip of Bell." At first, the scene is difficult to grasp, yet the extreme spatial disorientation, the detachment of the individual from world and self, and the isolation of the speaker — "I alone" — qualify this as an example of *micropsia*, a frightening aspect of derealization in which the surroundings appear to be small and distant.[30]

In poem 875, another dimension is explored. Here the speaker becomes "enormous, tall, the universe, equivalent to the universe."[31] This is an example of *macropsia*, another facet of derealization, in which the individual perceives his or her surroundings as enlarged and near.[32]

> I stepped from Plank to Plank
> A slow and cautious way
> The Stars about my Head I felt
> About my Feet the Sea.
>
> I knew not but the next
> Would be my final inch —
> This gave me that precarious Gait
> Some call Experience.

Suzanne Juhasz provides an interesting analysis of both 378 and 875, seeing them as types of "space-travel" in which the poet can "assert both the actuality of the mind and also its supremacy."[33] In poem 378, the explorer-speaker "at the edge of everything, anything" must deal with the uncharted provinces within her expanded mind. Juhasz's analysis coincides with a medical explanation, since the speaker, experiencing these altered perceptions due to depersonalization and derealization, sees herself literally in a new relation to the world. In one study, Dr. B. Ruddick writes of patients reporting "bodily sensations resembling those described in *Alice in Wonderland*, of shrinking and swelling which led to great difficulty in the actual delineation of the body scheme."[34] Autobiographical accounts of subjects who have experienced these phenomena correspond with the poems' imagery: "I feel unreal — as though I wasn't part of my surroundings, but watching from a distance." "I can see my body in the dark and it seems immensely long." "I feel by anatomy swell up to gigantic proportions."[35]

There are many episodes of depersonalization in the poems. In poem 351 (fasc. 17), the speaker "felt" her "life with both her hands / to see if it was there." There is a dramatic divorce between the person of the speaker and the self, as if the speaker were two separate people, one who does the weighing and the other who is weighed.

> I felt my life with both my hands
> To see if it was there —
> I held my spirit to the Glass,
> To prove it possibler —

> I turned my Being round and round
> And paused at every pound
> To ask the Owner's name —
> For doubt, that I should know the Sound —
>
> I judged my features — jarred my hair —
> I pushed my dimples by, and waited —
> If they — twinkled back —
> Conviction might, of me —
>
> I told myself, "Take Courage, Friend —
> That — was a former time —
> But we might learn to like the Heaven.
> As well as our Old Home!"

This account approximates the experience of other subjects who felt "distant, unreal, detached, alien or changed in size or shape," one explaining, "I feel unreal as though I wasn't part of my surroundings, but watching from a distance." Another complained that "I felt disembodied...only my mind seemed to exist."[36] The same sense of alienation and strangeness appears in poem 410 where the speaker is concerned she is insane. Here is the "odd" person looking at herself, asking who this is: "I turned my Being round and round / And paused at every pound / To ask the Owner's name — / For doubt, that I should know the Sound." Everything is strange and alien. The individual looks at herself as if she were someone from another place, hoping recognition would come. But it does not, only the admonition to "Take Courage, Friend."

Alienation is present in poem 470 where the opening line reveals "I am alive — I guess." Here the speaker is uncertain if she is alive or dead; she deduces she is living because there is a breath on the glass, no viewing of a corpse, no burial mound marked with her name. However, where the speaker can only be sure of life by the absence of death, the quality of life is questionable

Poems 761 (fasc. 23), 599 (fasc. 24), and 396 (fasc. 27) reveal further evidence of the numbness of depersonalization.

> From Blank to Blank —
> A Threadless Way
> I pushed Mechanic feet —
> To stop — or perish — or advance —
> Alike indifferent —
>
> If end I gained
> It ends beyond
> Indefinite disclosed —
> I shut my eyes — and groped as well
> 'Twas lighter — to be Blind —

In 761, the "Element of blank" that characterizes pain in 650 reappears, but here the poet visualizes herself moving along "A Threadless Way." Her feet are "Mechanic," like the felon in 414 who is "frozen led," attesting to the loss of muscular control the panic victim experiences. The speaker has neither control nor desire to move in any direction; she is apathetic since it doesn't seem to matter, "To stop—or perish—or advance— / Alike indifferent." In this respect, the speaker resembles the agoraphobic victim who during episodes of depersonalization admits to "an oppressive sense of loss of spontaneity in movement, thought and feeling" and to "automaton-like behavior."[37]

> There is a pain—so utter—
> It swallows substance up—
> Then covers the Abyss with Trance—
> So Memory can step
> Around—across—upon it—
> As one within a Swoon—
> Goes safely—where an open eye—
> Would drop Him—Bone by Bone.

The pain of poem 599 is "so utter," everything is dwarfed by it. The horror, indicated here by an "Abyss," is covered by a "Trance," so that the speaker can "step / Around—across—upon it" safely. This description of the trancelike effect of depersonalization brought on by the panic attack accurately describes its release function and the protective purpose it serves. By cutting the victim's feelings off, depersonalization prevents him or her from a more serious breakdown. Here the victim, like the speaker in poem 761 who walks with mechanical feet, moves "As one within a Swoon" and is protected from dropping into the Abyss "Bone by Bone."

In poem 396 (fasc. 27) we also witness this effect. Although the poem appears to concern death, it may reasonably be surmised that it refers to depersonalization.

> There is a Languor of the Life
> More imminent than Pain—
> 'Tis Pain's Successor—When the Soul
> Has suffered all it can—
>
> A Drowsiness—diffuses—
> A Dimness like a Fog
> Envelopes Consciousness—
> As Mists—obliterate a Crag.
>
> The Surgeon—does not blanch—at pain—
> His Habit—is severe—
> But tell him that it ceased to feel—
> The Creature lying there—

And he will tell you—skill is late—
A Mightier than He—
Has ministered before Him—
There's no Vitality

Here the victim is beyond feeling. Stanza 1 outlines the sequence: "There is a Languor of the Life / More imminent than Pain— / 'Tis Pain's Successor—When the Soul / Has suffered all it can—." When the suffering has reached its limit, then "A Drowsiness, A Dimness like a Fog" comes on and "Envelopes Consciousness." Here is that familiar landscape following pain. Between suffering and vitality, there is a softening, a muffling of pain that, like a shot of morphine, causes the patient to cease "to feel." It is a state of numbed suspension that makes life bearable. De Moor refers to the complex of "neuropsychological sensations" that accompany panic attack, one of which is "a haze before the eyes" corresponding to the "Dimness like a Fog" of poem 396.[38]

The numbness and deathlike state reported by victims who experience depersonalization remind us of poem 465 (fasc. 26), where the speaker describes the scene of her death. Although the poem, which was titled "Dying" in its appearance in 1896, details the "Stillness in the Room" and the behavior of the mourners, it is easy to sense the speaker's state of suspension as he or she moves between life and death.

I heard a Fly buzz—when I died—
The Stillness in the Room
Was like the Stillness in the Air—
Between the Heaves of Storm—

The Eyes around—had wrung them dry—
And Breaths were gathering firm
For that last Onset—when the King
Be witnessed—in the Room—

I willed my Keepsakes—Signed away
What portion of me be
Assignable—and then it was
There interposed a Fly—

With Blue—uncertain stumbling Buzz—
Between the light—and me—
And then the Windows failed—and then
I could not see to see—

The poem recalls a particular case history in which the patient "was dead from the neck down; she felt divided in two, one half was a passive spectator of the other's acts, her movements appeared forced, mechanical, her feelings dead."[39] Such descriptions of "an awareness suspended midway between the

levels of nervous function appropriate to voluntary and automatic ...
activities"[40] convey the experience of Dickinson's speakers as they move
trancelike through some devastating experience.

In the *Modern Idiom*, Porter writes that "the crucial affair for" Dickinson
"is living after things happen. It is a preoccupation with afterknowledge,
with living in the aftermath." "The vision repeatedly angles out of psychic
voids that follow crises."[41] In the poems that deal with aftermath, the
language and imagery document the "crisis" that unleashed psychic horror
and detail the speaker's readjustment to life. In each poem, we sense the
inherent difficulty of recovery and the delicate balance of mental health.

> I tie my Hat—I crease my Shawl—
> Life's little duties do—precisely—
> As the very least
> Were infinite to me—
>
> I put new Blossoms in the Glass—
> And throw the old—away—
> I push a petal from my Gown
> That anchored there—I weigh
> The time 'twill be till six o'clock
> I have so much to do—
> And yet—Existence—some way back—
> Stopped—struck—my ticking—through—
> We cannot put Ourself away
> As a completed Man
> Or Woman—When the Errand's done
> We came to Flesh—upon—
> There may be—Miles on Miles of Nought—
> Of Action—sicker far—
> To simulate—is stinging work—
> To cover what we are
> From Science—and from Surgery—
> Too Telescopic Eyes
> To bear on us unshaded—
> For their—sake—not for Our's
> 'Twould start them—
> We—could tremble—
> But since we got a Bomb—
> And held it in our Bosom—
> Nay—Hold it—it is calm—
>
> Therefore—we do life's labor—
> Though life's Reward—be done—
> With scrupulous exactness—
> To hold our Senses—on—

In poem 443 (fasc. 24), the speaker describes trying to "hold" her "Senses—on." We detect her fragility and vulnerability. Barely under control, she busies herself with matters like tying her hat, creasing her shawl—"Life's little duties," which she does "precisely." Although simple activities, they are "infinite—to me," the speaker admitting the difficulty of this transitional period between a state of shock and the semblance of normality. In stanza 2, she outlines the step-by-step procedure, the activities geared to bringing her back to life—putting flowers in a vase, throwing the old away—but before too long she refers to the event that "Stopped— struck—my ticking through." This imagery reminds us of the experience that was "like Midnight," "When everything that ticked—has stopped" (poem 510). Here she confides it was she who stopped, her "ticking," her existence "struck ... through." And although it appeared to be the end, something like death—also similar to poem 510—she could not put herself away as completed but must "simulate"—that is, play act, pretend that all is right and normal, even though it is not.

In the lines that continue she admits to trying to hide "what we are" from others' "Too Telescopic Eyes." This type of judgment appeared in poem 413 when God was "Himself—a Telescope." Here it is others who cannot bear the truth. She pretends for their sakes, so as not to "start them." The horror she refers to as a bomb, some explosive experience, is reminiscent of the sudden, threatening nature of panic attack. By choosing the past tense "held" and then switching to the present tense—"Nay—Hold it"—she admits it is not over but still continuing. The bomb, which "is calm" now, is still alive and might go off at any time. Thus, the speaker continues to "do life's labors" "With scrupulous exactness / To hold our Senses—on," to keep her sanity and mental control. The poem addresses its speaker's precarious state of mental health and the continuing threat posed by this bomblike terror.

Poems 617 And 618, both from fascicle 32, also testify to this state of precariousness.

> Dont put up my Thread & Needle—
> I'll begin to Sow
> When the Birds begin to whistle—
> Better Stitches—so—
>
> These were bent—my sight got crooked—
> When my mind—is plain
> I'll do seams—a Queen's endeavor
> Would not blush to own—
>
> Hems—too fine for Lady's tracing
> To the sightless Knot—
> Tucks—of dainty interspersion—
> Like a dotted Dot—

Leave my Needle in the furrow—
Where I put it down—
I can make the zigzag stitches
Straight—when I am strong—

Till then—dreaming I am sowing
Fetch the seam I missed—
Closer—so I—at my sleeping—
Still surmise I stitch—

                                        (617)

At leisure is the Soul
That gets a Staggering Blow—
The Width of Life—before it spreads
Without a thing to do—

It begs you give it Work—
But just the placing Pins—
Or humblest Patchwork—Children do—
To still it's noisy Hands—

                                        (618)

In poem 617, the speaker asks that her "Thread and Needle" not be put away. She refers to stitches that were "bent" and "zigzag" and that she will make "Straight—when I am strong" and "When my mind—is plain." In 618, there is that same attempt to "hold our Senses—on" as in 443. The Soul has received "a Staggering Blow" and, seeing the expanse of life before it, "It begs you give it Work." However, the simplest, menial job—"the placing Pins" that "Children do" appears to be all it can handle. A variant for the last line's "To still it's noisy Hands"—[To] "Help it's Vacant Hands"—emphasizes the speaker's needs.

In her journey back to health, one agoraphobe's experience recalls that of the speaker of poem 443—"Putting up with the constant, dragging terror of agoraphobia saps energy on a massive scale. This results in everyday jobs assuming gigantic proportions, where even to put a load of washing in a machine seems an almost insuperable task. The vicious circle of stress and fear leading to tiredness, leading to more stress . . . means that an agoraphobe forcing himself to lead a 'normal' life is burning himself up at an enormous rate."[42] Enormous energy is invested in trying to act "normal." In addition, the pretense of being "normal," the need to cover up her ailment for others, weighs heavily on her and reveals another characteristic of agoraphobics—the need to hide their illness—a quality Brita Lindberg-Seyersted called "privateness" in Dickinson's poetry.[43] Dickinson's family was a private one and, undoubtedly, took pains to cover up the poet's problem. It is probable that although they protected her from public view, they were confused and unsympathetic at times and accused her of posing. Their probable demands that she act normally, pull herself together—a common reaction of an agoraphobe's family—would necessitate the speaker's pretense. So, too, the fluctuations of agoraphobia make it even more difficult for the family to accept. There were probably times when Dickinson appeared to be fine, and others when more frequent attacks made her worse. The speaker's admission that the bomb is calm now reveals that the panic attacks are in remission, and although the bomb is still intact, she is in a state of relative ease, trying to appear normal.

Three other poems of aftermath—430, 584, and 739—deal with the concepts of wilderness and peace. Poem 430 is dramatic in its description of "Difference," the state of life the speaker must endure.

It would never be Common—more—I said—
Difference—had begun—
Many a bitterness—had been—
But that old sort—was done—

Or—if it sometime—showed—as 'twill—
Upon the Downiest—Morn—
Such bliss—had I—for all the years—
'Twould give an Easier—pain—

I'd so much joy—I told it—Red—
Upon my simple Cheek—
I felt it publish—in my Eye—
'Twas needless—any speak—

I walked—as wings—my body bore—
The feet—I former used—
Unnecessary—now to me—
As boots—would be—to Birds—

I put my pleasure all abroad—
I dealt a word of Gold
To every Creature—that I met—
And Dowered—all the World—

When—suddenly—my Riches shrank—
A Goblin—drank my Dew—
My Palaces—dropped tenantless—
Myself—was beggared—too—

I clutched at sounds—
I groped at shapes—
I touched the tops of Films—
I felt the Wilderness roll back
Along my Golden lines—

The Sackcloth—hangs upon the nail—
The Frock I used to wear—
But where my moment of Brocade—
My—drop—of India?

The bitterness of the past "was done" and the speaker begins to experience some new joy. However, as quickly as joy begins, it ends—that is how fleeting it is. A goblin creature appears, recalling poems 414 and 512, and "drank" her "Dew." She is "beggared" by the experience. In the last two stanzas, turmoil results, as the "moment of Brocade" recedes and is replaced by the sackcloth she "used to wear." In a sinking, maelstromlike image, the speaker is dragged down; she "clutched at sounds, . . . groped at shapes, . . . touched the tops of Films." She tries to make sense of the "Wilderness" opening up within. This graphic groping for survival recalls the process of self-fragmentation at the heart of 280 and 512, and the "complete vulnerability"[44] it brings as "the Wilderness" rolls back. The poem ends with the question, why has this happened?

In poem 584, the unsettling experience has passed. The wilderness has gone, and although grief abides, there is "almost Peace."

> It ceased to hurt me, though so slow
> I could not see the trouble go—
> But only knew by looking back—
> That something—had obscured the Track—
>
> Nor when it altered, I could say,
> For I had worn it, every day,
> As constant as the Childish frock—
> I hung upon the Peg, at night.
>
> But not the Grief—that nestled close
> As needles—ladies softly press
> To Cushions Cheeks—
> To keep their place—
>
> Nor what consoled it, I could trace—
> Except, whereas 'twas Wilderness—
> It's better—almost Peace—

The last poem that develops this imagery is 739, a despairing poem in which the speaker sees no peace, although "many times" she thought "Peace had come." However, she realizes there is no shore or harbor in sight. This last idea corresponds with the hopeless state after panic attack.

> I many times thought Peace had come
> When Peace was far away—
> As Wrecked Men—deem they sight the Land—
> At Centre of the Sea—
>
> And struggle slacker—but to prove
> As hopelessly as I—
> How many the fictitious Shores—
> Or any Harbor be—

Although the source of fears appears to be external to the victim of panic attack, the fears are rooted within. While the syndrome appears to be a "multiphobic condition," it is in reality "one central anxiety theme," the fear of fear itself.[45] Once the panic attack is triggered, the individual reacts by trying to avoid the scene of the attack. However, as the attacks recur in different locations and the individual's fears begin to generalize, the individual avoids more and more places. In actuality, what has happened is that the individual has a phobophobia—or fear of fear, the fear of his or her own physical and emotional response to panic. It is a fear the individual carries within and cannot control by avoidance.

This fear of fear is revealed in a number of powerful poems that suggest Dickinson suspected that the source of her fears was within. A conflict between the soul or spirit and the self is clearly evident in poem 642 (fasc. 33).

> Me from Myself—to banish—
> Had I Art—
> Invincible my Fortress
> Unto All Heart—
>
> But since Myself—assault Me—
> How have I peace
> Except by subjugating
> Consciousness?
>
> And since We're mutual Monarch
> How this be
> Except by Abdiction—
> Me—of Me?

In this poem, "Myself—assault Me," and the speaker admits that there will be no peace "Except by subjugating / Consciousness." But how can this be, since the speaker continues, "We're mutual Monarch." It is impossible to banish "Me from Myself." The problem is irresolvable; it reappears in poem 683 (fasc. 25), where the soul is an imperial friend "unto itself / Or the most agonizing Spy." The division between the two is clear; the soul can either be a friend or "An Enemy."

In poem 670, we glimpse the terrifying enemy within. Griffith and Mudge relate Dickinson's house imagery to the disunity within herself.

> One need not be a Chamber—to be Haunted—
> One need not be a House—
> The Brain has Corridors—surpassing
> Material Place—
>
> Far safer, of a Midnight Meeting
> External Ghost
> Than it's interior Confronting—
> That Cooler Host.

Far safer, through an Abbey gallop,
The Stones a'chase —
Than Unarmed, one's a'self encounter —
In lonesome Place —

Ourself behind ourself, concealed —
Should startle most —
Assassin hid in our Apartment
Be Horror's least.

The Body — borrows a Revolver —
He bolts the Door —
O'erlooking a superior spectre —
Or More —

Mudge calls poem 670 "the most chilling revelation of the severed self,"[46] while Griffith finds it unsuccessful because it is not "graphic enough to sustain our interest." He describes the confrontation of the self with the self as "a kind of jocular peek-a-boo."[47] However, if the poem is seen as the culmination of a series of poems in which the self and the soul — the "Me and Myself" — are pitted against each other, then it accurately presents the fear of fear within the panic victim. Agoraphobics "who experience the house as the only safe behavior territory often do not feel at peace there either."[48] This facet of the illness is clear in poem 670. Even in the house, within the safety of her own room, Dickinson may have been "haunted by the thought that 'it' might happen," the "it" identified by clinical psychologist De Moor as "the nameless anxiety attack."[49]

In the poem, Dickinson reveals her fear of being alone with herself: "Ourself behind ourself, concealed." It is this same fear of being alone and "vulnerable"[50] that the poet wrote about to Mrs. Havens: "Vinnie has been all, so long, I feel the oddest fright at parting with her for an hour, lest a storm arise, and I go unsheltered";[51] and later to her Norcross cousins: "The nights turned hot, when Vinnie had gone, and I must keep no window raised for fear of prowling 'booger,' and I must shut my door for fear front door slide open on me at the 'dead of night,' and I must keep 'gas' burning to light the danger up, so I could distinguish it — these gave me a snarl in the brain which don't unravel yet, and that old nail in my breast pricked me, these dear were my cause."[52]

Dickinson had used all of these images before: the house, the brain, the night. Here she arranges them differently. The brain has corridors, like rooms in a house, that are dangerous. The house, a place usually associated with safety by agoraphobics, is not as safe as "a Midnight Meeting" with an "External Ghost," or a ride through "an Abbey." In each stanza, the speaker reminds us of the terror that is within, the "interior Confronting," the "one's a'self encounters." Finally in the fourth stanza, we meet "Ourself behind ourself, concealed." We can protect ourselves from the "Assassin," but we cannot close "the Door" on the "superior spectre" of ourselves. The conclusion circles back to the perplexing question asked in poem 642: How can I banish me from myself— "Except by Abdication / Me of Me?" There is no way, short of suicide. What the poem underscores is the division, the rift, the "snarl in the brain" that Dickinson tried to heal through her poetry.

While agoraphobics seek safety at home in familiar surroundings and with trusted companions, they are attempting to run away from something internal rather than external. "The danger is not outside—it is in oneself." It is their own fear of panic that scares them and drives them to run from the world, yet it is "not something outside ... but ... within; you carry the object of your fear within you, and you have no escape from it."[53] "Psychologically speaking, the inner self is so frightened that it has to find some 'thing' to make sense of its fright."[54] Thus it runs home to safety, although even there no safety can be found.

14
"Then — Close the Valves of Her Attention Like Stone"

Dickinson's life of solitude has been variously interpreted by scholars. Wolff concludes that although Dickinson's life may be "described as a deviation from the norm," her choice of a poetic vocation "had a decidedly positive dimension." In other words, "her decision to lead a life devoid of significant event may well have been the necessary condition for her art."[1] Other critics believe that Dickinson lived in "a state of dislocation from her prosaic contemporaries" and that when her "expectation of marriage, of a family, and of a settled identity were over," she came to "the condition of afterward" and explored her isolation in her poems.[2]

Feminists argue that Dickinson did not want what the more traditional woman of the time wanted but chose solitude as a solution to the problem of being a woman in a restrictive age.[3] They believe that "slamming the door on the world was also a dramatic gesture of dissent. Born in the very patriachal nineteenth century, Emily Dickinson resoundingly rejected the priorities of her age."[4] In Juhasz's view Dickinson's seclusion was "strategy rather than debility."[5] "Given her temperament — her passionate intensity, her extreme sensitivity, her stubborn dedication to her sense of vocation; given the fate that awaited her as a normal woman of her class and era," she chose to live in her mind where she could explore its landscape and chart its dimensions.[6]

Despite the feminists' interpretation, the poet keenly sensed what her seclusion cost. In poem 944, she writes, "I learned — at least — what Home could be." In the final stanza she measures what she has against what she does not: "This seems a Home / And Home is not / But what that Place could be / Afflicts me — as a Setting Sun / Where Dawn — knows how to be." In her understanding of what home could be and what the reality of her own life would be, Dickinson realized she would never leave her father's home, except in death. In her admission that she never crossed her father's ground, she knew she would be the prisoner of that house. Agoraphobia is a chronic disease and left untreated will worsen until the last stages of complete withdrawal and depression are reached. Within the testimony of the poems is preserved the record of the poet's withdrawal and the evidence of a life turned to stone. Like some curious fossil, it speaks from another time and place about itself and its world. Within the stone imagery, Dickinson reveals the death-in-life that became her fate. She uses the word *stone* and particular types such as marble, alabaster, Carrara frequently in her poetry, letting them stand for death, hardness, and endurance. They also stand for protection, withdrawal, safety, and the speaker's own numbed state of being.

> The Soul selects her own Society—
> Then—shuts the Door—
> To her divine Majority—
> Present no more—
>
> Unmoved—she notes the Chariots—pausing—
> At her low Gate—
> Unmoved—an Emperor be kneeling
> Upon her Mat—
>
> I've known her—from an ample nation—
> Choose One—
> Then—close the Valves of her attention—
> Like Stone—

One of the most telling poems is 303 (fasc. 20). Here the female soul makes a choice "Then—shuts the Door" and though an "Emperor be kneeling / Upon her Mat" is "Unmoved." After the soul's selection, "One" is chosen and "the Valves of her attention" are closed "Like Stone." The variant word for *valves* is *lids*; however, valves is a better choice. Rather than simply dismiss the sight of another suitor, the soul in a mysterious, mechanical operation actually shuts off the channels through which life flows, becoming permanently stopped—inert, unfeeling, and lifeless like stone. By implication, the soul is keenly discriminating, "a divine Majority," beyond feeling, looking down "at her low Gate." Impervious and imperial in her disregard of "an Emperor," she makes her choice, which is forever fixed and inscrutable. Like death, this decision is final.

The withdrawal of the soul's attention in poem 303 expands to include a total withdrawal of the self in poem 341 (fasc. 18).

> After great pain, a formal feeling comes—
> The Nerves sit ceremonious, like Tombs—
> The stiff Heart questions was it He, that bore,
> And Yesterday, or Centuries before?
>
> The Feet, mechanical, go round—
> Of Ground, or Air, or Ought—
> A wooden way
> Regardless grown,
> A Quartz contentment, like a stone—

This is the Hour of Lead—
Remembered, if outlived,
As Freezing persons, recollect the Snow—
First—Chill—then Stupor—then the letting go—

This poem of "aftermath" deals with the time after crisis. Whatever the crisis, the pattern of reaction is here: the stasis after shock, the "formal feeling," the "Nerves like Tombs," the "stiff Heart," the "Feet, mechanical," "A Wooden Way," an "Hour of Lead," "Chill—then Stupor"—all summed up in one striking image: "A Quartz contentment, like a stone." The feeling is of rigor mortis, of a deathlike stiffening after the release of life, the reminder of death in the tombs, in "the letting go" of "Freezing persons." The speaker becomes stone before our eyes. She is beyond pain, unfeeling, like the soul in 303. There is a hardness, a durability to the quartz contentment that is also described as the "Hour of Lead," the heavy weight that crushes out life and leaves a diminished, nonfeeling self. This poem suggests the panic attack where the individual is numbed with anxiety and fear, feeling as if death has come.

In poem 1046 (set 6b) the words *stone, marble,* and *Carrara* describe some inexplicable experience that immobilizes and paralyzes the speaker, creating a condition analogous to being carved in stone.

I've dropped my Brain—My Soul is numb—
The Veins that used to run
Stop palsied—'tis Paralysis
Done perfecter on stone.

Vitality is Carved and cool.
My nerve in Marble lies—
A Breathing Woman
Yesterday—Endowed with Paradise.

Not dumb—I had a sort that moved—
A Sense that smote and stirred—
Instincts for Dance—a caper part—
An Aptitude for Bird—

Who wrought Carrara in me
And chiselled all my tune
Were it a Witchcraft—were it Death—
I've still a chance to strain

To Being, somewhere—Motion—Breath—
Though Centuries beyond,
And every limit a Decade—
I'll shiver, satisfied.

In stanza 1, the speaker complains that she "dropped" her brain and that her "Soul is numb." Her body has stopped functioning, too, because the "Veins" that "used to run" are "Done perfecter on stone." There is a frozen quality, as if death has occurred or the permanence of art been achieved. In stanza 2, *Carved* is used, and the speaker admits that her energy is "cool" and her "nerve in Marble lies." The speaker appears frozen in time, a state vastly different from yesterday when she was "A Breathing Woman." Thus, her soul is numb, her veins have stopped, her nerves and energy are cold. In stanza 3, the emphasis is on action and movement, what the speaker used to be, the verbs *smote* and *stirred* enhancing her quick, lively qualities. However, in stanza 4 there is a return to inactivity and to the question, "Who wrought Carrara in me / And chiselled all my tune." Who has done this to me and what has brought about this change? One question leads to another: Was it "Witchcraft" or death? In stanza 5, there are no answers, but only the hope that in the "Centuries beyond" she can again "strain / To Being, ... Motion—Breath."

The poem raises several questions. What has happened to bring on this numbed state? Was it an emotional crisis or a physical ailment? Whatever it was, the experience recalls poems from fascicles 15 and 16. Perhaps Dickinson's fear of fear left her afraid to engage in normal activities and created in her an isolation that was like death. Withdrawn, she became fixed in time, unchanging in her nature, despairing in her outlook, like some statue "wrought" in "Carrara." Dickinson may have felt that this was "witchcraft." She knew it was not death ("It was not death for I stood up"), although she had perhaps felt she was dying. According to Leonard, "phobic seizures at their worst approach any limits of terror that the human mind is capable of in the actual presence of death in its most horrible forms."[7] Dickinson certainly wondered why this terror happened. Without the medical information readily available today, she may have interpreted her ordeal as a religious judgment. This is not uncommon: "the central questions of 'Why me?' or 'Why?' at all, have never been satisfactorily answered." "Certainly the victim has no idea why it is happening" and sometimes puts "an entirely religious significance on it, since the attack comes like an avenging demon out of the blue."[8] "To the agoraphobic who is a sincere Christian, it must appear the ultimate folly that after years or even decades of existing in a living hell, there still exists the possibility of going to an even worse hell after death."[9] At the end of poem 1046, the speaker looks head to "Being," whatever that may be, as a contrast to this state of stony numbness.

The last stage of agoraphobia with panic attack, according to Sheehan, is depression. The individual who cannot deal with the real world, who has cut off all social ties with life beyond the front door, cannot look ahead to a promising future. Instead, unable to control life, he or she becomes chronically depressed: "depressive complaints" are "prominent"; they complain of "mood swings, apathy, crying spells, and sleeping difficulties."[10] Sheehan distinguishes between the depression of agoraphobia and a major depression. One difference is that while drugs alleviate other forms of depression, they have no effect on depression brought on by anxiety.[11] Thus, this depression, often mislabeled a "masked" or "latent" depression, is different and is the culminating stage of a chronic phobic disability.

Recent studies confirm "that patients who have anxiety disorders also have a high incidence of depression. The relationship appears particularly strong for panic disorder."[12] One study reports that as many as "seventy-five percent of patients who experience panic attacks went on to develop a depressive syndrome."[13] "This is not surprising," one researcher notes, "when one considers that these patients see themselves as helpless, dependent creatures and are often afraid of gradually drifting towards insanity."[14] The "low spontaneous recovery rate"[15] also accounts for the high incidence of depression. Dickinson knew depression intimately, describing its features in poem 258 (fasc. 13). In "a certain Slant of light," the poet feels a "Hurt" for which there is no "scar." She names it "Despair" and defines it as "An imperial affliction / Sent us of the Air."

In later fascicles, despair becomes more prominent. In poem 305 (fasc. 25), the poet distinguishes between fear and despair, describing the latter as a mind with "no Motion— / Contented as the Eye / Upon the Forehead of a Bust / That knows—it cannot see." Unlike fear, which spurs the soul in poem 770, despair is a permanent blindness without beginning or ending. Similarly, in poem 258 despair has "the look of Death," distant, unseeing, and uncaring. However, despair is most vividly portrayed in a poem that doesn't use the word, poem 458 in fascicle 32.

> Like Eyes that looked on Wastes—
> Incredulous of Ought
> But Blank—and steady Wilderness—
> Diversified by Night—
>
> Just Infinites of Nought—
> As far as it could see—
> So looked the face I looked upon—
> So looked itself—on Me—
>
> I offered it no Help—
> Because the Cause was Mine—
> The Misery a Compact
> As hopeless—as divine—
>
> Neither—would be absolved—
> Neither would be a Queen
> Without the Other—Therefore—
> We perish—tho' We reign—

The familiar images are present, the wilderness of emotional turmoil (430, 584, and 739) and the "Night" as a divider between days of pain or numbed grief (471). What is unique is the "Infinites of Nought" — the "Wastes" that define a despair brought about by a "hopeless" problem. The image is striking, anticipating the "gigantic" blank eyes of Doctor T. J. Eckleburg in F. Scott Fitzgerald's *The Great Gatsby*, which look out "above the gray land" and "brood on over the solemn dumping ground."[16] Here the tone is personal, voicing the ultimate despair of the speaker's "Cause." This despair is a "Grief of Cold," as she describes it in poem 561 (fasc. 27), where she measures her grief against others', wondering if "Some—are like My Own." However, in poem 477 (fasc. 33), the speaker concludes that despair cannot be compassed but is like a "Goalless Road" whose traveler is "Unconscious of the Width." In poem 405 (fasc. 28), the speaker, "accustomed to" her "Fate," realizes that it is better to live with a despair that she has grown comfortable with than with a hope she is "not used to."

The fears that controlled the poet's waking life and caused her to withdraw deeper into herself left her very lonely. The sixth stage of the agoraphobic syndrome is one in which "overall anxiety increases and confidence diminishes. At times the retreat can be so complete that patients will stay in one room of their house or restrict themselves to one piece of furniture in one room. The patient is now severely disabled."[17] At this point, Dickinson's world might have included none but family members. This loneliness resulting from limited social contacts is aggravated by the isolation of panic attack, which leaves its victim weakened and more fearful of the next. So too the effects of depersonalization and derealization further cut the victim off from natural surroundings and from his or her own feelings. "The loneliness of depersonalization is intense—after all, you have given up on everyone including yourself—and the pain and hurt is indescribable."[18] Isolation and the fear of it is "common to both agoraphobics and claustrophobics" where the individual is afraid of being "trapped," of being cut off without an exit.[19] If Dickinson were a victim of the agoraphobic syndrome, then how easy it is to understand the loneliness of which she speaks, a loneliness Mudge writes "probably terrorized Emily most." For Dickinson, "Loneliness towered above any other anxiety."[20]

This fear of loneliness is reflected in poems 590 (fasc. 29) and 777 (fasc. 39). Similar in their cavernous and dark landscapes, they exact a similar cost—a feeling of death, of being cut off from life.

> Did you ever stand in a Cavern's Mouth—
> Widths out of the Sun—
> And look—and shudder, and block your breath—
> And deem to be alone
>
> In such a place, what horror,
> How Goblin it would be—

And fly, as 'twere pursuing you?
Then Loneliness—looks so—

Did you ever look in a Cannon's face—
Between whose Yellow eye—
And your's—the Judgment intervened—
The Question of "To die"—

Extemporizing in your ear
As cool as Satyr's Drums—
If you remember, and were saved—
It's liker so—it seems—

In 590, the opening image objectifies the state of loneliness. It is dark— "in a Cavern's Mouth," cold "out of the Sun," and you are afraid— "what horror." This is loneliness "pursuing you." The second analogy is more life defying. You are looking into the cannon's "Yellow eye" and you are saved, "The Question of 'To Die' " still "in your ear." You are saved, but the hand of death has gripped you and left you numb and afraid.

The Loneliness One dare not sound—
And would as soon surmise
As in it's Grave go plumbing
To ascertain the size—

The Loneliness whose worst alarm
Is lest itself should see—
And perish from before itself
For just a scrutiny—

The Horror not to be surveyed—
But skirted in the Dark—
With Consciousness suspended—
And Being under Lock

I fear me this—is Loneliness—
The Maker of the soul
It's Caverns and it's Corridors
Illuminate—or seal—

In poem 777 the poet describes loneliness again. It is limitless, deeper than death. In stanza 2, she admits the worst fear is to see loneliness stretch before you. In stanza 3, the truth of loneliness, "The Horror not to be surveyed," should be avoided, and this reminds the reader of the abyss in poem 599 where memory steps "around—across—upon it / As one within a Swoon." Here too, the abyss of loneliness is "skirted in the Dark" in a numb, trancelike state with "Consciousness suspended / And Being under Lock." In the final stanza, loneliness is described as having "Caverns and ... Corridors," an architecture used in poems 670 and 590.

15

"Alone, I Cannot Be"

In *Plaintext*, a collection of autobiographical essays, writer Nancy Mairs considers agoraphobia. "Surprised" by the numbers who have the illness — "one in one hundred sixty people" — she remembers that when she first felt its effects there was "no label" for the disorder, and so she assumed she alone "experienced it. No one spoke of having symptoms like mine." She "denied them, disguised them" rather than admit them.[1] Emily Dickinson may have felt the same: "Wrecked, solitary here" (280), emotions she recorded in her poems. Dickinson's seclusion brings the poet to her mind, and Mairs realizes that "even confined to the house, a woman can always write. . . Emily did."[2] Mairs finds some connection among "womanness, poetry, depression, agoraphobia."[3] The fact "that at least two thirds of us are women"[4] does not surprise Mairs. Nevertheless, medical researchers are confused by the preponderance of women among agoraphobics and have tried within the last decades to understand why.

In *Fears and Phobias*, Marks notes that in certain neurotic disorders such as social anxieties, men and women are "equally represented."[5] However, this is not the case with agoraphobia. One of the startling facts of the disease is that it strikes more women than men. In a recent study "the rates are two-to-fourfold higher among women than men."[6] Estimates of the proportion of agoraphobics who are women range from a low of 64 percent to a high of 95 percent.[7] Ironically, when the illness was first diagnosed in 1872, it was based on the case histories of three male patients who displayed the primary symptoms of the disorder: a fear of walking across public squares and an imminent sense of dread with no apparent cause. Why then is agoraphobia predominantly a woman's illness, one that has been labeled the "housewives' disease"?[8] An examination of the research concerning the illness' uneven sexual distribution is enlightening.

The reasons may be categorized into biological and physiological factors, personality types, and differences in sex roles, parental patterns, and socialization processes. To begin, investigators such as Klein suspect that anxiety may be related to a "biologic control mechanism" that for some individuals may be more sensitive to alarm.[9] When it is triggered, as it is upon separation from the mother, panic results. Klein's theory of "biological propensity" and gender studies have recently been synthesized, some researchers now believing that "women might have a greater likelihood than men" to exhibit biological propensity, making them more prone to the illness.[10] This belief plus the fact that women show "higher frequency of panic in vivo" leads researchers to suggest that "the tendency to panic is sex-linked."[11]

Other studies suggest that hormonal differences also account for the higher proportion of women agoraphobics. "Estrogen disorders" are seen as one of the prime causes by some investigators, since the disorder is rare before puberty and intensifies during particular days of the menstrual cycle. One clinical psychologist notes that there is "an increase of ... agoraphobic symptoms during the premenstrual period," strongly suggesting hormonal involvement.[12] Researchers also believe that the "lower levels of testosterone, a hormone related to dominance and aggressive behavior," are also responsible for women's more fearful behavior.[13] In clinical studies of fear and timidity, it has been established that even in childhood, females "surpass males" in fear. Animal studies corroborate the "sexual differences in fear and avoidant behavior," suggesting that the different biologic and physiologic makeup of males and females contributes to the "differences in human fear behavior."[14] Once agoraphobia develops, the "more extreme avoidance behavior is found in agoraphobics who are higher in femininity and lower in masculinity."[15]

In his 1966 study of agoraphobia, J. D. Andrews states that "he has never heard of a phobic who is 'self-assertive, independent, or fearless.' "[16] It is generally believed that agoraphobes have a "hyperactive autonomous nervous system" and are prone to "acute anxiety." In general, they are more likely to suffer from anxiety and to be neurotic as well. Clinical psychologists Chambless and Goldstein believe this type of hysterical personality responsible for the higher incidence of agoraphobia in women.[17] Seeing relationships between agoraphobia and a conversion hysteria that "frequently emerges in women of hysterical personality type," the researchers realize that "women are particularly vulnerable to these problems as the sick, fearful role is an acceptable one for females in our culture."[18]

Researcher Thomas Rapp explains the higher incidence of women by looking at the difference in male and female social roles. In our society, it is accepted that men go out into the workplace, while women may stay at home. Men are accustomed to their roles and express their anxiety in different ways, perhaps turning in times of stress to alcohol or drugs. Despite their problems, however, they continue to force themselves to go out into the world. On the other hand, when women become anxious about going out, they become an extreme of their social stereotype, staying indoors in self-defense.[19]

The way women and men are socialized may also account for the uneven distribution in agoraphobia. Observe how girls and boys have been raised in our society. While boys are encouraged to be independent and daring, to explore the unknown, girls are protected and kept safe at home. This double standard teaches boys to be fearless and brave men in the outside world and trains girls to be secure only within the realm of the family. This system of education, undoubtedly more pronounced in Dickinson's day, "results in their [women's] finding psychological anchorage at home and in viewing the public world as one that allows little sense of safety control, or competence."[20]

We need not look far into Dickinson's life to recall how "well protected and safe" her parents kept her and her sister. Even at the age of twenty-one, Dickinson complains her parents would not leave the two of them alone. Recall Mrs. Dickinson's "objection" to leaving her daughters because she feared it wouldn't be "safe."[21] Such oversolicitous care causes Dickinson to doubt the outside world and to rely on the comforts and protection of her home. This "overprotective pattern of familial interaction is more congruent and thus more likely in dealing with a female child in our culture."[22]

According to Bowlby's exploration of separation anxiety, such overprotective behavior could "lead to anxious attachment in the form of agoraphobia."[23] In a study of female agoraphobics and female simple phobics, the former had higher levels of "childhood separation anxiety (sixty-three percent versus forty-four percent)."[24] Women are especially involved in "a lifelong struggle with their mothers over issues of dependency and autonomy."[25] One recent study confirmed that in agoraphobic subjects "Parent-related events (especially mother-related events) were significantly overrepresented."[26] In fact, in some families "mild independence in women is equated with rebellion by some mothers."[27] The research shows that agoraphobic women have a "special relationship with their mothers." In one study, two thirds of the agoraphobic women involved had "ambivalent feelings toward their mothers,"[28] and this is a category in which Dickinson's letters clearly place her. Other data reveal that women who achieve are women who have experienced "maternal rejection."[29] In some instances, the child may be taught "however covertly to remain at home as the companion to the parent and to feel anxious if she wishes to do otherwise."[30] In Dickinson's case, this may have been true, especially after 1855 when her mother's illness forced her to stay home and to cater to her family's demands. In 1858, Dickinson wrote to Mrs. Joseph Haven: I should love to pass an hour with you, and the little girls, could I leave home, or mother. I do not go out at all, lest father will come and miss me, or miss some little act, which I might forget, should I run away—."[31] Eight years earlier Dickinson had written to Abiah Root about her service to her family, a type of "martyrdom" she satirized: "I am yet the Queen of the court, if regalia be dust, and dirt, have three loyal subjects, whom I'd rather relieve from service. Mother is still an invalid tho' a partially restored one—Father and Austin still clamor for food, and I, like a martyr am feeding them."[32]

One familial pattern of agoraphobia fits Dickinson's situation perfectly. In this constellation "a parent's illness, especially mother's," triggers in the child an overwhelming fear that if he or she leaves "something dreadful might happen" and that "if at home the child can save the parent."[33] This fear is spelled out in a letter to Jane Humphrey: "I'm afraid I'm growing selfish in my dear home, but I do love it so, as when some pleasant friend invites me to pass a week with her, I look at my father and mother and Vinnie, and all my friends, and I say no — no, can't leave them, what if they die when I'm gone."[34] The role of the family is especially important in agoraphobia, for were it not for their "support," their need to keep the woman a child, the individual could not become agoraphobic. "One must conclude that the pattern of parental reinforcement, childhood learning, and socialization experience may provide the clues to our understanding of the phobic symptoms and their associated personality traits in women, particularly the propensity to develop agoraphobia."[35]

In a comprehensive examination of gender imperatives, which he defines as "the only one [model] that addresses the frequently observed sex difference in the prevalence of agoraphobia," Barry Wolfe writes that "the traditional ideology of femininity is phobogenic, inculcating in women a fundamentally dependent perspective concerning themselves and the world."[36] "In fact, women may learn that independence (symbolized by leaving home) is bad or unsafe."[37] In their acceptance of a female identity, women come to accept several ancillary beliefs: (1) "they cannot function on their own"; (2) that they must rely on a man to "protect them"; (3) that because they are women there are "difficult life experiences and challenges" they can "avoid mastering"; and (4) that "it is inappropriate to feel or express powerful feelings such as anger or rage."[38] This last point can easily be related to Chambless and Goldstein's determination that the agoraphobic victim, rather than assert herself and deal with the interpersonal conflict that triggers the panic attack, "concentrates on avoidance of those situations where future panic attacks are anticipated."[39] Thus the conflict is unresolved and keeps the individual dependent and trapped.

The socialization process, then, teaches women to "avoid autonomy, initiative or assertiveness"[40] and keeps them in the role of children. As soon as female infants are born, parents treat them as "fragile," even though they may be "sturdier than male infants."[41] In school, readers portray females as "helpless and incompetent." Girls are more afraid, expressing their fears "three times more often than boys." While boys "master fear," little girls give in to it.[42] The female identifying with her gender sees herself as helpless and unprotected, unable to cope on her own. When a problem arises or a stage in life is reached that calls for an assertive or independent act, the woman may become phobic in an attempt to avoid "defiance of someone" close to her rather than risk losing his or her love and support. "For many the phobia was a way out of a difficult situation in which two or more people were exerting equally dominating but conflicting pressures on the patient, parents vs. husband, and the other alternative would have been open defiance of someone."[43] Untrained to deal with defiance, guilt-ridden for justifiable feelings of anger, the woman remains the child she has been taught to be — passive, unassertive, and helpless. As I have noted, Dickinson presented herself as a child. In her letters, she "identifies the role of women in social relationships with that of the little girl, or daughter, perceiving that if adults are people with authority, autonomy, maturity, then women are not adults." As Barbara Mossberg points out, "she uses the pose of the dutiful daughter in which she downgrades her capabilities in order to gain love."[44]

There are other consequences of female identity outlined by Nancy Roeske in her discussion of gender imperatives. One is that since women place greater value on "relationships and attachment" than do men, they may be more sensitive to any changes — "real or imagined" — within these relationships. In addition to being psychologically dependent on relationships, women are "financially dependent on them" as well. Thus, the reality of women's economic status limits their control and makes them more vulnerable. Another issue is a social one; it is more acceptable for a woman to be dependent than a man, and since her place "is in the home,"[45] it is not noticed if she avoids leaving it. She can more easily disappear into the house, hiding in the role of homemaker. This is reminiscent of Dickinson's case: in the death records at the Amherst town clerk's office, hers reads, "Occupation: At Home."[46]

Current feminist theory takes the concept of gender identity a step further. It interprets the illness of agoraphobia as an act of rebellion, "a living and acting metaphor . . . a sit-in strike."[47] This position is not unlike that of Susie Orbach who in *Hunger Strike* describes "the anorectic's struggle as a metaphor for our age." Hysteria in the nineteenth century and eating disorders in the twentieth century are both expressions of "rebellion and the accommodation that women come to make in the context of a social role lived within circumscribed boundaries."[48] Like the sufferer of anorexia, the agoraphobe takes control of her life in the only way she can, a way that is ultimately destructive of the self. In *Women Who Marry Houses*, agoraphobia is portrayed "as a paradigm for the historical intimidation and oppression of women. The self-hate, self-limitation, self-abnegation, and self-punishment of agoraphobia is a caricature of centuries of childhood instructions to women. Only when society gives just value to the work women do at home, and makes it easier for them to leave the home to do fully accepted and compensated work, will women no longer need to be agoraphobic."[49]

In a chapter devoted to Emily Dickinson, "A Woman Who Chose to Stay at Home," Robert Seidenberg and Karen DeCrow examine the life of the poet and suggest that her seclusion was brought about not by an "unrequited love" but by "her keen awareness of the difficulties, of the lack of place for her, in entering the world." If she were not a recluse, "she probably would have married, had several children and several miscarriages, spent her days at the market and at the stove," and "in all probability would not have written a line of poetry."[50] Agoraphobia, seen as a socially conditioned disease, engages its victim in "a most subtle aspect of passive resistance by playing the feminine role. By complete acquiescence the agoraphobe becomes the complete homebody."[51]

In 1979, *The Madwoman in the Attic* addressed the female literary tradition and found that women writers used metaphors of starvation, madness, and enclosure both consciously and unconsciously to describe their struggle with the male-dominated literary world. These metaphors dramatize the high price creativity exacts. Sandra Gilbert describes how Dickinson "became a madwoman—became ... both ironically a madwoman (a deliberate impersonation of a madwoman) and truly a madwoman (a helpless agoraphobic, trapped in a room in her father's house)."[52] Here agoraphobia is characterized as a defense rather than a disorder, one she turned to because of "the 'double bind' of the woman poet: on the one hand, the impossibility of self-assertion for a woman, on the other hand, the necessity of self-assertion for a poet."[53]

While there is some validity to these views, there are also obvious omissions. The question of why more women than men are agoraphobic is complex, one that must take into account the fact that "all human beings are biologic, psychological, and sociologic creatures" and that agoraphobia must be understood within "these three areas."[54] Seeking answers to the question, researchers must explore these three overlapping and intersecting areas, being especially wary of a simplistic or one-dimensional solution. While many see Dickinson's withdrawal as a symbolic gesture, a defiant slam of the door on her repressive, chauvinistic society, they interpret agoraphobia primarily as a metaphor and ignore that it is an illness with debilitating effects. Thus they overlook the true nature of her seclusion and its impact on her personality. Dickinson's agoraphobia may have been influenced by the male-dominated culture in which she felt she had no place, but her withdrawal was neither a conscious decision nor a voluntary rebellious act.

The poet was in a no-win position. From her early years, she was dominated by a strict father who never encouraged independence. Instead she was raised to be dependent and helpless, someone to be protected. From her mother, she learned a pattern of fear, of timidity, which was her mother's way of dealing with life in a male-dominated world. Although Dickinson had a normal desire to break free, she was unable to do so and probably felt guilty for even wanting to. In the 1860s, some unidentified trigger set off a panic attack, similar to the attack of January 1854, and left her afraid. Although Dickinson tried to avoid her fears, she could not and, consequently, did not improve but grew worse. According to research, a feedback loop is set up:

the individual, rather than getting better by getting out of the situation that initiated the conflict, stays in it and has more attacks. Dickinson stayed within the unhealthy home atmosphere and became more deeply enmeshed in it. Sometimes "family members ... inadvertently, or perhaps intentionally, reinforce a patient's fears."[55] Dickinson's family may have reinforced her need for them, her illness convincing them that she needed their care.

Depression and loneliness are the normal outgrowths of such a situation. However, there are also unconscious psychological benefits. For one, Dickinson did not have to resolve the conflict between her family and herself, nor did she have to deal with the guilt that was a by-product of this conflict. So, too, she received the attention and love she needed. Lastly, she got control. Someone who felt powerless to direct her own life could now control her family's life, since she created a situation wherein they must do her bidding. "As a result of the limited mobility," the agoraphobe is "dependent on others not only to fulfill the role of companions, but also to take over the various kinds of daily obligations. It is not always easy to distinguish this dependency from secondary-gain manipulation. The call on service of others may degenerate into veiled tyranny."[56] However, we must also bear in mind that "It is presumably impossible to become an agoraphobic without the aid of someone who will submit to the inevitable demands imposed upon them by the sufferer."[57] In a way, it was her punishment of her family. It was the price they had to pay for discouraging her independence. Now they had to deal with her total dependence.

If we overlook this explanation, we defuse the poetry of torment, of the horror Dickinson faced and the attempts she made to understand herself. Dickinson's personality and heredity, her home and culture created the circumstances that caused her illness and made her the person we know. The poet transformed her weakness into strength, transcending her limitation of space through the liberation of words. However, if we disregard her illness and interpret her seclusion as a symbolic act, then Dickinson becomes a parody of herself and the force behind her poems is lost.

16

"The Soul Achieves — Herself"

After 1865, Dickinson withdrew further into a seclusion not unlike that described in poem 216: "Safe in their Alabaster Chambers." She was "safe" too from the world outside, under her own "Roof of stone." Withdrawn into her own alabaster chamber, she severed connections with the larger world. Porter writes that "When she went into reclusion in her father's house, she took her language with her."[1] Her language thus becomes enigmatic, "language talking to itself, not negotiating with the outside world." Her poems are "removed from sensation into words of a privately encoded intent."[2] In an attempt to explain Dickinson's art, Porter explores "some technical mysteries" and claims that the "most basic of all" is "the absence of connective webbing in her works."[3] Here the diagnosis of agoraphobia can help. Although it cannot provide the "connective webbing" for all her poetry, it dispels the mystery of some poems written during the crisis years.

These poems do not present an "ordinary observation of experience," because the agoraphobic syndrome is not ordinary and creates vast confusion for its victim. Dickinson saw through a veil of fears; her disorder colored her life. So wide-ranging were its symptoms and effects that Dickinson was unaware of what was happening to her and reflected this bafflement in her nameless, seemingly "non-referring" poems.[4] However, at the poetry's core, she described the physical, mental, and emotional devastation she was undergoing. With the advantage of today's medical and scientific advances, we can discover what Dickinson herself could not possibly have known in her own day — that she suffered from a crippling illness which would fluctuate in intensity throughout her life, leaving her a victim of its assaults. The fact that we can detect the illness from her descriptions is a credit to her ability to clearly and accurately articulate what was happening to her.

Dickinson wielded the written word as a potent wedge against her fears, words bringing her a measure of control over a life she must have felt powerless to change. Poetry served as a channel through which her fears could be transformed into something positive and lasting. In poem 544 (fasc. 30), Dickinson referred to this aspect of creativity, the suffering that became art: "The Martyr Poets — did not tell / But wrought their Pang in syllables / That when their mortal name be numb / Their mortal fate — encourage Some."

Dickinson carved a life out of words, words gained through "the gift of Screws" (poem 675). She controlled her fears, tamed them through her poetic skill, and healed herself as effectively as she could. She knew she would be heard despite the fact of her seclusion. Why else thread the fascicles together and refer to them self-consciously: "But this—in Lady's Drawer / Make Summer—When the Lady lie / In Ceaseless Rosemary—." For Dickinson the art of writing was speaking, saying aloud what she experienced in her life, making an invisible life visible to later generations, making it understandable to herself. She tolerated the pain that composition exacted during those painful crisis years because the poems that would become her legacy also provided the healing balm that allowed her "to hold" her senses on.

For Dickinson words had power; they held the magic she needed to release herself spiritually and mentally from the emotional torments she felt. Dickinson knew what "she had wrought." Although Porter believes that the poet wrote "furiously with a language ... removed from its representational and responsive function,"[5] Dickinson's language helped her accommodate herself to a world of loneliness and withdrawal. Readers know her suffering firsthand; we experience it directly through her descriptions of the physical changes, the fear of insanity, the bafflement and confusion she felt in the face of an unknown assailant. Although she records her own condition, she also tells the story of others who suffer, her work testifying to the capacity of the mind to overcome and master its demons. In two poems Dickinson details this strength, this self-endurance.

> On a Columnar Self—
> How ample to rely
> In Tumult—or Extremity—
> How good the Certainty
>
> That Lever cannot pry—
> And Wedge cannot divide
> Conviction—That Granitic Base—
> Though None be on our Side—
>
> Suffice Us—for a Crowd—
> Ourself—and Rectitude—
> And that Assembly—not far off
> From furthest Spirit—God—

Poem 789 (fasc. 31) celebrates "a Columnar Self"—an extension of the stone imagery discussed in chapter 14—here seen as reliable and secure. Nothing can divide or move "That Granitic Base" which supports her. In poem 306 (fasc. 31), she sees the advantage of being alone: "The Soul's Superior instants" that "Occur to Her" when she is "withdrawn." From her "remote" "Hight," she is privy to "Eternity's disclosure" of "Immortality," insights she undoubtedly preserves in her poems.

Many critics agree that Dickinson used her poetry as therapy. Cody sees the poet exorcising her psychic terrors in the production of that watershed year 1862.[6] Mudge writes that "When Emily examined, analyzed and labelled her fears . . . she could temporarily overcome them."[7] Patricia Meyer Spacks sees this quality as common to women writers: "women dominate their own experience by imaging it, giving it form, writing about it."[8] Thus, Dickinson was able to take control of her life and fears through writing and focusing on them. Griffith, in his study of the poet, believes that her poetry reads like "a personal diary," one in which the poet addressed herself and kept "counselling herself on how best to resist the wounds and the outrages, the frustration and disillusionment, which life is always terrifyingly eager to impose."[9] Finally Sewall recognizes the "healing power" in the verses and states that Dickinson understood "how necessary they were to her own health of mind and spirit."[10]

For agoraphobics, one technique of self-knowledge and insight into their illness is a journal or diary wherein they write down what happens, what they feel and are afraid of. It is a technique suggested by doctors, who believe this will help them gain control over panic and fear. In one description of therapy, the recommendation for "record keeping" is given so that "the individual can begin to observe himself and try to see a cause/effect relationship between the panic and its trigger."[11] Behavioralist Marks credits the autobiographical accounts of agoraphobic patients as a method to learn "the hidden, enduring distress so often found in this condition."[12] During the crisis years, Dickinson was writing out of terror, a terror that appeared to focus on death, or insanity, or physical collapse. Lost and afraid, she clung to words for survival. They were her raft, the spar to the drowning person, that gave her the support to go on.

If we look at certain poems, we catch a glimpse of the poet as she viewed herself self-consciously in the act of creating. In poem 1275, she portrays "the Spider as an Artist" and sees his creation as "surpassing Merit." In poem 605 (fasc. 24), the spider holds his gift like a "Silver Ball" that no one notices, yet he performs, "dancing softly" for himself, as he "unwinds His Yarn of Pearl." Dickinson, like the spider, knows what she is about and creates out of herself; unwinding, expending her yarn, she aims for "Immortality" (poem 1138).

When Dickinson withdrew into her father's house, into the circumference of herself — her "circle of safety" — she became a certain type of woman. Just as deep within the earth, geologic forces exert pressures that mold molten liquid into rock, so too Dickinson became what she had to due to the disorder she suffered. She experienced its horrors, adjusted to those "Evenings of the

Brain," and although her life became rigid and inflexible to those around—
the lifeline to society "closing like stone"—Dickinson's spirit remained free.
Perhaps she expressed it best in poem 384 (fasc. 31). Despite her disability
and suffering, she claimed freedom as her own: "No Rack can torture
me / My Soul—at Liberty"; "Captivity is Consciousness— / So's Liberty."

> No Rack can torture me—
> My Soul—at Liberty—
> Behind this mortal Bone
> There knits a bolder One—
>
> You Cannot prick with saw—
> Nor pierce with Cimitar—
> Two Bodies—therefore be—
> Bind One—The Other fly—
>
> The Eagle of his Nest
> No easier divest—
> And gain the Sky
> Than mayest Thou—
>
> Except Thyself may be
> Thine Enemy—
> Captivity is Consciousness—
> So's Liberty.

Thus, paradoxically, Dickinson, a prisoner in her father's house, knew
freedom better than most, just as she had written in poem 67 that "Success
is counted sweetest / By those who ne'er succeed." Dickinson exulted in her
soul's freedom. Although her life-style left her lonely and isolated, it offered
moments of transcendence. In several poems she celebrates the state of
solitude that allowed her to accept her life and to triumph over its pain:
"Exhiliration [sic]—is within—" (poem 383). The life she knew, based on
"Renunciation"—"the Choosing / Against itself" (poem 745)—would give
her other advantages, one spoken of in poem 746: "Never for Society / He
shall seek in vain / Who His own acquaintance / Cultivate—Of Men / Wiser
Men may weary— / But the Man within / Never knew Satiety—." And in
750, she knew what her life's work was to be. Hers was not the natural life
given to most, but she accommodated herself to her situation and achieved
"it's difficult Ideal."

> Growth of Man—like Growth of Nature—
> Gravitates within—
> Atmosphere, and Sun endorse it—
> But it stir—alone—

> Each—it's difficult Ideal
> Must achieve—Itself—
> Through the solitary prowess
> Of a Silent Life—
>
> Effort—is the sole condition—
> Patience of Itself—
> Patience of opposing forces—
> And intact Belief—
>
> Looking on—is the Department
> Of it's Audience—
> But Transaction—is assisted
> By no Countenance—

As early as 1862 Dickinson may have known that the only way she would leave her home completely would be through death. In poem 649, the speaker envisions a funeral complete with carriages and guests. It is a celebration that "Never Bride had," an allusion to her own unmarried state. She is finally out of the house, out of the control of a father who overshadowed her life. He was powerless now, unable to reach her, unless he "pass the Crystal Angle / That obscure Her face—." Dickinson finally achieves an adult selfhood, one unclaimed in her own life. Through her poetry she would experience the "Paradise" denied her in life.

> Her Sweet turn to leave the Homestead
> Came the Darker Way—
> Carriages—Be sure—and Guests—True—
> But for Holiday
>
> 'Twas more pitiful Endeavor
> Than did Loaded Sea
> O'er the Curls attempt to caper
> It had cast away—
>
> Never Bride had such Assembling—
> Never kinsmen kneeled
> To salute so fair a Forehead—
> Garland be indeed—
>
> Fitter Feet—of Her before us—
> Than whatever Brow
> Art of Snow—or Trick of Lily
> Possibly bestow
>
> Of Her Father—Whoso ask Her—
> He shall seek as high
> As the Palm—that serve the Desert—
> To obtain the Sky—

Distance be Her only Motion—
If 'tis Nay—or Yes—
Acquiescence—or Demurral—
Whosoever guess—

He—must pass the Crystal Angle
That obscure Her face—
He—must have achieved in person
Equal Paradise—

Notes

Preface

1. Jay Leyda, *The Years and Hours of Emily Dickinson*, 2 vols. (Hamden, Conn.: Archon Books, 1970), 1:319.
2. Richard Sewall, *The Life of Emily Dickinson*, 2 vols. (New York: Farrar, Straus & Giroux, 1974), 1:7.
3. John Cody, *After Great Pain: The Inner Life of Emily Dickinson* (Cambridge: Harvard University Press, Belknap Press, 1971), 294–95.
4. Ibid., 295.
5. Ralph W. Franklin, ed., *The Manuscript Books of Emily Dickinson*, 2 vols. (Cambridge: Harvard University Press, Belknap Press, 1981), xv.
6. Ibid., xvi.
7. Cody, *After Great Pain*, 357.
8. Ibid., 295.
9. Ibid., 294.
10. Ibid., 291–92.
11. Franklin, *Manuscript Books*, xii–xiii.
12. Cody, *After Great Pain*, 293.
13. Franklin, *Manuscript Books*, ix.
14. Sewall, *Life* 2:491.
15. Clark Griffith, *The Long Shadow: Emily Dickinson's Tragic Poetry* (Princeton: Princeton University Press, 1964), 77.
16. Ibid., 78.
17. Ibid., 78.
18. Ibid., 282.
19. Ibid., 13.
20. Ibid., 29.
21. Ibid., 297.
22. Ibid., 11.
23. Ibid., 12.
24. Ibid., 40.
25. Thomas H. Johnson, *Emily Dickinson: An Interpretative Biography* (Cambridge: Harvard University Press, Belknap Press, 1955), 31.
26. Cynthia Griffin Wolff, *Emily Dickinson* (New York: Alfred A. Knopf, Inc., 1986), 167.
27. Ibid., 168.
28. Ibid., 54.
29. David Porter, *Dickinson: The Modern Idiom* (Cambridge: Harvard University, 1981), 125.
30. *The Letters of Emily Dickinson*, 3 vols., ed. Thomas Johnson and Theodora Ward (Cambridge: Harvard University Press, Belknap Press, 1958), 2:412.
31. Porter, *Modern Idiom*, 129.
32. Ibid., 254.

33. Ibid., 292.

34. David Porter, "Dickinson's Readers," *The New England Quarterly* 57 (March 1984): 114.

35. Richard Sewall, *The Lyman Letters: New Light on Emily Dickinson and Her Family* (Amherst: University of Massachusetts, 1966), 63.

36. Lionel Trilling, "Art and Neurosis," in *The Liberal Imagination* (New York: Viking Press, 1950), 169.

37. Cody, *After Great Pain*, 292.

38. Quoted in Porter, *Modern Idiom*, 116.

39. Griffith, *Long Shadow*, 274.

40. Ibid., 275.

41. *The Poems of Emily Dickinson*, 3 vols., ed. Thomas Johnson (Cambridge: Harvard University Press, Belknap Press, 1955), poem 365. Subsequent poems will be cited by number in the text.

42. Trilling, "Art and Neurosis," 160.

43. George Pickering, *Creative Malady* (New York: Oxford University Press, 1974), 19.

44. Ibid., 17.

45. Ibid., 18.

46. Trilling, "Art and Neurosis," 179–80.

47. Nina Baym, "Review of *Emily Dickinson*," *The New England Quarterly* 60 (June 1987): 322.

48. Sewall, *Life* 1:11.

Chapter 1. The Impression

1. Dickinson, *Letters* 2:473.

2. Ibid., 411.

3. Ibid., 408.

4. Ibid., 414.

5. Ibid., 473.

6. Thomas Wentworth Higginson, "Emily Dickinson's Letters," in *Jubilee — One Hundred Years at the Atlantic*, ed. Edward Weeks and Emily Flint (Boston: Little Brown, 1957), 196.

7. Sewall, *Life* 1:6.

8. Dickinson, *Letters* 2:473.

9. Ibid., 476.

10. Ibid.

11. Paul H. Wender and Donald F. Klein, *Mind, Mood, and Medicine: A Guide to the New Biopsychiatry* (New York: Farrar, Straus & Giroux, 1981), 98.

12. Ibid., 98.

13. Dickinson, *Letters* 2:415.

14. Ibid., 461.

15. Ibid., 462.

16. Ibid., 450.

17. Ibid., 460.

18. Ibid., 461.

19. Ibid.

20. R. P. Snaith, "A Clinical Investigation of Phobias," *British Journal of Psychiatry* 114 (1968): 673.

21. Ibid., 673.

22. Isaac Marks, *Fears and Phobias* (New York: Academic Press, 1969), 7–8.

23. Ibid., 3.

24. Ibid., 8.

25. Ibid., 8–9.

26. Ibid., 9.

27. Paul Laybourne, Jr., and Joann Redding, "Agoraphobia: Is Fear the Basis of Symptoms," *Postgraduate Medicine* 78 (October 1985): 109.

28. Ibid.

29. Wender and Klein, *Mind, Mood*, 333.

30. Pickering, *Creative Malady*, 29.

31. J. G. Mendel and Donald F. Klein, "Anxiety Attacks with Subsequent Agoraphobia," *Comprehensive Psychiatry* 10 (1969): 194.

32. Edoardo Weiss, *Agoraphobia in the Light of Ego Psychology* (New York: Grune and Stratton, 1964), 5.

33. Laybourne and Redding, "Agoraphobia," 109.

34. "Fear Itself," television episode of "Innovation" (New York: PBS, WNET), 2 February 1985.

35. Laybourne and Redding, "Agoraphobia," 110–11.

36. Dickinson, *Letters* 2:376.

37. Leyda, *Years and Hours* 1:369.

38. Ibid., 283.

39. James Ballenger, "Psychopharmacology of the Anxiety Disorders," *Psychiatric Clinics of North America* 7 (December 1984): 759.

40. Thomas Uhde and J. Maser, "Current Perspectives on Panic Disorder and Agoraphobia," *Hospital and Community Psychiatry* 36 (November 1985): 1153.

41. Wilfried De Moor, "The Topography of Agoraphobia," *American Journal of Psychotherapy* 39 (July 1985): 371.

42. Thomas Horn, "Agoraphobia," *American Academy of Family Physicians* 32 (July 1985): 165.

43. *Diagnostic and Statistical Manual of Mental Disorders*, 3d ed. (Washington, D.C.: American Psychiatric Association, 1980), 227. Subsequent references will be to the *DSM*.

44. Ibid., 226.

45. Wender and Klein, *Mind, Mood*, 94.

46. Marks, *Fears*, 119.

47. Ibid.

48. Dianne L. Chambless and Alan J. Goldstein, "Anxieties: Agoraphobia and Hysteria," in *Women and Psychotherapy*, ed. Annette Brodsky and Rachel Hare-Mustin (New York: The Guilford Press, 1980), 119.

49. R. S. Hallam and R. Hafner, "Fears of Phobic Patients," *Behavioral Research and Therapy* 16 (1978): 314.

50. Ibid., 1.

51. Dianne L. Chambless and Alan J. Goldstein, *Agoraphobia: Multiple Perspectives on Theory and Treatment* (New York: John Wiley & Sons, 1982), 186.

Chapter 2. "My Life Was Made a Victim"

1. *DSM*, 230.

2. Marks, *Fears*, 126.

3. Marjorie Gelfond, "Agoraphobia and Personal Crisis," in *Emotion and Adult*

Development, ed. Carol Malatesta and Karol Izard (New York: Sage Press, 1984), 134.

4. *DSM*, 226.

5. Robert Hicks, Anna Okonek, and John M. Davis, "The Psycho-pharmacological Approach," in *The Handbook on Stress and Anxiety*, ed. Irwin Kutash et al. (San Francisco: Jossey-Bass, 1980), 434.

6. Bruce Thyer et al. "A Comparison of Panic Disorder and Agoraphobia with Panic Attacks," *Comprehensive Psychiatry* 26 (March–April 1985): 212.

7. *DSM*, 230.

8. David V. Sheehan and Kathy Sheehan, "Diagnostic Classification of Anxiety and Phobic Disorders," *Psychopharmacology Bulletin* 18, no. 4 (October 1982): 40.

9. Dickinson, *Letters* 1:80.

10. Ibid., 184.

11. Ibid., 236.

12. Ibid., 254.

13. Ibid., 283.

14. *DSM*, 230.

15. Thomas Uhde et al., "Longitudinal Course of Panic Disorder," *Progress in Neuro-Psychopharmacology and Biological Psychiatry* 9 (1985): 44.

16. Dickinson, *Letters* 1:291.

17. Ibid. 2:315.

18. Leyda, *Years and Hours* 2:478.

19. Chambless and Goldstein, *Agoraphobia*, 187.

20. Leyda, *Years and Hours*, 1:298.

21. Ibid., 302–3.

22. Dickinson, *Letters* 1:298.

23. Leyda, *Years and Hours*, 1:319.

24. Chambless and Goldstein, *Agoraphobia*, 3.

25. Dickinson, *Letters*, 2:317.

26. Ibid., 324.

27. Ibid., 337.

28. Ibid., 1:98.

29. Ibid., 2:335.

30. Ibid., 345.

31. Ibid., 348.

32. Ibid., 407.

33. Chambless and Goldstein, *Agoraphobia*, 186.

Chapter 3. "The World Looks Staringly"

1. Chambless and Goldstein, *Agoraphobia*, 8.

2. Marks, *Fears*, 124.

3. Chambless and Goldstein, *Agoraphobia*, 8.

4. Walter Blum, "The Thirteenth Guest," *San Francisco Sunday Examiner and Chronicle*, 17 April 1977, 8.

5. Chambless and Goldstein, *Agoraphobia*, 8.

6. Marks, *Fears*, 80.

7. R. P. Snaith, "Clinical Investigation," 674.

8. W. B. Terhune, "The Phobic Syndrome," *Archives of Neurology and Psychiatry* 62 (1949): 162.

9. Ibid., 163.
10. Ibid., 163–64.
11. Marks, *Fears*, 80.
12. Richard Sewall, *Life* 2:370.
13. Dickinson, *Letters* 1:53.
14. Ibid., 62.
15. Ibid., 66.
16. Ibid., 65.
17. Ibid., 82.
18. Ibid., 104.
19. Ibid., 148.
20. Ibid., 160.
21. Ibid., 175.
22. Ibid., 167.
23. Ibid., 197.
24. Ibid., 249.
25. Chambless and Goldstein, *Agoraphobia*, 183.
26. Ibid., 184.
27. Ibid.
28. Dickinson, *Letters* 1:83.
29. Ibid., 132.
30. Ibid., 150.
31. Ibid., 152.
32. Ibid., 155.
33. Ibid., 145.
34. Ibid., 169.
35. Ibid., 177.
36. Ibid., 181.
37. Ibid., 193.
38. Ibid., 194.
39. Ibid., 211.
40. Ibid., 215–16.
41. Ibid., 221.
42. Ibid., 223.
43. Ibid., 229.
44. Ibid., 229.
45. Ibid., 304.
46. Chambless and Goldstein, *Agoraphobia*, 184.
47. Wolff, *Emily Dickinson*, 114.

Chapter 4. "I Love So to Be a Child"

1. Alan Goldstein and Edna B. Foa, *The Handbook of Behavioral Intervention: A Clinical Guide* (New York: John Wiley & Sons, 1980), 324.
2. Ibid.
3. Ibid.
4. Dickinson, *Letters* 1:104.
5. Sewall, *Life* 1:39.
6. Gelfond, "Agoraphobia and Personal Crisis," 131.
7. Snaith, "Clinical Investigation," 674.

8. Goldstein and Foa, *Handbook*, 325.
9. Chambless and Goldstein, *Agoraphobia*, 8.
10. Goldstein and Foa, *Handbook*, 325.
11. Ibid., 326.
12. Ibid.
13. Dickinson, *Letters* 1:111.
14. Ibid., 231.
15. Ibid.
16. Ibid., 136.
17. Ibid., 243.
18. Ibid., 152.
19. Ibid., 132.
20. Wolff, *Emily Dickinson*, 167.
21. Dickinson, *Letters* 1:184.
22. Ibid., 161.
23. Ibid., 197.
24. Ibid., 241.
25. Ibid., 245.
26. Leyda, *Years and Hours* 1:136.

Chapter 5. "What If They Die When I'm Gone?"

1. Donald F. Klein and Judith G. Rabkin, eds., *Anxiety: New Research and Changing Concepts* (New York: Raven Press, 1981), 295–96.
2. Gordon Parker, "Reported Parental Characteristics of Agoraphobics and Social Phobics," *British Journal of Psychiatry* 135 (1979): 555.
3. Ibid.
4. Blake H. Tearnan, Michael J. Telch, and Peter Keefe, "Etiology and Onset of Agoraphobia," *Comprehensive Psychiatry* 25, no. 1 (February 1984): 53.
5. Willem A. Arrindell et al., "The Role of Perceived Parental Rearing Practices in the Aetiology of Phobic Disorders: A Controlled Study," *British Journal of Psychiatry* 143 (August 1983): 185.
6. Ibid.
7. Leyda, *Years and Hours* 2:224.
8. Ibid., 231.
9. Ibid.
10. Dickinson, *Letters* 1:237.
11. Ibid., 250.
12. Leyda, *Years and Hours*, 1:332.
13. Ibid., 2:231.
14. Dickinson, *Letters*, 1:180.
15. Cody, *After Great Pain*, 50.
16. Ibid., 51.
17. Ibid.
18. Nancy Roeske, "Commentary on 'Gender Imperatives, Separation Anxiety, and Agoraphobia in Women,'" *Integrative Psychiatry* 2 (March 1984): 62.
19. Ibid., 63.
20. Dorothy Buglass, et al., "A Study of Agoraphobic Housewives," *Psychological Medicine* 7 (1977): 85.
21. Parker, "Reported Parental Characteristics," 559.

22. Wolff, *Emily Dickinson*, 53.
23. Ibid.
24. Ibid.
25. Ibid., 54.
26. Cody, *After Great Pain*, 53.
27. Wolff, *Emily Dickinson*, 58.
28. Ibid.
29. Ibid., 109.
30. Dickinson, *Letters* 1:97.
31. Ibid., 204.
32. Ibid., 2:324.
33. Ibid., 335.
34. Ibid., 1:336.
35. Leyda, *Years and Hours* 2:7.
36. Wolff, *Emily Dickinson*, 134.
37. Ibid., 578.
38. Blake H. Tearnan, "The Etiology of Agoraphobia: An Examination of Critical Life Events," *Dissertation Abstracts International* 43 (May 1983) 3745B.
39. Dickinson, *Letters* 1:180.
40. Chambless and Goldstein, *Agoraphobia*, 12.
41. Terhune, "Phobic Syndrome," 162.
42. A. Frances and P. Dunn, "The Attachment-Autonomy Conflict in Agoraphobia," *International Journal of Psycho-Analysis* 56 (1975): 436.
43. Tearnan, Telch, and Keefe, "Etiology and Onset," 53.
44. Terhune, "Phobic Syndrome," 168.
45. Tearnan, Telch, and Keefe, "Etiology and Onset," 54.
46. Wolff, *Emily Dickinson*, 64.
47. Ibid., 61.
48. Ibid., 63.
49. Marks, *Fears*, 89.
50. Wolff, *Emily Dickinson*, 554.
51. Ibid.
52. Millicent Todd Bingham, *Emily Dickinson's Home* (New York: Harper & Brothers, 1955), 179.
53. Roeske, "Commentary," 62.
54. Dickinson, *Letters* 1:82.
55. Wolff, *Emily Dickinson*, 121.
56. Ibid., 97.
57. Dickinson, *Letters* 1:44.
58. Ibid., 65.
59. Wolff, *Emily Dickinson*, 68.
60. Dickinson, *Letters* 1:66.
61. Leyda, *Years and Hours* 1:215.
62. Ibid., 218.
63. Dickinson, *Letters* 1:98–99.
64. Ibid., 197.
65. Wolff, *Emily Dickinson*, 124.
66. Leyda, *Years and Hours* 1:240.
67. James C. Ballenger, ed., *The Biology of Agoraphobia* (Washington, D. C.: American Psychiatric Press, 1984), 100.
68. Tearnan, Telch, and Keefe, "Etiology and Onset," 53.

69. Ballenger, *Biology*, 3.

70. Ibid., 100.

71. Alan Breier, et al., "The Diagnostic Validity of Anxiety Disorders and Their Relationship to Depressive Illness," *The American Journal of Psychiatry* 142 (July 1985): 790.

72. David V. Sheehan, "Current Concepts in Psychiatry: Panic Attacks and Phobias," *The New England Journal of Medicine* 307, no. 3 (July 1982): 157.

73. Sheehan and Sheehan, "Diagnostic Classification," 44.

74. Chambless and Goldstein, *Agoraphobia*, 186.

75. Ballenger, *Biology*, 66.

76. Laybourne and Redding, "Agoraphobia," 118.

77. Jennifer Pyke and M. Longdon, "Agoraphobia," *The Canadian Nurse* 6 (June 1985): 19.

Chapter 6. "Newton Is Dead"

1. *DSM*, 226.

2. Marks, *Fears*, 97.

3. Barry Wolfe, "Gender Imperatives, Separation Anxiety, and Agoraphobia in Women," *Integrative Psychiatry* 2 (March 1984): 57.

4. Marjorie Raskin et al., "Panic and Generalized Anxiety Disorders," *Archives of General Psychiatry* 39 (June 1982): 687.

5. Carlo Faravelli et al., "Prevalence of Traumatic Early Life Events in 31 Agoraphobic Patients with Panic Attacks," *American Journal of Psychiatry* 142 (December 1985): 1493.

6. John Bowlby, *Separation: Attachment and Loss* (New York: Basic Books, Inc., 1973), 2:292.

7. Ibid., 258.

8. Ibid., 313.

9. Gelfond, "Agoraphobia and Personal Crisis," 127.

10. Frances and Dunn, "Attachment-Autonomy Conflict," 437.

11. Ibid., 436.

12. Gelfond, "Agoraphobia and Personal Crisis," 127.

13. Raskin et al., "Panic," 689.

14. Joan Dittrich et al., "Panic Disorder: Assessment and Treatment," *Clinical Psychology Review* 3 (1983): 219.

15. Klein and Rabkin, *Anxiety*, 325.

16. Ibid., 246.

17. Dittrich et al., "Panic Disorder," 219.

18. Bruce Thyer et al., "Agoraphobia: A Test of the Separation Anxiety Hypothesis," *Behavior Research and Therapy* 23 (1985): 75.

19. Horn, "Agoraphobia," 166.

20. Cody, *After Great Pain*, 273.

21. Wolff, *Emily Dickinson*, 109.

22. Ibid., 110.

23. Bowlby, *Separation*, 309.

24. Chambless and Goldstein, "Anxieties," 126.

25. Raskin et al., "Panic," 687.

26. *DSM*, 231.

27. Dickinson, *Letters* 1:236.

28. Ibid., 241.
29. Ibid., 249.
30. Ibid., 273–74.
31. Ibid., 277–78.
32. Ibid., 277.
33. Wolff, *Emily Dickinson*, 114.
34. Dickinson, *Letters* 1:282–83.
35. Raskin et al., "Panic," 687.
36. Wolff, *Emily Dickinson*, 109.
37. Ibid.
38. Ibid., 110.
39. Dickinson, *Letters* 1:282.
40. Ibid., 285.
41. Ibid., 229.
42. Bingham, *Emily Dickinson's Home*, 179–80.
43. De Moor, "Topography," 378.
44. Ibid., 379.
45. Tearnan, Telch, and Keefe, "Etiology and Onset," 55.
46. Ballenger, *Biology*, 66.
47. Sheehan and Sheehan, "Diagnostic Classification," 40.
48. Ibid.
49. Wolff, *Emily Dickinson*, 167.
50. Dickinson, *Letters* 2:551.
51. Ibid., 1:405.
52. Several poems are believed to refer to Newton: poem 299 written to celebrate the ninth anniversary of his death; poem 360, which alludes to a gift "a friend gave" who is now "At Rest"; and poem 622, which paraphrases the poet's letter to Newton's minister.

Chapter 7. "I Have Never Seen Anyone ..."

1. Chambless and Goldstein, *Agoraphobia*, 2.
2. Ibid.
3. Otto Fenichel, "Remarks on the Common Phobias," *Psychoanalytic Quarterly* 13 (1944): 315.
4. Marks, *Fears*, 133.
5. Isaac Marks, *Living with Fear* (New York: McGraw-Hill, 1978), 86.
6. Frances and Dunn, "Attachment-Autonomy Conflict," 438.
7. Chambless and Goldstein, "Anxieties," 119.
8. Dickinson, *Letters* 2:404.
9. Ibid. 1:92.
10. Ibid. 2:358.
11. Ibid., 416.
12. Ibid., 427.
13. Ibid., 450.
14. Ibid., 408.
15. Ibid., 415.
16. Ibid., 374.
17. Leyda, *Years and Hours* 1:367.
18. Ibid., 358.

19. Ibid., 2:21.
20. Dickinson, *Letters* 2:431.
21. Ibid., 449.
22. Ibid., 454.
23. Ibid., 461.
24. Sewall, *Life* 1:129.
25. Dickinson, *Letters* 1:310.
26. Ibid., 297.
27. Ibid., 311.
28. Leyda, *Years and Hours* 1:213.
29. Ibid., 163.
30. Ibid., 283.
31. Ibid., 301.
32. Ibid., 215.
33. Chambless and Goldstein, "Anxieties," 130.
34. Dickinson, *Letters* 1:83.
35. Ibid., 218.
36. Ibid., 2:353.
37. Ibid., 346.
38. Ibid., 351.
39. Sewall, *Lyman Letters*, 70.
40. Dickinson, *Letters* 2:424.
41. Ibid. 1:284.
42. Leyda, *Years and Hours* 1:298.
43. Dickinson, *Letters* 2:348.
44. De Moor, "Topography," 376.
45. Dickinson, *Letters* 1:311.
46. Ibid. 2:419.
47. Ibid., 430.
48. Ibid., 435.
49. De Moor, "Topography," 376.
50. Sewall, *Life* 1:142.
51. Dickinson, *Letters* 2:508.
52. Leyda, *Years and Hours* 2:471.
53. Ibid., 472.

Chapter 8. "I Had a Terror ..."

1. Dickinson, *Letters* 2:404.
2. Sewall, *Life* 2:543.
3. David V. Sheehan and Kathy Sheehan, "The Classification of Phobic Disorders," *The International Journal of Psychiatry in Medicine* 12 (1983): 250.
4. Ballenger, "Psychopharmacology," 759.
5. Horn, "Agoraphobia," 167.
6. Bruce Thyer, "Temporal Relationships Between Panic Attack and Phobic Avoidance in Agoraphobia," *Behavior Research and Therapy* 23 (1985): 608.
7. Uhde et al., "Longitudinal Course," 44.
8. Sewall, *Life* 2:443.
9. Ibid.
10. Dickinson, *Letters* 2:360.
11. Ibid., 362.

12. Ibid., 363.
13. Sewall, *Life* 2:489.
14. Dickinson, *Letters* 2:376.
15. William Ellery Leonard, *The Locomotive-God* (New York: D. Appleton-Century Co., 1942), 321.
16. Ruth H. Vose, *Agoraphobia* (London: Faber & Faber, 1981), 81.
17. Ibid., 46.
18. Nancy Mairs, *Plaintext* (Tucson: University of Arizona Press, 1986), 101–2.
19. Tearnan, Telch, and Keefe, "Etiology and Onset," 52.
20. Sheehan, "Current Concepts," 156.
21. Laybourne and Redding, "Agoraphobia," 111.
22. Breier et al., "Diagnostic Validity," 787.
23. Pickering, *Creative Malady*, 29–31.
24. Marks, *Fears*, 126.
25. Wolff, *Emily Dickinson*, 164–65.
26. Ibid., 165.
27. Ibid.
28. Ibid.
29. Henry P. Laughlin, *The Neuroses in Clinical Practice* (Philadelphia, Pa.: W. B. Sanders Co., 1956), 54.
30. Ibid., 56.
31. Vose, *Agoraphobia*, 40.
32. Leonard, *Locomotive-God*, 251.
33. Ibid., 248.
34. Ibid., 249–50.
35. Dickinson, *Letters* 2:439.
36. Ibid., 448.
37. John Cody, "Watchers Upon the East: The Ocular Complaints of Emily Dickinson," *Psychiatric Quarterly* 42, no. 3 (1968): 548.
38. Ibid., 550.
39. Ibid., 551.
40. Ibid., 554.
41. Dickinson, *Letters* 2:439.
42. Ibid., 430.
43. Vose, *Agoraphobia*, 141.
44. Peter Blythe and David McGlown, "Agoraphobia—Is It Organic?" *World Medicine* 10 (July 1982): 57.
45. Ibid., 58.
46. Vose, *Agoraphobia*, 153.
47. Ibid., 154.
48. "Did Emily Dickinson Suffer from Eye Disease?" *The New York Times*, 11 December 1979, sec. B; p. 14.
49. Sewall, *Life* 2:606.
50. Mary Elizabeth Bernhard, "A Response to 'Eyes Be Blind, Heart Be Still,' " *The New England Quarterly* 55 (1982): 112–14.
51. Dickinson, *Letters* 2:351.
52. Blythe and McGlown, "Agoraphobia," 57.
53. Dickinson, *Letters* 1:284.
54. Vose, *Agoraphobia*, 141.
55. Ibid., 76.
56. Blythe and McGlown, "Agoraphobia," 58.
57. Vose, *Agoraphobia*, 154.

58. Ibid., 160–61.

59. Blythe and McGlown, "Agoraphobia," 57.

60. Vose, *Agoraphobia*, 160.

61. Ibid., 162.

62. Harold N. Levinson, M.D., with Steve Carter, *Phobia Free* (New York: M. Evans and Co., Inc., 1986), 60–61.

Chapter 9. "I Told My Soul to Sing"

1. Isaac Marks, "Agoraphobic Syndrome," *Archives of General Psychiatry* 23 (December 1970): 546.

2. Dickinson, *Letters* 2:439.

3. Marks, *Fears*, 123.

4. "Anonymous: Recovery from a Long Neurosis," *Psychiatry* 15 (1952): 163.

5. Ibid., 164.

6. Vose, *Agoraphobia*, 141.

7. Dickinson, *Letters* 1:81.

8. Ibid., 102.

9. Ibid., 298.

10. Ibid., 2:315.

11. Ibid., 328.

12. Ibid., 344.

13. Ibid., 460.

14. Ibid., 408.

15. Ibid., 404.

16. Franklin, *Manuscript Books*, ix.

17. Dickinson, *Letters* 2:408.

18. Ralph W. Franklin, *The Editing of Emily Dickinson*: *A Reconsideration* (Madison: University of Wisconsin Press, 1967), 147.

19. Franklin, *Manuscript Books*, ix–xii.

20. Ruth Miller, *The Poetry of Emily Dickinson* (Middletown, Conn.: Wesleyan University Press, 1968), 261.

21. William Shurr, *The Marriage of Emily Dickinson*: *A Study of the Fascicles* (Lexington: University of Kentucky Press, 1983), 30.

22. Ibid., 194–195.

23. M. L. Rosenthal and Sally M. Gall, *The Modern Poetic Sequence* (New York: Oxford University Press, 1983), 53.

24. Sewall, *Life* 2:538.

25. R. W. Franklin, "The Emily Dickinson Fascicles," *Studies in Bibliography* 36 (1983): 2.

26. Rosenthal and Gall, *Modern Poetic Sequence*, 73.

27. Franklin, "Fascicles," 17.

28. Franklin, *Manuscript Books*, ix.

29. Franklin, "Fascicles," 17.

Chapter 10. "A Prison Gets to Be a Friend"

1. Dolores Lucas, *Emily Dickinson and Riddle* (De Kalb, Illnois: Northern Illinois University Press, 1969), 8.

2. Wolff, *Emily Dickinson*, 163.

3. Robert Weisbuch, *Emily Dickinson's Poetry* (Chicago: University of Chicago Press, 1975), 173.

4. Pyke and Longdon, "Agoraphobia," 18.

5. Muriel Frampton, *Agoraphobia—Coping with the World Outside* (Wellingborough, Northamptonshire: Turnstone Press, 1984), 17.

6. Ibid., 78.

7. Ibid., 79.

8. Dickinson, *Poems* 1.254–55.

9. Fraser Kent, *Nothing to Fear: Coping with Phobias* (Garden City, New York: Doubleday, 1977), 47.

10. Dickinson, *Letters* 1:283.

11. Frampton, *Agoraphobia*, 17.

12. Marks, *Living with Fear*, 79.

13. Sewall, *Life* 1:146.

14. Frampton, *Agoraphobia*, 34.

15. Dickinson, *Poems* 1:256.

16. Ibid.

17. Ibid., 257.

18. David V. Sheehan, "Age of Onset of Phobic Disorders: A Reevaluation," *Comprehensive Psychiatry* 22, no. 6 (December 1981): 550.

19. Jean Mudge, *Emily Dickinson and the Image of Home* (Amherst: University of Massachusetts Press, 1975), 230.

20. Ibid., 1.

21. Laybourne and Redding, "Agoraphobia," 111.

22. Marks, *Fears*, 4.

23. Vose, *Agoraphobia*, 22–23.

24. Ibid., 79.

25. Ibid., 81.

26. David Diamond, M.D. "Panic Attacks, Hypochondriasis, and Agoraphobia: A Self-Psychology Formulation," *American Journal of Psychotherapy* 39 (January 1985): 122.

27. Kent, *Nothing to Fear*, 50.

28. Ibid., 59–60.

29. "Anonymous: Recovery," 167.

30. Diamond, "Panic Attacks," 122.

31. Dickinson, *Letters* 1:111.

32. Wolff, *Emily Dickinson*, 123.

33. Vose, *Agoraphobia*, 25.

34. Frampton, *Agoraphobia*, 79.

35. Ibid., 4.

36. "Anonymous: Recovery," 168–69.

37. Diamond, "Panic Attacks," 121.

38. Dianne Chambless and Alan Goldstein, "The Treatment of Agoraphobia," in *Handbook of Behavioral Intervention*, ed. A. Goldstein and E. Foa (New York: John Wiley and Sons, 1980), 335.

39. De Moor, "Topography," 375.

40. Marks, *Fears*, 113.

41. Ibid., 110.

42. Ibid., 120.

43. Ruth Miller, *Poetry of Emily Dickinson*, app. 2, 333.

44. Linda Huf, *A Portrait of the Artist as a Young Woman: The Writer as Heroine in American Literature* (New York: Frederick Unger, 1983), 12.
45. Alexandra Symonds, "Phobias After Marriage," in *Psychoanalysis and Women*, ed. Jean B. Miller (Baltimore: Penguin, 1973), 301–2.
46. Mudge, *Image of Home*, 218.
47. Porter, *Modern Idiom*, 289.
48. Ibid., 2.
49. Cody, *After Great Pain*, 297.
50. Dickinson, *Letters* 2:111.

Chapter 11. "A Thing So Terrible"

1. Franklin, *Manuscript Books*, xvi.
2. Franklin, "Fascicles," 13.
3. Rosenthal and Gall, *Modern Poetic Sequence*, 48.
4. Ibid., 73.
5. Porter, *Modern Idiom*, 24.
6. Ibid., 8.
7. Cody, *After Great Pain*, 315.
8. Griffith, *Long Shadow*, 102.
9. Rosenthal and Gall, *Modern Poetic Sequence*, 54–55.
10. Dickinson, *Letters* 2:404.
11. Kent, *Nothing to Fear*, 53.
12. De Moor, "Topography," 383.
13. Dianne L. Chambless et. al., "Assessment of Fear of Fear in Agoraphobics: The Body Sensations Questionnaire and the Agoraphobic Cognitions Questionnaire," *Journal of Consulting and Clinical Psychology* 5 (1984): 1093.
14. Vose, *Agoraphobia*, 38.
15. Ibid., 37.
16. Ibid., 43.
17. Kent, *Nothing to Fear*, 54.
18. De Moor, "Topography," 374–75.
19. Uhde et. al., "Longitudinal Course," 42.
20. Chambless and Goldstein, "Treatment," 354.
21. "Fear Itself," television episode of "Innovation" (New York: PBS, WNET), 2 February 1985.
22. Laybourne and Redding, "Agoraphobia," 111.
23. Klein and Rabkin, *Anxiety*, 228.
24. Kent, *Nothing to Fear*, 53.
25. Claire Weekes, *Simple, Effective Treatment of Agoraphobia* (New York: Bantam, 1979), 52.
26. Kent, *Nothing to Fear*, 52.
27. Chambless and Goldstein, "Treatment," 350.
28. Weekes, *Treatment of Agoraphobia*, 58.
29. Klein and Rabkin, *Anxiety*, 298.
30. Goldstein and Foa, *Handbook*, 325.
31. *DSM*, 230.
32. Hicks, Okonek, and Davis, "Psycho-pharmacological Approach," 430–32.
33. Wender and Klein, *Mind*, 325.
34. Leonard, *Locomotive-God*, 322–23.

35. Marks, *Fears*, 121.
36. Ibid., 142.
37. Ibid., 141.
38. Leonard, *Locomotive-God*, 300–303.
39. Ibid., 304–8.
40. Vose, *Agoraphobia*, 39.
41. Leonard, *Locomotive-God*, 321.
42. Laughlin, *Neuroses*, 55.
43. Claire Weekes, *Peace from Nervous Suffering* (New York. Bantam, 1978), 20.
44. De Moor, "Topography," 377–78.
45. Leyda, *Years and Hours*, xxi.
46. Chambless and Goldstein, "Treatment," 325.
47. Laybourne and Redding, "Agoraphobia," 111.
48. Sheehan and Sheehan, "Classification," 249–50.
49. Uhde et al., "Longitudinal Course," 4.
50. Chambless and Goldstein, "Treatment," 325.
51. Vose, *Agoraphobia*, 53.
52. Ibid., 54.
53. Weekes, *Peace*, 54.
54. "Anonymous: Recovery," 167–68.
55. M. Roth, "The Phobic Anxiety Depersonalization Syndrome," *Proceedings of the Royal Society of Medicine* (1959), 589.
56. Ibid., 590.
57. Griffith, *Long Shadow*, 202.
58. "Anonymous: Recovery," 171.
59. Chambless and Goldstein, *Agoraphobia*, 122.
60. Ibid., 130.
61. Ibid.
62. Ibid.
63. Vose, *Agoraphobia*, 54.
64. Marks, "Agoraphobic Syndrome," 552.
65. David Gelman with Pamela Abramson, "Home Behind Bars," *Newsweek*, 23 April 1984, 70.
66. Vose, *Agoraphobia*, 54–55.
67. Uhde and Maser, "Current Perspectives," 1154.
68. Margaret West, letter to author, 29 March 1985.
69. Dickinson, *Letters* 2:594.
70. De Moor, "Topography," 375.
71. Marks, *Living With Fear*, 85.
72. De Moor, "Topography," 375.

Chapter 12. "I Dropped Down and Down"

1. Dickinson, *Letters* 2:438–39.
2. Sewall, *Lyman Letters*, 74.
3. Laughlin, *Neuroses* 54; Weekes, *Treatment of Agoraphobia*, 51; Roth, "Depersonalization Syndrome," 590.
4. De Moor, "Topography," 383.
5. Vose, *Agoraphobia*, 40.

6. Leonard, *Locomotive-God*, 250.
7. "Anonymous: Recovery," 162.
8. Ibid., 176.
9. Ibid., 167.
10. Marks, "Agoraphobic Syndrome," 546.
11. Kent, *Nothing to Fear*, 51.
12. Vose, *Agoraphobia*, 83.
13. Marks, "Agoraphobic Syndrome," 546.
14. Leyda, *Years and Hours* 2:357.
15. Sheehan and Sheehan, "Classification of Phobic Disorders," 255.
16. Griffith, *Long Shadow*, 247.
17. Leonard, *Locomotive-God*, 278.
18. Ibid., 312.
19. Laughlin, *Neuroses*, 54–56.
20. Weekes, *Peace*, 23.
21. Sheehan and Sheehan, "Classification," 261.
22. Weekes, *Treatment of Agoraphobia*, 47.
23. Ibid., 58.
24. Griffith, *Long Shadow*, 199.
25. Cody, *After Great Pain*, 293.
26. Leonard, *Locomotive-God*, 238.
27. Ibid., 308.
28. Sewall, *Life* 2:502.
29. C. H. Harding Branch, *Aspects of Anxiety*, 2d ed. (Philadelphia, Pa.: J. D. Lippincott Co., 1968), 102.
30. Vose, *Agoraphobia*, 46.
31. Ibid., 22.
32. Diamond, "Panic Attacks," 116.
33. Ibid., 119.
34. Dickinson, *Letters* 1:284.
35. Chambless and Goldstein, "Treatment," 355–56.
36. Franklin, "Fascicles," 17.
37. Ibid., 19.
38. Sewall, *Life* 2:538.
39. Weekes, *Peace*, 52.
40. Sheehan and Sheehan, "Classification," 250–55.
41. Rosenthal and Gall, *Modern Poetic Sequence*, 96.
42. Ibid., 26.

Chapter 13. "Blank—and Steady Wilderness"

1. Sheehan and Sheehan, "Classification," 256.
2. Chambless and Goldstein, Treatment," 351.
3. Dickinson, *Letters* 2:361.
4. Ibid., 333.
5. Ibid.
6. Ibid., 363.
7. Diamond, "Panic Attacks," 120–21.
8. Kent, *Nothing to Fear*, 52–53.
9. Uhde et. al., "Longitudinal Course," 42.

10. Diamond, "Panic Attacks," 123.

11. Chambless and Goldstein, "Treatment," 325.

12. Ibid., 337.

13. Ibid., 343.

14. Leon Grunhaus et. al., "Panic Attacks: A Review of Treatments and Pathogenesis," *The Journal of Nervous and Mental Disease* 169 (1981): 612.

15. Sheehan and Sheehan, "Classification," 255.

16. Weekes, *Peace*, 21.

17. Peter E. Hodgkinson, "Far from the Madding Crowd," *Nursing Mirror* 153 (1 July 1981): 38.

18. Vose, *Agoraphobia*, 43.

19. Sheehan and Sheehan, "Classification," 251.

20. De Moor, "Topography," 378.

21. Dickinson, *Letters* 2:424.

22. Alan Goldstein and Dianne L. Chambless, "A Reanalysis of Agoraphobia," *Behavior Therapy* 9 (1978): 55.

23. Weekes, *Peace*, 35.

24. Griffith, *Long Shadow*, 194.

25. Roth, "Depersonalization Syndrome," 589.

26. Chambless and Goldstein, "Treatment," 343.

27. Ibid., 350.

28. Roth, "Depersonalization Syndrome," 587.

29. Sheehan and Sheehan, "Classification," 254.

30. D. H. Myers and G. Grant, "A Study of Depersonalization in Students," *British Journal of Psychiatry* 121 (1972): 62.

31. Suzanne Juhasz, "The Undiscovered Continent: Emily Dickinson and the Space of the Mind," *The Missouri Review* 3 (Fall 1979): 94.

32. Myers and Grant, "Depersonalization in Students," 62.

33. Juhasz, "Undiscovered Continent," 95.

34. B. Ruddick, "Agoraphobia," *International Journal of Psychoanalysis* 42 (1962): 542.

35. Myers and Grant, "Depersonalization in Students," 60.

36. Ibid.

37. Roth, "Depersonalization Syndrome," 589.

38. De Moor, "Topography," 377.

39. Roth, "Depersonalization Syndrome," 588.

40. Ibid., 589.

41. Porter, *Modern Idiom*, 9.

42. Vose, *Agoraphobia*, 55.

43. Quoted in James Woodress, "Emily Dickinson," in *Fifteen American Authors before 1900*, ed. Earl Herbert (Madison: University of Wisconsin Press, 1985). 165.

44. Diamond, "Panic Attacks," 119.

45. De Moor, "Topography," 373.

46. Mudge, *Image of Home*, 220.

47. Griffith, *Long Shadow*, 201.

48. De Moor, "Topography," 375.

49. Ibid., 375–77.

50. Ibid., 375.

51. Dickinson, *Letters* 2:346.

52. Ibid., 424.

53. Frampton, *Agoraphobia*, 29.

54. Vose, *Agoraphobia*, 68.

Chapter 14. "Then—Close the Valves ..."

1. Wolff, *Emily Dickinson*, 167–68.
2. Porter, *Modern Idiom*, 19.
3. Juhasz, "Undiscovered Continent," 87.
4. Barbara Williams, "A Room of Her Own: Emily Dickinson as Woman Artist," in *Feminist Criticism*: *Essays on Theory, Poetry and Prose*, ed. Cheryl Brown and Karen Olson (Metuchen, N.J.: Scarecrow Press, 1978), 70.
5. Juhasz, "Undiscovered Continent," 86.
6. Ibid., 87.
7. Vose, *Agoraphobia*, 37.
8. Ibid., 26–27.
9. Ibid., 37.
10. Mendel and Klein, "Anxiety Attacks," 192.
11. Sheehan and Sheehan, "Classification," 255.
12. Breier et al., "Diagnostic Validity," 790.
13. Ibid.
14. De Moor, "Topography," 376.
15. Ibid., 371.
16. F. Scott Fitzgerald, *The Great Gatsby* (New York: Scribners, 1925), 23.
17. Sheehan and Sheehan, "Classification," 254.
18. Vose, *Agoraphobia*, 54.
19. Frampton, *Agoraphobia*, 42.
20. Mudge, *Image of Home*, 108.

Chapter 15. "Alone, I Cannot Be"

1. Mairs, *Plaintext*, 102.
2. Ibid., 103.
3. Ibid., 98.
4. Ibid., 103.
5. Marks, *Fears*, 124.
6. Myrna Weissman et al., "The Epidemiology of Anxiety Disorders," *Psychopharmacology Bulletin* 21 (1985): 539.
7. Wolfe, "Gender Imperatives," 57.
8. Chambless and Goldstein, "Anxieties," 122.
9. Klein and Rabkin, *Anxiety*, 247.
10. Leon Salzman et al., "Commentary on 'Gender Imperatives, Separation Anxiety and Agoraphobia in Women'," *Integrative Psychiatry* 2 (March 1984): 61.
11. Roeske, "Commentary," 64.
12. De Moor, "Topography," 375.
13. Chambless and Goldstein, "Anxieties," 123.
14. Salzman et al., "Commentary," 68.
15. Ibid., 64.
16. Violet Franks and V. Burtle, eds., *Women in Therapy* (New York: Bruner/Mazel, 1974), 140.
17. Chambless and Goldstein, "Anxieties, 122.

18. Ibid., 131.

19. Hodgkinson, "Madding Crowd," 38.

20. Gelfond, "Agoraphobia and Personal Crisis," 132.

21. Dickinson, *Letters* 1:180.

22. Salzman et al., "Commentary," 64.

23. Wolfe, "Gender Imperatives," 60.

24. Salzman et al., "Commentary," 66.

25. Ibid., 61.

26. Faravelli et al., "Traumatic Early Life Events," 1494.

27. Iris Fodor, "The Phobic Syndrome in Women," in *Women in Therapy*, ed. Violet Franks and V. Burtle (New York: Bruner/Mazel, 1974), 147.

28. De Moor, "Topography," 380.

29. Fodor, "Phobic Syndrome," 142.

30. Salzman et al., "Commentary," 61.

31. Dickinson, *Letters* 2:337

32. Ibid. 1:99.

33. Roeske, "Commentary," 62.

34. Dickinson, *Letters* 1:197.

35. Fodor, "Phobic Syndrome," 140.

36. Wolfe, "Gender Imperatives," 57.

37. Ibid., 61

38. Ibid., 60.

39. Ibid.

40. Fodor, "Phobic Syndrome," 133.

41. Ibid., 142.

42. Ibid., 145.

43. Ibid., 151.

44. Suzanne Juhasz, "Reading Emily Dickinson's Letters," *English Studies Quarterly* 30 (1984): 183.

45. Fodor, "Phobic Syndrome," 158.

46. Leyda, *Years and Hours* 2:474.

47. Robert Seidenberg and K. DeCrow, *Women Who Marry Houses* (New York: McGraw-Hill, 1983), 209.

48. Judith Moore, "The New Hysteria," review of *Hunger Strike, The Anorectic's Struggle as a Metaphor for Our Age*, by Susie Orbach, *The New York Times Book Review*, 23 March 1986, 41.

49. Seidenberg and DeCrow, *Women Who Marry Houses*, 6.

50. Ibid., 52–53.

51. Ibid., 214.

52. Sandra Gilbert and Susan Gubar, *The Madwoman in the Attic* (New Haven: Yale University Press, 1979), 583.

53. Ibid., 584.

54. Laybourne and Redding, "Agoraphobia," 118.

55. Ibid., 117.

56. De Moor, "Topography," 376.

57. Cited in Fodor, "Phobic Syndrome," 158.

Chapter 16. "The Soul Achieves—Herself"

1. Porter, *Modern Idiom*, 116.

2. Ibid., 116–17.
3. Ibid., 137.
4. Ibid., 138–39.
5. Ibid., 141–42.
6. Cody, *After Great Pain*, 438.
7. Mudge, *Image of Home*, 109.
8. Juhasz, "Undiscovered Continent," 96.
9. Griffith, *Long Shadow*, 42.
10. Sewall, *Life* 2:546.
11. Chambless and Goldstein, "Treatment," 339.
12. Marks, *Fears*, 121.

Bibliography

Agras, Stewart, et al. "The Epidemiology of Common Fears and Phobias." *Comprehensive Psychiatry* 10 (1969): 151–56.

Allen K. W. "Behavioural Treatment of an Agoraphobic." *Nursing Times* 77 (12 February 1981): 268–72.

Anderson, Charles R. *Stairway of Surprise*. New York: Holt, Rinehart & Winston, 1960.

"Anonymous: Recovery from a Long Neurosis." *Psychiatry* 15 (1952):161–77.

Arrindell, Willem, and Paul Emmelkamp. "A Test of the Repression Hypothesis in Agoraphobics." *Psychological Medicine* 15 (1985): 125–29.

Arrindell, Willem A., et al. "The Role of Perceived Parental Rearing Practices in the Aetiology of Phobic Disorders: A Controlled Study." *British Journal of Psychiatry* 143 (August 1983): 183–87.

Bachtold, Louise, and Emmy Werner. "Personality Characteristics of Creative Women." *Perceptual and Motor Skills* 36 (1973): 311–19.

Ballenger, James C. "Psychopharmacology of the Anxiety Disorders." *Psychiatric Clinics of North America* 7 (December 1984): 757–71.

Ballenger, James. C., ed. *The Biology of Agoraphobia*. Washington, D.C.: American Psychiatric Association Press, 1984.

Barlow, David, et al. "The Phenomenon of Panic." *Journal of Abnormal Psychology* 94 (August 1985): 320–28.

Baumgold, Julie. "Agoraphobia: Life Ruled by Panic." *New York Times Magazine*, 4 December 1977.

Baym, Nina. Review of *Emily Dickinson*, by Cynthia G. Wolff. *The New England Quarterly* 60 (June 1987): 320–22.

Berg, Ian, et al. "School Phobia and Agoraphobia." *Psychological Medicine* 4 (1974): 428–34.

Bernhard, Mary Elizabeth. "A Response to 'Eyes Be Blind, Heart Be Still.' " *The New England Quarterly* 55 (1982): 112–14.

Bingham, Millicent Todd. *Emily Dickinson's Home*. New York: Harper & Brothers, 1955.

Blum, Walter. "The Thirteenth Guest." *San Francisco Sunday Examiner and Chronicle*, 17 April 1977.

Blythe, Peter, and David McGlown. "Agoraphobia—Is It Organic?" *World Medicine* 10 (July 1982): 57–59.

Bowlby, John. *Separation: Attachment and Loss* 2 vols. New York: Basic Books, Inc., 1973.

Branch, C. H. Hardin. *Aspects of Anxiety*. 2d ed. Philadelphia, Pa.: J. D. Lippincott Co., 1968.

Breier, Alan, et al. "The Diagnostic Validity of Anxiety Disorders and Their Relationship to Depressive Illness." *The American Journal of Psychiatry* 142 (July 1985): 787–97.

Brodsky, Annette M., and Rachel T. Hare-Mustin, eds. *Women and Psychotherapy: An Assessment of Research and Practice.* New York: The Guilford Press, 1980.

Brown, Cheryl, and Karen Olson, eds. *Feminist Criticism.* Metuchen, N. J.: Scarecrow Press, 1978.

Buglass, Dorothy, et al. "A Study of Agoraphobic Housewives." *Psychological Medicine* 7 (1977): 73–86.

Cameron, Oliver. "The Differential Diagnosis of Anxiety." *Psychiatric Clinics of North America* 8 (March 1985): 3–23.

Chambless, Dianne L., and Alan J. Goldstein. *Agoraphobia: Multiple Perspectives on Theory and Treatment.* New York: John Wiley & Sons, 1982.

_____. *"Anxieties: Agoraphobia and Hysteria."* In *Women and Psychotherapy*, edited by Annette M. Brodsky and Rachel T. Hare-Mustin, 113–34. New York: The Guilford Press, 1980.

_____. "The Treatment of Agoraphobia." In *Handbook of Behavioral Intervention*, edited by Alan Goldstein and Edna B. Foa, 322–415. New York: John Wiley and Sons, 1980.

Chambless, Dianne L., et al. "Assessment of Fear of Fear in Agoraphobics: The Body Sensations Questionnaire and the Agoraphobic Cognitions Questionnaire." *Journal of Consulting and Clinical Psychology* 5 (1984): 1090–97.

Cody, John. *After Great Pain: The Inner Life of Emily Dickinson.* Cambridge: Harvard University Press, Belknap Press, 1971.

_____. "Mourner Among the Children I." *Psychiatric Quarterly* 41, no. 1 (1967): 12–37.

_____. "Mourner Among the Children II." *Psychiatric Quarterly* 41, no. 2 (1967): 233–63.

_____. "Watchers Upon the East: The Ocular Complaints of Emily Dickinson." *Psychiatric Quarterly* 42, no. 3 (1968): 548–76.

Coryell, William, et al. "Excess Mortality in Panic Disorder." *Archives of General Psychiatry* 39 (June 1982): 701–3.

Costello, C. G. "Fears and Phobias in Women: A Community Study." *Journal of Abnormal Psychology* 91 (August 1982): 280–86.

Cott, Jonathan. "A Neurology of the Soul." *New Age* (March 1986): 38–42, 99.

Curtis, George C. "New Findings in Anxiety." *Psychiatric Clinics of North America* 8 (March 1985): 169–75.

De Moor, Wilfried. "The Topography of Agoraphobia." *American Journal of Psychotherapy* 39 (July 1985): 371–88.

de Swaan, Abram. "The Politics of Agoraphobia: On Changes in Emotional and Relational Management." *Theory and Society* 10 (1981): 359–85.

Deutsch, Helene. "The Genesis of Agoraphobia." *International Journal of Psychoanalysis* 10 (1929): 51–69.

De Voge, J. T., et al. "Effects of Behavioral Intervention and Interpersonal Feedback on Fear and Avoidance Components of Severe Agoraphobia: A Case Analysis." *Psychological Reports* 49 (1981): 595–605.

Diagnostic and Statistical Manual of Mental Disorders. 3d ed. Washington, D. C.: American Psychiatric Association, 1980.

Diamond, David, M. D. "Panic Attacks, Hypochondriasis, and Agoraphobia: A Self-Psychology Formulation." *American Journal of Psychotherapy* 39 (January 1985): 114–25.

Dickinson, Emily. *The Letters of Emily Dickinson*. Edited by Thomas H. Johnson and Theodora Ward. 3 vols. Cambridge: Harvard University Press, Belknap Press, 1958.

_____. *The Poems of Emily Dickinson*. Edited by Thomas H. Johnson. 3 vols. Cambridge: Harvard University Press, Belknap Press, 1955.

"Did Emily Dickinson Suffer From an Eye Disease?" *The New York Times*, 11 December 1979.

Dittrich, Joan, et al. "Panic Disorder: Assessment and Treatment." *Clinical Psychology Review* 3 (1983): 215–25.

Faber, M. D. "Psychoanalytic Remarks on a Poem by Emily Dickinson." *Psychoanalytic Review* 56 (1969): 247–64.

Faravelli, Carlo, et al. "Prevalence of Traumatic Early Life Events in 31 Agoraphobic Patients with Panic Attacks." *American Journal of Psychiatry* 142 (December 1985): 1493–94.

"Fear Itself." Episode of "Innovation." New York: PBS, WNET, 2 February 1985. Television program.

Fenichel, Otto. "Remarks on the Common Phobias." *Psychoanalytic Quarterly* 13 (1944): 313–26.

Fier, Morton. "Agoraphobia: The 'What If' Syndrome." *The Journal of the Medical Society of New Jersey* 78 (April 1981): 206–8.

Fitzgerald, F. Scott. *The Great Gatsby*. New York: Scribners, 1925.

Fodor, Iris. "The Phobic Syndrome in Women." In *Women in Therapy*, edited by Violet Franks and V. Burtle, 132–68. New York: Bruner/Mazel, 1974.

Frampton, Muriel. *Agoraphobia—Coping with the World Outside*. Wellingborough, Northamptonshire: Turnstone Press, 1984.

Frances, A., and P. Dunn. "The Attachment-Autonomy Conflict in Agoraphobia." *International Journal of Psycho-Analysis* 56 (1975): 435–39.

Franklin, Ralph W. "The Dickinson Packet 14 and 20, 10 and 26." *Papers of the Bibliographical Society of America* 73 (1979): 348–55.

_____. *The Editing of Emily Dickinson: A Reconsideration*. Madison: University of Wisconsin Press, 1967.

_____. "The Emily Dickinson Fascicles." *Studies in Bibliography* 36 (1983): 1–20.

_____. "Emily Dickinson's Packet 27 (and 80, 14, and 6)." *Harvard Library Bulletin* 27 (July 1979): 342–48.

_____. "The Houghton Library Dickinson Manuscript I 57." *Harvard Library Bulletin* 28 (July 1980): 245–57.

_____. "Three Additional Dickinson Manuscripts." *American Literature* 50 (March 1978): 109–16.

_____. ed. *The Manuscript Books of Emily Dickinson*. 2 vols. Cambridge: Harvard University Press, Belknap Press, 1981.

Franks, Violet, and V. Burtle, eds. *Women in Therapy*. New York: Bruner/Mazel, 1974.

Friedman, Daniel, and Arnold Jaffe. "Anxiety Disorders." *The Journal of Family Practice* 16 (1983): 145–52.

Frye, Northrup. *Fables of Identity*. New York: Harcourt, Brace, 1963.

Gallipeo, Paul T. "The Amherst Fascicles of Emily Dickinson." *Dissertation Abstracts International* 45 (September 1984): 844A.

Garakani, Houshang, et al. "Treatment of Panic Disorder with Imipramine Alone." *American Journal of Psychiatry* 141 (March 1984): 446–48.

Gelfond, Marjorie. "Agoraphobia and Personal Crisis." In *Emotion and Adult Development*, edited by Carol Malatesta and Karol Izard, 125–37. New York: Sage Press, 1984.

_____. "Agoraphobia and the Meaning of Home." In *Knowledge for Design*. Proceedings of Environmental Design Research Association 13, edited by Polly Bart, Alexander Chin, and Guido Francescato, 348–53. College Park: University of Maryland, 1982.

____. "Agoraphobia in Women and Environmental Meaning." City University of New York, 1983. Photocopy.

Gelman, David, with Pamela Abramson. "Home Behind Bars." *Newsweek*, 23 April 1984, 70.

Gelpi, Albert J. *The Mind of the Poet*. Cambridge: Harvard University Press, 1965.

Gilbert, Sandra, and Susan Gubar. *The Madwoman in the Attic*. New Haven: Yale University Press, 1979.

Gleed, Elizabeth. "Some Psychological Mechanisms in Agoraphobia." *British Journal of Projective Psychology and Personality Study* 19 (December 1974): 27–33.

Gloger, Sergio, et al. "Treatment of Spontaneous Panic Attacks with Chlomipramine." *American Journal of Psychiatry* 138 (September 1981): 1215–7.

Goldney, Robert D. "Agoraphobia: The Clinical Problem." *Australian Family Physician* 9 (April 1980): 272–78.

Goldstein, Alan, and Edna B. Foa. *The Handbook of Behavioral Intervention: A Clinical Guide*. New York: John Wiley & Sons, 1980.

Goldstein, Alan, and Dianne L. Chambless. "A Reanalysis of Agoraphobia." *Behavior Therapy* 9 (1978): 47–59.

Griffith, Clark. *The Long Shadow: Emily Dickinson's Tragic Poetry*. Princeton: Princeton University Press, 1964.

Grunhaus, Leon, et al. "Panic Attacks: A Review of Treatments and Pathogenesis." *The Journal of Nervous and Mental Disease* 169 (1981): 608–13.

Hallam, R. S. "Agoraphobia: A Critical Review of the Concept." *British Journal of Psychiatry* 133 (1978): 314–19.

Hallam, R. S. and R. Hafner. "Fears of Phobic Patients." *Behavioral Research and Therapy* 16 (1978): 1–6.

Harvey, Vera. "How to Recognise and Help Agoraphobics." *The Australasian Nurses Journal* 11 (1981): 29.

Henry, Diane. "Did Eye Ailment Add to Emily Dickinson's Woes? *The New York Times*, 18 December 1979.

Hicks, Robert, Anna Okonek, and John M. Davis. "The Psycho-pharmacological Approach." In *The Handbook on Stress and Anxiety*, edited by Irwin Kutash et al., 428–35. San Francisco: Jossey-Bass, 1980.

Higginson, Thomas Wentworth. "Emily Dickinson's Letters." In *Jubilee—One Hundred Years at the Atlantic*, edited by Edward Weeks and Emily Flint, 184–99. Boston: Little Brown, 1957.

Hoch, Paul, and Phillip Polatin. "Pseudoneurotic Forms of Schizophrenia." *Psychiatric Quarterly* 23 (1949): 246–76.

Hodgkinson, Peter E. "Far from the Madding Crowd." *Nursing Mirror* 153 (1 July 1981): 37–38.

Hoehn-Saric, Rudolph, and D. McLeod. "Generalized Anxiety Disorder." *Psychiatric Clinics of North America* 8 (March 1985): 73–88.

Horn, Thomas, M. D. "Agoraphobia." *American Academy of Family Physicians* 32 (July 1985): 165–73.

Howard, Elizabeth. "Too Scared to Face the World." *McCalls*, September 1984, 82.

Huf, Linda. *A Portrait of the Artist as a Young Woman: The Writer as Heroine in American Literature.* New York: Frederick Unger, 1983.

Jacob, Rolf G., et al. "Otoneurological Examination in Panic Disorder and Agoraphobia with Panic Attacks." *American Journal of Psychiatry* 142 (June 1985): 715–20.

Johnson, Thomas H. *Emily Dickinson: An Interpretative Biography.* Cambridge: Harvard University Press, Belknap Press, 1955.

_____. "Establishing a Text: The Emily Dickinson Papers." *Studies in Bibliography* 5 (1952–53): 21–32.

Juhasz, Suzanne. "Reading Emily Dickinson's Letters." *English Studies Quarterly* 30 (1984): 170–92.

_____. "The Undiscovered Continent: Emily Dickinson and the Space of the Mind." *The Missouri Review* 3 (Fall 1979): 86–97.

Kent, Fraser. *Nothing to Fear: Coping with Phobias.* Garden City, N. Y.: Doubleday, 1977.

King, Malcolm. "A Woman in Need: Dependency in Agoraphobia." *Nursing Mirror* 152 (22 January 1981): 34–36.

Klein, Donald F., and John M. Davis. *Diagnosis and Drug Treatment of Psychiatric Disorders.* Baltimore: The Williams & Wilkins Co., 1969.

Klein, Donald F., and Judith G. Rabkin, eds. *Anxiety: New Research and Changing Concepts.* New York: Raven Press, 1981.

Last, Cynthia, et al. "The Relationship Between Cognitions and Anxiety." *Behavior Modification* 9 (April 1985): 253–41.

Laughlin, Henry P. *The Neuroses in Clinical Practice.* Philadelphia, Pa.: W. B. Sanders Co., 1956.

Laybourne, Paul, Jr., and Joann Redding. "Agoraphobia: Is Fear the Basis of Symptoms?" *Postgraduate Medicine* 78 (October 1985): 109–18.

Leckman, James, et al. "Anxiety Disorders and Depression: Contradictions Between Family Study Data and DSM III Conventions." *American Journal of Psychiatry* 140 (July 1983): 880–82.

Leonard, William Ellery. *The Locomotive-God.* New York: D. Appleton-Century Co., 1942.

Levinson, Harold N., M. D., with Steve Carter. *Phobia Free.* New York: M. Evans and Co., Inc. 1986.

Leyda, Jay. *The Years and Hours of Emily Dickinson.* 2 vols. 1960. Reprint. Hamden, Conn.: Archon Books, 1970.

Liebowitz, Michael, et al. "Lactate Provocation of Panic Attacks II." *Archives of General Psychiatry* 42 (July 1985): 709–19.

Lim, Daniel. "Behind Closed Doors." *Nursing Mirror* 154 (21 April 1982): 50–51.

Lucas, Dolores. *Emily Dickinson and Riddle*. De Kalb, Ill.: Northern Illinois University Press, 1969.

Mc Conaghy, Nathaniel. "Behavior Completion Mechanisms Rather Than Primary Drives Maintain Behavioral Patterns." *Activitas Nervosa Superior* (Praha) 22 (1980): 138–51.

Mairs, Nancy. *Plaintext*. Tucson: University of Arizona Press, 1986.

Marks, Isaac. "Agoraphobic Syndrome." *Archives of General Psychiatry* 23 (December 1970): 538–53.

_____. "The Classification of Phobic Disorders." *British Journal of Psychiatry* 116 (1970): 377–86.

_____. *The Cure and Care of Neuroses: Theory and Practice of Behavioral Psychotherapy*. New York: John Wiley & Sons, 1981.

_____. *Fears and Phobias*. New York: Academic Press, 1969.

_____. *Living With Fear*. New York: McGraw-Hill, 1978.

Marks, I. M., and E. Herst. "A Survey of 1,200 Agoraphobics in Britain." *Social Psychiatry* 5 (1970): 16–24.

Martin, Wendy, *An American Triptych: Anne Bradstreet, Emily Dickinson, Adrienne Rich*. Chapel Hill: University of North Carolina Press, 1984.

Mathews, Andrew M., et al. *Agoraphobia: Nature and Treatment*. New York: The Guilford Press, 1981.

Mavissakalian, Matig, and Larry Michelson. "Patterns of Psycho-physiological Change in the Treatment of Agoraphobia." *Behavior Research and Therapy* 20 (1982): 347–56.

Mendel, J. G., and Donald F. Klein. "Anxiety Attacks with Subsequent Agoraphobia." *Comprehensive Psychiatry* 10 (1969): 190–95.

Miller, Jean Baker, ed. *Psychoanalysis and Women*. Baltimore: Penguin, 1973.

Miller, Milton. "On Street Fear." *International Journal of Psychoanalysis* 32 (1953): 232–40.

Miller, Ruth. *The Poetry of Emily Dickinson*. Middletown, Conn.: Wesleyan University Press, 1968.

Moore, Judith. "The New Hysteria." Review of *Hunger Strike, The Anorectic's Struggle as a Metaphor for Our Age*, by Susie Orbach. *The New York Times Book Review*, 23 March 1986, 41.

Mossberg, Barbara. *When a Writer is a Daughter*. Bloomington: Indiana University Press, 1982.

Mudge, Jean. *Emily Dickinson and the Image of Home*. Amherst: University of Massachusetts Press, 1975.

Myers, D. H., and G. Grant. "A Study of Depersonalization in Students." *British Journal of Psychiatry* 121 (1972): 59–65.

Parker, Gordon. "Reported Parental Characteristics of Agoraphobics and Social Phobics." *British Journal of Psychiatry* 135 (1979): 555–60.

Persson, G., and C. Nordlund. "Agoraphobics and Social Phobics." *Acta Psychiatrica Scandinavica* 71 (February 1985): 148–59.

Pickering, George. *Creative Malady*. New York: Oxford University Press, 1974.

Pitts, Ferris N., Jr. "The Biochemistry of Anxiety." *Scientific American* 220, no. 2 (February 1969): 69–75.

Polk, Mary Lynn. "Emily Dickinson: A Survey of the Criticism and Selective Annotated Bibliography." *Dissertation Abstracts International* 45 (November 1984): 1399A.

Porter, David. *Dickinson: The Modern Idiom*. Cambridge: Harvard University Press, 1981.

———. "Dickinson's Readers." *The New England Quarterly* (March 1984): 106–17.

Pyke, Jennifer, and M. Longdon. "Agoraphobia." *The Canadian Nurse* 6 (June 1985): 18–21.

Rachman, S. "The Experimental Analysis of Agoraphobia." *Behaviour Research and Therapy* 22 (1984): 631–40.

Rapp, Morton and M. R. Thomas. "Agoraphobia." *Canadian Journal of Psychiatry* 27 (1982): 419–25.

Raskin, Marjorie, et al. "Panic and Generalized Anxiety Disorders." *Archives of General Psychiatry* 39 (June 1982): 687–89.

Ravaris, C. Lewis. "Current Drug Therapy for Agoraphobia." *American Family Physician* 23 (January 1981): 129–31.

Roberts, A. H. "Housebound Housewives—a Followup Study of Phobic Anxiety." *British Journal of Psychiatry* 110 (1964): 191–97.

Rock, Martin, and L. Goldberger. "Relationship between Agoraphobia and Field Dependence." *The Journal of Nervous and Mental Disease* 166 (November 1978): 781–86.

Roeske, Nancy. "Commentary on 'Gender Imperatives, Separation Anxiety, and Agoraphobia in Women.' " *Integrative Psychiatry* 2 (March 1984): 62–63.

Rosenbaum, S. P., ed. *A Concordance to the Poems of Emily Dickinson*. Ithaca: Cornell University Press, 1964.

Rosenthal, M. L. and Sally M. Gall. *The Modern Poetic Sequence*. New York: Oxford University Press, 1983.

Roth, M. "The Phobic Anxiety Depersonalization Syndrome." *Proceedings of the Royal Society of Medicine* (1959): 587–95.

Ruddick, B. "Agoraphobia." *International Journal of Psychoanalysis* 42 (1962): 537–43.

Salzman, Leon, et al. "Commentary on 'Gender Imperatives, Separation Anxiety and Agoraphobia in Women.' " *Integrative Psychiatry* 2 (March 1984): 61–68.

Schmideberg, Melitta. "A Note on Claustrophobia." *Psychoanalytic Review* 35 (1948): 309–11.

Seidenberg, Robert. "The Trauma of Eventlessness." In *Psychoanalysis and Women*, edited by Jean B. Miller, 350–62. Baltimore: Penguin, 1973.

Seidenberg, Robert, and K. DeCrow. *Women Who Marry Houses*. New York: McGraw-Hill, 1983.

Sewall, Richard B. "In Search of Emily Dickinson." *Michigan Quarterly Review* 23 (Fall 1984): 514–28.

———. *The Life of Emily Dickinson*. 2 vols. New York: Farrar, Straus & Giroux, 1974.

———. *The Lyman Letters: New Light on Emily Dickinson and Her Family*. Amherst: University of Massachusetts Press, 1966.

Shands, Harley. "Malinowski's Mirror: Emily Dickinson as Narcissus." *Contemporary Psychoanalysis* 12 (July 1976): 300–334.

Sheehan, David V. "Age of Onset of Phobic Disorders: A Reevaluation." *Comprehensive Psychiatry* 22, no. 6 (December 1981): 544–53.

_____. "Current Concepts in Psychiatry: Panic Attacks and Phobias." *The New England Journal of Medicine* 307, no. 3 (July 1982): 156–58.

Sheehan, David V., and Kathy Sheehan. "The Classification of Phobic Disorders." *The International Journal of Psychiatry in Medicine* 12 (1983): 243–66.

_____. "Diagnostic Classification of Anxiety and Phobic Disorders." *Psychopharmacology Bulletin* 18, no. 4 (October 1982): 35–44.

Shurr, William. *The Marriage of Emily Dickinson: A Study of the Fascicles.* Lexington: University of Kentucky Press, 1983.

Sinnott, Austin, et al. "Agoraphobia: A Situational Analysis." *Journal of Clinical Psychology* 37 (January 1981): 123–27.

Snaith, R. P. "A Clinical Investigation of Phobias." *British Journal of Psychiatry* 114 (1968): 673–97.

Solyom, L., and M. Silberfeld. "Maternal Overprotection in the Etiology of Agoraphobia." *Canadian Psychiatric Association Journal* 21 (1976): 109–13.

Stamm, J. T. "Infantile Trauma, Narcissistic Injury and Agoraphobia." *Psychiatric Quarterly* 46 (1972): 254–72.

Stanworth, H. M. "Agoraphobia—An Illness or Symptom?" *Nursing Times* 78 (10 March 1982): 399–403.

Symonds, Alexandra. "Phobias After Marriage." In *Psychoanalysis and Women*, edited by Jean B. Miller, 288–303. Baltimore: Penguin, 1973.

Taylor, Harold, et al. "A Patient Homebound by Panic." The Journal of Family Practice 16 (1983): 1071–84.

Tearnan, Blake H. "The Etiology of Agoraphobia: An Examination of Critical Life Events." *Dissertation Abstracts International* 43 (May 1983), 3745B.

Tearnan, Blake H., Michael J. Telch, and Peter Keefe. "Etiology and Onset of Agoraphobia." *Comprehensive Psychiatry* 25, no. 1 (February 1984): 51–62.

Teghtsoonian, R., and R. Frost. "The Effects of Viewing Distance on Fear of Snakes." *Journal of Behavioral Therapy and Experiential Psychiatry* 13 (1982): 181–90.

Terhune, W. B. "The Phobic Syndrome." *Archives of Neurology and Psychiatry* 62 (1949): 162–72.

Thyer, Bruce. "Temporal Relationships Between Panic Attack and Phobic Avoidance in Agoraphobia." *Behavior Research and Therapy* 23 (1985): 607–8.

Thyer, Bruce, et al. "Agoraphobia: A Test of the Separation Anxiety Hypothesis." *Behavior Research and Therapy* 23 (1985): 75–78.

_____. "A Comparison of Panic Disorder and Agoraphobia with Panic Attacks." *Comprehensive Psychiatry* 26 (March–April 1985): 208–14.

Trilling, Lionel. "Art and Neurosis." In *The Liberal Imagination*, 160–80. New York: Viking, 1950.

Turns, Danielle M. "Epidemiology of Phobic and Obsessive-Compulsive Disorders." *American Journal of Psychotherapy* 39 (1985): 360–70.

Uhde, Thomas, and J. Maser. "Current Perspectives on Panic Disorder and Agoraphobia." *Hospital and Community Psychiatry* 36 (November 1985): 1153–54.

Uhde, Thomas, et al. "Longitudinal Course of Panic Disorder." *Progress in Neuro-Psychopharmacology and Biological Psychiatry* 9 (1985): 39–51.

Vose, Ruth H. *Agoraphobia*. London: Faber & Faber, 1981.

Wand, Martin, and Richard B. Sewall. "Eyes Be Blind, Heart Be Still." *The New England Quarterly* 52 (1979): 400–406.

Weekes, Claire. *Peace from Nervous Suffering*. New York: Bantam, 1978.

———. *Simple, Effective Treatment of Agoraphobia*. New York: Bantam, 1979.

Weisbuch, Robert. *Emily Dickinson's Poetry*. Chicago: University of Chicago Press, 1975.

Weiss, Edoardo. *Agoraphobia in the Light of Ego Psychology*. New York: Grune and Stratton. 1964.

Weissman, Myrna, et al. "The Epidemiology of Anxiety Disorders." *Psychopharmacology Bulletin* 21 (1985): 538–41.

Wells, Anna May. "Was Emily Dickinson Psychotic?" *American Imago* 19 (Winter 1962): 309–21.

Wender, Paul H., and Donald F. Klein. *Mind, Mood, and Medicine: A Guide to the New Biopsychiatry*. New York: Farrar, Straus, and Giroux, 1981.

West, Margaret. Letter to author, 29 March 1985.

White, William. "Emily Dickinson: Bibliography for 1981–1984." *Dickinson Studies* 54 (1984): 3–25.

Whittle, Amberys R. "Second Opinion: Diagnosing Emily Dickinson." *Dickinson Studies* 52 (1984): 22–31.

Williams, Barbara. "A Room of Her Own: Emily Dickinson as Woman Artist." In *Feminist Criticism: Essays on Theory, Poetry and Prose*, edited by Cheryl Brown and Karen Olson, 69–91. Metuchen, N. J.: Scarecrow Press, 1978.

Winokur, George, and E. Holemon. "Chronic Anxiety Neurosis: Clinical and Sexual Aspects." *Acta Psychiatrica Scandinavica* 39 (1963): 384–412.

Witken, N. "Psychological Differentiation and Forms of Pathology." *Journal of Abnormal Psychology* 70 (1965): 317–36.

Wolfe, Barry. "Gender Imperatives, Separation Anxiety, and Agoraphobia in Women." *Integrative Psychiatry* 2 (March 1984): 57–61.

Wolff, Cynthia Griffin. *Emily Dickinson*. New York: Alfred A. Knopf, Inc., 1986.

Wolpe, Joseph. "Identifying the Antecedents of an Agoraphobic Reaction: A Transcript." *Journal of Behavioral Therapy and Experiential Psychiatry* 1 (1970): 299–304.

Wolpe, Joseph, and David Wolpe. *Our Useless Fears*. Boston: Houghton Mifflin Company, 1981.

Woodress, James. "Emily Dickinson." In *Fifteen American Authors before 1900*, edited by Earl Herbert, 139–68. Madison: University of Wisconsin Press, 1985.

General Index

Agoraphobia, 68
Agoraphobia, 31–32, 69, 79; age and, 34, 67, 69; causes of, 49, 51, 53–54, 61, 141, 143–45; depersonalization and derealization in, 94, 98–99, 106, 119–24, 121–22; and depression, 100–101, 136–38, 146; and eye disorder, 70, 75, 104–5; fears of victims of, 46, 83, 130; genetics and, 55–56, 58, 140–41; importance of home in, 29, 85; and insanity, 68–69, 93, 120; misdiagnosis of, 30–31, 69; and panic attack, 68, 92–100, 102, 105, 107, 115–17, 129; personality of victim of, 39–41; safety zone in, 62, 86, 149; self-fragmentation in, 107, 114–15, 129; and separation anxiety, 57–58; shame of, 82–83; stages of, 34, 45–46, 61, 98, 112; statements of victims of, 96–97, 99, 149; symptoms of, 32, 70, 75, 87, 97; terminology of, 28, 30, 69; trusted companion in, 62; and women, 140–41, 143–44, 146
Anatomy of Melancholy, 29
Anderson, Charles, 77
Andrews, J. D., 141
Arrindell, Willem, 49–50
Aspects of Anxiety, 107
Atlantic Monthly, The, 27
Autobiography of David, The, 107

Ballenger, James, 56
Benedikt, M., 29, 72
Bernhard, Mary Elizabeth, 72
Bingham, Millicent Todd, 54
Biology of Agoraphobia, The, 56
Blythe, Peter, 72–73
Bowlby, John, 49, 57–59, 142
Bowles, Mary, 113
Bowles, Samuel, 68, 113

Branch, C., 107
Burton, Robert, 29

Carlo, 62–3
Chambless, Dianne, 38, 59, 93, 120, 141, 143
Claustrophobia, 87
Cody, John, 30, 50–52, 58, 71, 88, 91, 107, 149
Complex agoraphobia, 38–39. *See also* Agoraphobia

Da Costa's syndrome, 69. *See also* Agoraphobia
Darwin, Charles, 69
DeCrow, Karen, 144
De Moor, Wilfried, 61, 124, 131
Depression, 100–101, 136–37. *See also* Agoraphobia
Diagnostic and Statistical Manual, 31–32, 34, 57, 59
Diamond, David, 107, 114
Dickinson, Austin (brother), 41–42, 47–48, 59
Dickinson, Edward (father), 47, 50, 55, 84
Dickinson, Emily: her anxieties, 28, 35, 41; and Benjamin Newton, 58–61, 76; and Carlo, 62–63; her conflict with father, 47–48, 84, 88; her dependence on Lavinia, 63–66, 131; description of, 27, 38; early years of, 35, 40; her eye disorder, 29, 70–71, 75, 103–4; her fear of separation, 41–44, 59–61; her home life, 45, 50, 54–56, 142–46; importance of siblings to, 58, 60, 68; at Mount Holyoke, 40; her move to Homestead, 37, 68; her need for close attachments, 41, 58; and panic attack, 35–36, 60, 73, 80, 82, 92; her pattern of avoidance, 36–38, 59, 80–81; her

poetry, 76–77, 90, 149–51; her relationship with mother, 37–38, 50–55, 142–43, 145; her "Terror since September," 67, 91; her withdrawal and seclusion, 28, 81, 133–34, 138, 143–49; writing as therapy for, 76, 79, 132, 147–49. *See also* Letters of ED; Poetry of ED

Dickinson, Emily Norcross (mother), 50–53, 55, 142–43

Dickinson, Lavinia (sister), 63–66, 71

Die Agoraphobia, 29, 62

Diethelm, O., 39

DSM. See Diagnostic and Statistical Manual

Dunn, P., 57

Dwights, 66

Editing of Emily Dickinson, The, 77

Emblems, Divine and Moral, 77

Emily Dickinson and the Image of Home, 82

Emily Dickinson's Home, 54

Fascicles, 77–78, 90. *See also* Poetry of ED

Fears and Phobias, 140

Fowler, Emily, 47–48

Frances, A., 57

Franklin, Ralph, 77, 90, 109

Freud, Sigmund, 57

Gall, Sally, 78, 90

Gilbert, Sandra, 145

Gilbert, Susan (Mrs. Austin Dickinson), 42–43

Goldstein, Alan, 33, 38, 44, 56, 59, 93, 141, 143

Griffith, Clark, 91, 99, 106, 119, 131, 149

Hale, Edward Everett, 60

Havens, Mrs., 38

Hestiaphilia, 85

Higginson, Thomas Wentworth, 27–28, 63, 67, 76–77, 82, 92, 101, 104

Holland, Elizabeth (Mrs. Josiah), 72–73

Hollands, 37

Huf, Linda, 87

Humphrey, Jane, 40, 48, 75, 143

Hunger Strike, 144

James, William, 55

Johnson, Thomas, 113

Juhasz, Suzanne, 121, 133

Kent, Fraser, 93, 115

Klein, Donald F., 58, 93–94, 140

Laughlin, Henry, 70

Leonard, William, 68, 70, 96, 106, 136

Letters of ED: on Benjamin Newton's death, 60, 76; on desire for independence, 46–48; on fear of leaving home, 38, 143; on loneliness, 41–42, 47, 59; on martyrdom to family, 38, 40, 142; Master letters, 68; on mother's illness, 38, 52; on need for close attachments, 42–43, 48; on panic attack, 35–36; phobic behavior, 38, 72–73, 75; on "Terror since September," 67. *See also* names of individual recipients, i.e., Bowles, Mary; Bowles, Samuel; Dickinson, Austin; Dickinson, Lavinia; Fowler, Emily; Gilbert, Susan; Hale, Edward Everett; Havens, Mrs.; Higginson, Thomas Wentworth; Holland, Elizabeth; Humphrey, Jane; Norcross, Louise; Root, Abigail; Sweetser, Joseph

Leyda, Jay, 97

Lindberg-Seyersted, Brita, 127

Locomotive God, The, 107

Lyman Letters, The, 104

McClure, J. N., 55–56

McGlown, David, 72

Macropsia, 121

Madwoman in the Attic, The, 145

Mairs, Nancy, 69, 140

Manuscript Books of Emily Dickinson, The, 77

Marks, Isaac, 32, 53–54, 62, 69, 102, 140, 149

Marriage of Emily Dickinson, The, 77–78

Micropsia, 121

Miller, Ruth, 68, 77

Mother at Home, The, 88

Mount Holyoke, 40, 45, 54
Mudge, Jean, 37, 82, 88, 131, 138, 149

New England Journal of Medicine, 56
Newton, Benjamin, 58, 61, 76
Nightingale, Florence, 69
Norcross, Louise, 38

OBD. *See* Organic Brain Dysfunction
Orbach, Susie, 144
Organic Brain Dysfunction, 72–73
Ovesey, L., 62

Panic attack, 34, 36, 46, 61, 68, 73–74
Panic phobia, 32. *See also* Agoraphobia; Panic attack
Parker, Gordon, 49
Phobia Free, 73–74
Phobias, 29, 32
Phobic partner, 62
Phobogenic process, 99–100
Pitts, F. N., 55–56
Plaintext, 69, 140
Platzschwindel, 29
Poems, 105
Poetry of ED: arrangement of by theme, 77; arrangement of by fascicle, 77–78, 90, 109–11; despair and loneliness in, 137–39; drowning and the sea in, 113; experience of "aftermath" in, 90, 117–18, 125–28, 135–38; "goblin" creature in, 98–99, 116, 129; house imagery in, 82, 85, 106, 131; "omitted center" in, 97; panic attack in, 96–97, 105, 112, 119–24, 130–31, 147; pattern of agoraphobic in, 79, 82, 83, 91, 109–11, 147; prison imagery in, 84–88; stone imagery in, 134–36, 148; suicide in, 88–89, 132; transcendence in, 149–51
Poetry of Emily Dickinson, The, 77
Porter, David, 90, 125, 147
Portrait of the Artist as a Young Woman, 87

Quarles, Francis, 77

Rapp, Thomas, 141
Raskin, Marjorie, 59
Roeske, Nancy, 51, 144
Root, Abigail, 38, 40–41, 142
Rosenthal, M. L., 78, 90–91, 111
Roth, M., 119–20
Ruddick, B., 121

Seidenberg, Robert, 144
Separation and Loss, 49
Separation anxiety, 34, 57–58, 142
Sewall, Richard, 104, 109, 149
Sheehan, David, 34–35, 56, 61, 97, 136–37
Shurr, William, 77–78
Snaith, R. P., 39
Spacks, Patricia Meyer, 149
Springfield Republican, 68
Subpanic symptoms, 35
Sweetser, Joseph, 38
Symonds, Alexandra, 87

Tate, Allen, 79
Tearnan, Blake H., 53
Terhune, W. B., 39–40, 49, 53
Todd, Mabel Loomis, 77
Tucker, W., 49

Uhde, Thomas, 55

Vose, Ruth, 68, 70, 100–101

Wand, Martin, 72
Webster, A., 49
Weekes, 98
Weiss, Edoardo, 31
Westphal, C., 29, 62
Williams, Henry, 70
Wolfe, Barry, 143
Wolff, Cynthia Griffin, 44, 51–53, 70, 79, 84, 133
Women Who Marry Houses, 144

Zane, Manual, 99–100
Zitrin, Charlotte, 58

Index of First Lines

The Johnson number follows in parentheses.

A Charm invests a face (421) 110–11
A Day! Help! Help! Another Day! (42) 84
A Night—there lay the days between— (471) 117, 138
A Secret told— (381) 83
A Prison gets to be a friend (652) 85–87
A Spider sewed at Night (1138) 149
Afraid! Of whom am I afraid? (608) 109
After Great pain, a formal feeling comes— (341) 134–35
At leisure is the Soul (618) 127

Before I got my eye put out (327) 103–4, 110–11
Bring me the sunset in a cup (128) 88

Did you ever stand in a Cavern's Mouth (590) 138–39
Dont put up my Thread and Needle— (617) 126–27
Doom is the House without the Door— (475) 88

Essential Oils—are wrung— (675) 148
Exhiliration—is within— (383) 150

From Blank to Blank— (761) 122–23

Growth of Man—like Growth of Nature (750) 150–51

Her Sweet turn to leave the Homestead (649) 151–52

Like Eyes that looked on Wastes— (458) 137–38

I am alive—I guess— (470) 122
I breathed enough to take the Trick— (272) 89, 119
I felt a Cleaving in my Mind— (937) 107, 120
I felt a Funeral, in my Brain (280) 105–7, 109–11, 129
I felt my life with both my hands (351) 121–22
I heard a Fly buzz—when I died— (465) 124
I hide myself within my flower (903) 83
I learned—at least—what Home could be— (944) 133
I lived on Dread— (770) 118
I many times thought Peace had come (739) 129, 138

I measure every Grief I meet (561) 138
I never felt at Home—Below— (413) 83, 126
I read my sentence—steadily— (412) 82
I saw no Way—The Heavens were stitched— (378) 120
I stepped from Plank to Plank (875) 121
It ceased to hurt me, though so slow (584) 89, 129, 138
I tie my Hat—I crease my Shawl— (443) 125, 127
It might be lonelier (405) 138
It struck me—every Day— (362) 116–17
It was not Death, for I stood up (510) 112–13, 117, 119, 126
It would have starved a Gnat— (612) 88
It would never be Common—more—I said— (430) 128, 138
I've dropped my Brain—My Soul is numb— (1046) 135–36

Me from Myself—to banish— (642) 130, 132
My Portion is Defeat—today— (639) 84

Never for Society (746) 150
No Man can compass a Despair— (477) 138
No Rack can torture me— (384) 150

Of Tribulation—these are They (325) 81
On a Columnar Self— (789) 148
One need not be a Chamber—to be Haunted— (670) 130–32

Papa above! (61) 84

Renunciation—is a piercing Virtue— (745) 150

Safe in their Alabaster Chambers— (216) 147
Some keep the Sabbath going to Church— (324) 80
Success is counted sweetest (67) 84, 150
Sunset at Night—is natural— (415) 101, 110
Suspense—is Hostiler than Death— (705) 118–19

The Battle fought between the Soul (594) 84
The Brain, within it's Groove (556) 120
The Color of the Grave is Green— (411) 94, 109–10
The difference between Despair (305) 137
The first Day's Night had come— (410) 91–94, 107, 109–10, 122
The Loneliness One dare not sound— (777) 139
The Martyr Poets—did not tell— (544) 147
The Months have ends—the Years—a knot— (423) 89
There is a Languor of the Life (396) 123–24
There is a pain—so utter— (599) 123
There's a certain Slant of light (258) 137
The Soul has Bandaged moments— (512) 113–16, 129
The Soul selects her own Society— (303) 134, 150
The Soul's Superior instants (306) 148–49
The Soul unto itself (683) 130
The Spider as an Artist (1275) 149

The Sun kept setting—setting—still (692) 115–16
They shut me up in Prose— (613) 87–88
Tie the Strings to my Life, My Lord (279) 105, 110
'Tis so appalling—it exhilirates— (281) 107–8, 111
'Tis true—They shut me in the Cold— (538) 87–88
To my quick ear the Leaves—conferred— (891) 83
'Twas just this time, last year, I died (445) 108–10
'Twas like a Maelstrom, with a notch (414) 94–101, 106–14,
                                                              116, 118, 123, 129
Two swimmers wrestled on the spar— (201) 113

We dont cry—Tim and I (196) 83
We grow accustomed to the Dark— (419) 101–2, 111, 118, 149–50
What if I say I shall not wait! (277) 89
When we stand on the tops of Things— (242) 111